**DENIS CAULFEILD HERON**

# *AN INTRODUCTION TO THE HISTORY OF JURISPRUDENCE*

**BOOK I-III**

Elibron Classics
www.elibron.com

Elibron Classics series.



ISBN 1-4021-9686-5 (paperback)
ISBN 1-4212-9776-0 (hardcover)

This Elibron Classics book contains the complete text of the edition published in 1860 by John W. Parker & Son, London.

# AN INTRODUCTION

TO THE

# HISTORY OF JURISPRUDENCE.

BY

D. CAULFEILD HERON, LL.D.

LONDON:
JOHN W. PARKER AND SON, WEST STRAND.

1860.

# CONTENTS

# PREFACE

I have written the following pages as an Introduction to the History of Jurisprudence.

I have attempted to give an historical review of the great authors who have scientifically cultivated Law, combined with a sketch of its internal development. Some biographical details are added.

A great portion of the book is a compilation. Following the example of distinguished authorities, "I have taken whatever appeared most valuable from the works of former writers."

In a volume embracing so large a portion of human knowledge in one of its most difficult branches, I have necessarily been obliged to rely much upon the labours of my predecessors. I acknowledge my many obligations to the works of TENNEMANN, HALLAM, J. S. MILL, WHEATON, LERMINIER, and JANET.

D. C. HERON.

# BOOK I
# PRINCIPLES OF JURISPRUDENCE

*"Ου γαρ οι ακροαται του νομου δικαιοι παρα τω θεω, αλλ' οι ποιηται του νομου δικαιωθησονται. "Οταν γαρ εθνη τα μη νομον εχοντα, φυσει τα του νομου ποιη, ουτοι νομον μη εχοντες, εαυτοις εισι νομος. Οιτινες ενδεικνυνται το εργον του νομου γραπτον εν ταις καρδιαις αυτων, συμμαρτυρουσης αυτων της συνειδησεως, και μεταξυ αλληλων των λογισμων κατηγορουντων, η και απολογουμενων"*

*'Επιστολη προς 'Ρωμαιους*, cap. ii., 13, 14, 15.

"Not the hearers of the Law are just before God, but the doers of the Law shall be justified. For when the Gentiles, who have not the Law, do by nature those things that are of the Law, those having not the Law, are a Law unto themselves, which show the works of the Law written in their hearts, their consciences bearing witness to them, and their thoughts between themselves accusing or else defending one another."

*St. Paul's Epistle to the Romans*, cap. ii., 13, 14, 15.

## *CHAPTER I*
## *INTRODUCTION: THE SOCIAL SCIENCES*

Jurisprudence is the Science of Positive Laws. It has been observed that Laws are by the public considered as something distinct from common life, and the common affairs of society — as a sort of intellectual Japan, all access to which is prohibited, and the coasts of which are guarded by the gloom of an inexorable exclusion. Yet, even Japan in our own time has been opened. And to one truly reflecting upon the nature of Laws, few subjects ought to be more interesting. The whole fabric of society rests chiefly on the Law. The social and political life in which we live, the freedom which we enjoy, all result from the labours of the wise and good in this department of human intelligence. And the science of Jurisprudence concerns not individuals, but the community. The pleasures of knowledge, the glories of the refined arts are known to few; Laws are praised or cursed by every fireside. Each nation lives in the cottage as well as in the castle; and unless the beauty of legislature and the excellence of statesmanship dwell in the feelings and condition of the common people, our Government acts like the Epicurean gods, who enjoyed their existence careless of humanity.

The object of a History of Jurisprudence is to exhibit the circumstances which have attended the establishment of existing positive Laws. But the exposition of the dead laws which have been superseded is inseparably interwoven with that of the living laws which have superseded them. And in this investigation are furnished the great examples for the Art of Legislation.[1]

Bolingbroke has observed, that to enable one to take a commanding view of the field of Law and Legislation there are two principal vantage grounds on which it is necessary to mount — History and Metaphysics. The road is smooth and flowery to that vantage ground offered by History. There has been no want of those who have ascended to it, and taken post upon it. To that which belongs to the region of Metaphysics, the road is rugged and full of thorns. Few have attempted to gain it; fewer have succeeded in placing themselves in a position whence a view at once clear and extensive could be obtained.

Many of the definitions which I shall adopt may be controverted. They are attempts to give some precision and accuracy to the most difficult department of Social Science. Lord Bacon has said that civil knowledge is conversant about a subject which, above all others, is most immersed in matter the hardest to be reduced to axiom. Aristotle, in the Politics, condemns the pursuit of a delusive geometrical accuracy in moral reasoning. Still, the first principles of Jurisprudence are maxims of reason which pervade all human laws, and the observance of which is discovered by experience to be essential to happiness and security.

I have attempted to sketch an outline of the subjects and divisions of Jurisprudence, its limits and province.

The word Law, in its widest sense, is used to designate those natural principles which are incident to, and govern all things, animate and inanimate. The entire of physical nature is subject to certain laws — the laws of gravitation, of light, of heat. In the Institutes of Justinian, the term Law is extended to

---

[1] Bentham.

the instincts of animals, and natural Law is therein defined to be that which nature has implanted in all living things "For this is not proper to men exclusively, but belongs to all animals, whether produced in the earth, in the air, or in the water." Hooker says: "That which doth assign unto each thing the kind, that which doth moderate the force and power, that which doth appoint the form and measure of working, the same we term a Law." All nature obeys certain rules, and animals are governed by fixed instincts. The bee and the beaver have built for thousands of years with the same degree of perfection. The celestial bodies have from the period of creation rolled in their orbits, subject to the laws of matter. And the term Law, in its general philosophical sense, is no less applicable to the phenomena of mind than to the phenomena of matter. The processes of the mind are as uniform as the processes of matter. The mode in which the mind arrives at a conclusion is as fixed and unalterable as the mode in which an apple falls to the ground. But, in Jurisprudence, the meaning of the word *Law* is limited. Law is a rule of civil conduct prescribed and enforced by the State.

A Science is a collection of the fundamental truths concerning the same subject matter, arranged in methodical order.

Philosophy is the explanation of the phenomena of the universe. With the ancients Philosophy was the love of wisdom; with us it implies the search after truth. The objects of Philosophy are the discovery of what is true, and the practice of what is good.

The explanation of a phenomenon is the reference of the fact to be explained to some known principle.

The properties and motions of matter form the subject of Natural Philosophy and its sub-divisions; thus the science of Astronomy treats of the laws which govern the heavenly bodies; the science of Mechanics treats of the laws of weight and motion.

Similarly, Mental Philosophy treats of the laws which regulate the powers, faculties, and affections of the human mind and its development.

Mental Philosophy has been divided into two parts; one treats of man in his individual capacity, the other of man as a member of society. But these parts are divided by an uncertain line, and each encroaches upon the distinct province of the other. The first branch of Mental Philosophy discusses the individual mind, its intellectual as well as its moral and active powers, the faculties of the understanding and those of the will. The second branch of Mental Philosophy treats of the social development of the human race, and has been termed the Political Science, or the Social Science, or Sociology.

Moral Duties, Exchanges, and Laws are the three subjects of the Social Science.

Ethics, Political Economy, and Jurisprudence, form the three subdivisions of the Social Science.

Notwithstanding considerable progress has been made in some of the physical sciences, especially in Astronomy, still, of many common occurrences in nature, the laws are either unknown, or at least are not reduced to that precision to which science ought to aspire.

Prevision is the test of science. Few branches of knowledge as yet can bear that test. An eclipse may be predicted; who shall foretell the hour of a revolution?

But the possibility of a science which can treat of the laws of society is denied. Even in the nineteenth century our writers maintain the exploded doctrines of the ancient Sophists, and insist that, in the domain of Laws and Politics, there exist no laws of laws — *leges legum.* Mr. Hallam says, "If it is meant that any systematic science, whether by the name of Jurisprudence or Legislation, can be laid down as to the principles which ought to determine the institutions of all nations, or that, in other words, the laws of each separate community ought to be regulated by any universal standard in matters not depending upon Eternal Justice, we must demur to receiving so very disputable a proposition."

This passage is obscure. If the term "Eternal Justice" be intended to apply only to those principles of right which can be enforced in the most advanced state of society, then the doctrine is erroneous. Many things are right in one state of society which are wrong in another. Slavery appears to have been suited to some ancient systems, and not to have worked the horrors of Tennessee and Kentucky. Trial by Jury is adapted for a people, honest, fair-dealing, tolerant, and free; it does not produce unmixed good amongst a people divided into fanatical parties, hostile to one another, and who disregard the obligation of an oath for the purpose of acquitting their friends and convicting their religious or political enemies. Trial by Jury, although abstractedly right, cannot be introduced into every country. Slavery, although abstractedly wrong, cannot be at once abolished.

Similarly, Professor Sedgwick, in his discourse on the Studies in the University of Cambridge, says — "If, in moral reasoning, it be mere mockery to use the language of abstraction, and to build up systems by trains of *a priori* reasoning, it is assuredly not less absurd to affect the forms of inductive proof in political speculation. Every political as well as every moral principle practically involves the determination of the will, and thereby becomes at once separated from that class of investigations in which we consider the immutable relations of physical phenomena." The various causes of obstruction to the progress of the scientific cultivation of Laws have been frequently enumerated, Modern jurists have fallen into confusion, vagueness, and obscurity of thought from not having distinguished at the outset Ethics or Morals from compulsory human law; and they have considered both under one general appellation. They have adopted a kind of *a priori* method of investigation, instead of the inductive method; they have assumed general principles, not warranted by actual observation of facts; they have invented systems of law and government by inductions from careless or imperfect observation, or even by the mere force of imagination, and then adapted the facts of history to these ideal or fictitious systems.

However, it is a great step in the progress of science that the existence of laws is admitted in those operations of nature which form the subject of the physical sciences. But, even where men have the choice of different modes of action, certain consequences follow from adopting one course of action or the other. Nor are such laws observable merely in the conduct of the individual. They are more to be observed in the conduct of multitudes, and in the rise and fall of great nations, in the records of crimes, and the annals of justice. If one army be marshalled confusedly — if the general have no sympathy with his soldiers — if they do not obey him with promptitude, zeal, and fidelity, there will be but an unsuccessful campaign against the force where order, discipline, and enthusiasm prevail. Faith, labour, honesty, and perseverance have, as they always had, their power to elevate in the scale of humanity the men and nations which adopt them. God is great: His mercy and goodness endure for ever; the fertile lands smile in verdure beneath the heavens; the seed multiplies; the summer sun ripens the bountiful harvest"; the Process of Life goes on; millions of the human race become more prosperous, better educated, better fitted to serve their Creator; others, by their own deserts, sink in filth and degradation. The words God, Liberty, and Truth, find a response in the hearts of men, even during the saddest days of Atheism, Despotism, and Dishonesty. "Neither is it the part of a well-regulated, but rather of a perverse mind to seek glory rather than practise virtue, and for one to desire to be crowned before he hath contended. In vain does one endeavour to rise to the height of glory who has not first been illustrious in virtue."[2]

Illustrations will occur to every student of history.

At the present period of philosophy, therefore, it is not pretended that the Science of Society is in a very advanced state. It is easier for the Astronomer by observation to ascertain the rules of celestial mechanics — it is easier for the Geologist to discover the history of the earth's mutations, than for the Jurist to trace those circumstances in human affairs which guide men to truth in Politics and Laws. "The man of real science recognises more than the superficial observer the concord between physical and moral laws, between science and religion. Both come from one great source, and every step that we make in the investigation of the physical laws, and of their principles, ought to lead us only to a nearer and better acquaintance with those of the moral universe, and with the majesty and grandeur of Him who has wished to grant us the growing evidence of Himself and of his attributes, by allowing His works, perfect from the beginning, to be gradually unveiled and explained to our researches."[3] In all human probability, Sociology will be the last science to be perfected. Of its three component parts the domain of Ethics alone has been scientifically cultivated by the greatest intellects for a long period in history. But Adam Smith, late in the eighteenth century, gave the first great impulse to the study of Political Economy. Bentham and Savigny, names of very recent memory, have, in the present generation, analyzed and historied Jurisprudence.

---

[2] St Bernard's Sermon on St. Victor.

[3] Cardinal Wiseman.

Yet, though the Physical Sciences have been first cultivated with some degree of success, the study of the Social Sciences appears more important with regard to human progress. Most of the processes of nature, the subjects of the Physical Sciences, are beyond the dominion of man; and though he may be affected by their result still he cannot control them. The earth sweeps through space round the sun, careless of the populations which it bears; the sun revolves round some distant and unknown centre of gravitation; the causes of light and heat are mysteries. The earth, with all its millions of the human race, inspired by Love, Genius, and Ambition, is in creation but a whirling speck of dust; and were it this moment to vanish into nothingness, its loss would be unfelt, unseen by the galaxies which throng the firmament. But most of the subjects of the Social Sciences are within our dominion; and with ourselves alone it rests whether we will use and combine the materials of civilization, or leave those materials unused, and remain in ignorance, poverty, and misery. "It would be clearly an inversion of the order which Providence has established were we to regard science and its progress as the essential basis of man's happiness and of society's, and the moral duties as merely secondary and subsidiary, instead of assisting that great and salutary principle which we must always keep inviolate, that the true and real basis of all human happiness is the observance of the moral law; while, science, literature, and art — every thing, indeed, that ennobles, every thing that engentles, every thing that makes more graceful, or touches with higher perfection human nature in the individual, or in any form of society — may be made, and ought to be made, subservient to its progress, and thereby to its perfection."[4]

It is, therefore, idle to declare an aversion to Political Science: in so doing, persons state their indifference to the happiness of mankind. It is true that the moral and legal sentiments of mankind are various in different stages of civilization. At the present day, in every country, all opposing parties, Conservatives and Progressists alike, contest the first principles upon which Political Science is founded; but a similar strife has occurred in the infancy of all sciences. What varied theories have existed in Astronomy! The boundaries between the virtue of Justice and the

---

[4] Cardinal Wiseman.

other virtues are not yet so distinctly defined as to fix the limits of compulsory law. Time will fix those limits. In legislation, the Historical and Analytical Schools have hitherto been opposed. But it is the business of Science to unite them. For actual legislation ought always to be a compromise between history and philosophy. Since all our external actions react upon our fellow-men, we ought to strive to regulate them according to the laws of human association, by the aid of those very Political Sciences which some persons despise. All legitimate interests are in harmony. And the healthful prosperity of one promotes the prosperity of all. The study of the Social Sciences will foster disinterestedness, sympathy, patriotism, enthusiasm for all that is good and great. Even if the study of the Political Sciences were prohibited, their practice could not for a single moment be suspended. There are nations in which the theory of Government has never been the subject of reflection or discussion; nevertheless they are governed. If, then, the Social Sciences be obscure, let us throw light upon them; if they be uncertain, let us endeavour to fix them; if they be speculative, let us establish them upon reason and experience.[5]

In every science the principles are natural and fixed. Very few principles as yet have been discovered in any science. There are natural and fixed principles of legal Right and illegal Wrong, as there are natural and fixed principles of Gravitation. If the laws of Exchanges were properly understood, legislative interference would no more attempt to control the rise and fall of prices than the rise and fall of the barometer, or of the tides. If the true principles of Jurisprudence were acted upon, absurd and wicked legislation would disappear.

The study of Jurisprudence is so intimately connected with its kindred branches of Sociology, that it is necessary to compare and define their several limits. The three Social Sciences, Ethics, Political Economy, and Jurisprudence, are so united that it is difficult to treat of their subjects without the equal assistance of the jurist, the economist, and the moral philosopher.

The object of the Science of Jurisprudence is the discovery of the relations which ought to be established by the Positive Law, and the best means to enforce such relations.

---

[5] Mignet.

The object of Political Economy is the discovery of the laws which regulate the exchangeable value of commodities, and the discovery of the best means to determine the distribution of wealth.

Thus, each science, as to its own subject matter, strives to attain the true objects of Philosophy, the Discovery of Truth, and the Practice of Good.

Many kindred branches of knowledge assist these studies. Of all the sciences which aid the progress of Sociology, the most important is Statistics.

Statistics is the science of social facts expressed in numerical terms. It is most intimately allied to the three Social Sciences. All have for their end the amelioration of the social state, in guiding by the light of an exalted reason, administrative and political powers; but the Social Sciences proceed with boldness into the most elevated region of speculative systems, whilst Statistics is a science of facts which, in rapid figures, enumerates the wants of nations, their daily progress, and all the fortunate or unhappy individualities of their destinies.

The science of Statistics aids the practice of the Social Sciences in detailing the population of a country, its fertility, its means of communication and defence. This science fixes the numbers of the army which guarantees the independence of the State. It assists in the just imposition of Taxes. It tells the quantity and value of the productions of Agriculture and Manufactures. It traces the progress of the National Education, which makes men better by enlightening them. It gives the details of the machinery and cost of justice. It traces the history and causes of diseases, and points out the true course for sanitary reform. It illustrates, by novel and exact truths, a crowd of objects which arise from day to day, agitate public opinion, and exhibit problems to be solved by the Social Science.

Working steadfastly at these subjects, wise men have developed the Social Sciences, and the human race has progressed in civilization. Civilization is that condition of social life possessed by a moral, educated, and wealthy community, enjoying public security and liberty under the protection of law. The first requisite of society is security. When property is not secure from foreign ambition or civil commotion, or from crime, accumulation cannot proceed, nor can wealth remain in that degree which is necessary to provide persons with the luxuries and decencies of civilized life. No one would till the earth unless under the certainty that a reasonable share of the harvest would be enjoyed by himself. No one would voluntarily live and work in that country which is continually ravaged by foreign armies. Public Liberty is as essential an ingredient of Civilization as Public Security or Order. By Public Liberty I mean freedom of discussion, freedom of action, including absolute personal liberty, a free press, and a representative government. Such liberty is enjoyed by England and the United States; such liberty is not enjoyed by Russia. But, wherever there is tolerable security, even without any high degree of liberty, morality, or knowledge, wealth may still accumulate. Thus, in China, Northern India, Egypt, and the fertile provinces of Asiatic Turkey, many of the inhabitants enjoy a considerable amount of wealth. Still, morality or the sense of Right is the essential ingredient of a high order of civilization, and exercises the most remarkable influence on the prosperity of nations, and their success in art and war. Facility of communication is also an important part of advanced civilization. A country cannot be considered united, nor can it possess the stability of centralized government, unless there be easy and ready means of communicating from the capital to the different parts of the empire. The Romans were well aware of this when they constructed the roads which remain to the present day memorials of the Roman greatness. But the recent triumphs of mechanical science have surpassed the rude efforts of ancient times; and the railway, the steamboat, and the electric telegraph are among the most important agents in the diffusion of knowledge and the maintenance of freedom. In nothing, however, have the civilized nations of modern times more surpassed the civilization of the ancients than in the knowledge and education of the people. Hence it is reasonable to entertain a hope that our present civilizations will not be lost, like those of Egypt, Greece, or Rome. The first literary state was Athens, possessed of the little territory of Attica, containing a population inferior to that of some English and Irish counties. Although books then were enormously dear — and it is recorded of Plato that he once paid £300 for an indifferent volume — still there was in Athens a popular education of a high order. Thus, Homer and the Rhapsodists publicly recited their poems; the plays of Æschylus and Sophocles were performed in the presence of 30,000 spectators; the history of Herodotus was read at the Olympic games; the odes of Pindar were sung at Delphi; Æschines and Demosthenes addressed the people in the assembly; the glorious statues and temples of the Ionian race were another and a splendid part of their education. In Rome there was no popular literature. The military aristocracy encouraged the people in their warlike spirit by wild-beast shows and gladiatorial combats. The early Romans organized Government and War, but left Art for other races. The Northern conquerors of the Roman Empire despised learning. The great majority of their kings, counts, and dukes were unable to write their names. Their signature was a seal, *signum,* impressed on their deeds. In effect, the improvement of the mechanical arts, the invention of printing, and the general use of paper first rendered a cheap literature and popular education possible. There is a great difference between the first Gazette published at Venice, and the *Times* of the latter half of the nineteenth century. The first Gazette contained fragments of doubtful news; now, more than by any thing else in England, the people are educated by the newspapers, that with such industry collect, and with such rapidity disperse, information every morning to the working intelligence of the empire. The education of the people is increasing every day among all the nations most advanced in civilization. It was even recently the fashion to discuss whether education ought to be extended to the people; but, whilst learned men discussed these things, the labouring classes have become comparatively educated, and are an element in society. And, by the aid of printing and the diffusion of education, one clever man can now speak: to tens of thousands more than Demosthenes ever electrified in the popular assembly.

Such are the present prospects of civilization. It is plain that if the civilized nations of Europe and America were left to themselves, untrammelled by the feudal forms, and freed from despotism whether monarchical or demoratic, a long career of progress would be before us. But the same cause which has so often checked civilization for centuries may again devastate Europe. War is the greatest foe of Progress. War has often annihilated the most magnificent civilizations. Foreign aggression ruined Egypt. A foreign war destroyed Carthage; and the northern coast of Africa has never recovered from the devastations committed two thousand years ago by the Roman soldiers. Rome, by war, destroyed the Grecian civilization. The northern barbarians annihilated the Roman Empire. The Mahometans conquered the civilization which, under the Greek emperors, a second time arose on the banks of the Hellespont. In every country the ruins of lost civilizations appear destroyed by War.

As nations advance in knowledge and enjoy self-government, wars for the sake of mere conquest between states in the same stage of civilization become more difficult. A shop-keeper in London or Paris is unwilling to pay armies; and, personally, has more dislike to serve as a soldier than a Zouave, a Cossack, or a Croat. The United States of America, by the absence of a standing army, appear incapable of carrying on a foreign war of aggression with a distant and powerful country. Foreign aggression is easiest when the strength of a nation can be wielded by one man under a military despotism. Such power was possessed by Attila. Such power is possessed by the three emperors of Europe, or, to speak more correctly, by the Governments of Russia, Austria, and France. The barbarian soldiery of Russia are now as fierce, ignorant, and savage as they were a thousand years ago; still they are not the rude spear-armed militia of Totila. Clothed from the looms of England, armed with Prussian muskets and spring-bayonets, skilled in the science of the French engineers and artillery, the Russian battalions crossed the Carpathians under Nicholas I., and in our own memory annihilated the representative government and the free institutions of the Magyar aristocracy.

The present system of the military empires of Europe leaves the most beautiful portions of the earth without representative government, either central or local — without freedom of thought — without liberty of the press — without that personal security which Englishmen have, that, on the trial where the Government prosecutes a political accusation, the judges shall be impartially chosen from the people themselves. Under these despotical systems the whole energy of the State is centralized in the metropolis, and the only check upon arbitrary power is the fear of assassination.

The project of perpetual peace was prominently brought forward by Kant towards the close of the eighteenth century. Some of the articles of his theoretical treaty of a perpetual peace are essential to study. One of the most important is the disbanding of those vast armies which now consume the wealth of the most powerful states. Standing armies — *miles perpetuus* — ought to disappear entirely with time. For these appearing always ready for the combat incessantly threaten other powers with war, and excite states to surpass one another in the quantity of their troops. This rivalry is a source of expense, which ends by rendering peace more burdensome than a short war. National debts ought not to be contracted for the purpose of interests external to the State. This system of credit is a treasure always ready for war. The only security for the preservation of universal peace is in the freedom of the Constitution of each State. Where citizens are free and have in their own hands the government, they hesitate to declare against themselves the calamities of war; but where the subjects are not citizens, the sovereign and the governing classes having little to fear for their personal comforts, may declare war upon the most frivolous reasons.

The abolition of standing armies, the restriction of national debts, and the independence of representative constitutions are the only guarantees of peace.

# *CHAPTER II*
# *ETHICS IN RELATION TO JURISPRUDENCE*

Ethics is the Science of Moral Duties.

The purpose of the physical sciences throughout all their provinces is to answer the question "what is?" They consist only of facts, arranged according to their likeness, and expressed by general names given to every class of similar facts. The purpose of the moral sciences is to answer both the questions, "what is?" and "what ought to be?" They aim at ascertaining the rules which ought to govern voluntary action, and to which those habitual dispositions of mind which are the source of voluntary action ought to be adapted.[6]

The possibility of erecting Ethics into a science can be consistently disputed by those only who question the veracity of that consciousness, which immediately shows to us the existence and operation of a moral faculty.

---

[6] Sir James Mackintosh.

The arguments against the existence of a moral faculty are generally founded upon the gross insensibility to moral distinctions exhibited by uneducated children or savage nations; or upon instances of persons who, from various causes, have counted those things right which we deem wrong, or esteemed actions as praiseworthy which we regard with abhorrence. But such exceptional and anomalous cases are nothing to the purpose. When we are told of the absurdities and self-contradictions believed, or at least professed, by whole nations as certain truths — when we are reminded that children and uneducated peasants do not readily assent at first hearing to the very axioms of science, we are not apt to be greatly disconcerted by such cavils against the existence of reason. The case is similar with respect to imperfect or diseased manifestations of our moral nature. Moral blindness, if it really exist at all, is a phenomenon far too rare to be taken into account in the psychology of man. The gootre is, indeed, a melancholy instance of the evil results of a depressing physical condition; the Chinese woman's foot displays remarkably the power of bad training; but the anatomist of healthy humanity does not describe gootres and club-feet as our normal condition. Hume, who industriously traversed the history of our race to collect all the instances of aberration which have resulted from neglect or imperfect study of the moral consciousness, is constrained to conclude that the principles upon which men reason in morals are always the same, though their conclusions are often very different: and Dugald Stewart observes, no less beautifully than ingeniously, that the histories of human imbecility are, in truth, the strongest testimonies which can be produced to prove how wonderful is the influence of the fundamental principles of morality over the belief, when they are able to sanctify in the apprehension of mankind every extravagant opinion which early education has taught us to associate with them. Such are their opinions. Though the obscure character of psychological law, the influence of predominating passions, or the capricious action of human volition, may interfere with the inferential process in morals — and though the peculiar difficulties by which the moral philosopher is embarrassed, arising from the unavoidable use of a terminology impressed with the laxity of colloquial language, may render futile the attempt to compete with the geometrician in the simplicity and lucidity of his deductions, yet his process is identical with the geometrical method. Could we, indeed, shut out human volition, and the action of disturbing fancies, mankind would no more differ about the conclusions to be drawn from the primary elements of Ethics than about the deductions from geometrical postulates and definitions. Nor are the moral sciences alone exposed to the uncertainty arising from disturbing influences. There are elements in meteorology and in the laws of the tides which are unaccountable, and for which allowance must be made in the calculations which compute their effects in any given instance. We are not, then, to relinquish, on account of these disturbing influences and great obstacles, the erection of an imposing group of moral sciences on grounds quite as solid as those which refer to the material world. We find a scientific basis furnished to Ethics in the laws of our moral constitution; their nature, value, and the truths guaranteed by them, can be determined only by inductive investigation — the common method of "The Athenian Verulam and the British Plato."

It is quite evident that Bacon meant his method to be applicable to psychology and morals as well as to physics; he expressly declares it. In the one branch of philosophy as in the other there should be an orderly observation of facts, accompanied by analysis, or, as he expresses it, the necessary exclusions of things indifferent. This should be followed by a process of generalization in which we seize on the points of agreement. The only essential difference between the two lies in this, that in the one we take the senses, and in the other consciousness as our informant.

The only question of any difficulty respecting an inductive treatment of morals seems to be this: Does such a treatment mean that there are no *a priori* or intuitive principles of moral guidance, which, instead of deriving their authority from experience, are fitted and intended to sanction experience? Does not such a procedure expose us to the danger of substituting empirical generalizations and accidental associations for necessary truths and eternal principles? — of confounding, like the Athenian sophists, an average morality with an absolute standard of rectitude?

This objection is based on a misapprehension of the scientific process. To identify ethical truth with vulgar credence, or to adjust it to the fluctuating standard which the popular market supplies in every age to the demands of each succeeding generation, would be fatal to the very idea of a real moral law. A series of facts brought forward to show the general acknowledgement among men of a moral truth, must be carefully distinguished from an induction of a physical law from facts observed. The principles operate *a priori,* and independently of experience; they cannot become known to us, or be employed as philosophic principles, till we have determined their nature, rule, and limits by methodized observation. The distinction between moral good and evil — the obligation to shun the evil and do the good — are laws which, like the laws of logic, man discovers in his own nature, and which have their origin in himself, as they have their application in his actual life.[7] Moral laws are put into a man's soul or mind as into a treasure or repository, some in his very nature, some in after actions, by education and positive sanction.[8] The moralist refers for judgment on the necessary truths he enounces, not to voluminous statistics, however undeniably useful such records may be as a definite expression of certain facts in our social economy, and entitled as they are to an intermediate place between morals and politics; he bids the student descend into his own consciousness — the depths of his own personality — and observe what he finds there: —

> "To search through all he felt or saw,
> The springs of life, the depths of awe,
> And reach the law within the law."

Mental laws thus inductively determined are henceforward to be regarded as primary principles, and are open at once to the sweeping range of direct deduction. And again, experience has its part, in which there is an immensity to be done, not in the way of invading the domain of the exact science, but in that of extending our knowledge of the facts to which it is to be applied. Where the science of intuitive morals ends, there the science of the experimentalist meets it; and by a process which modern logicians have named traduction we pass from one order of reasoning to the other, and complete a science of Ethics practically applicable to every detail of life. And thus a method, constructed

---

[7] Guizot.
[8] Jeremy Taylor.

after the aphorism of Bacon, secures to the experimental as well as to the purely rational element its own approximate value, assigns to each its own place, and shows how the two are inseparably united, and how they mutually confirm and illustrate each other.

"Alterius sic
Altera poscit opem res, et conjurat amice."

The preceding general views may be illustrated by the following passage from Kant: — "It is more particularly in the region of morals that Plato discovers his ideas. Moral truth rests upon liberty, and liberty is under the government of laws which spring from the reason itself. Whoever would rest the idea of virtue upon experience, and establish as a model that which can Scarcely serve as an example in any important practical application, would render virtue altogether uncertain, make it dependent upon time and circumstances, and render the formation of any rules impossible. Every one on the contrary, can see that if any person were held up to him as a model of virtue, it is only in himself that the true type exists, to which the proposed model might be compared, and, consequently, appreciated. Now, this type is the idea of virtue; the objects of experience may, indeed, serve as examples to show that what the reason demands is, up to a certain point, possible in practice; but the archetype itself is not there. Because a man never acts in accordance with the pure idea he has of virtue, it does not follow that the idea itself is a mere chimera; for it is only by means of this idea that moral judgments are formed at all; it is, consequently, the foundation of moral perfection, so far at least as this is possible, considering the obstacles which human nature presents, which are, however, indeterminate. The Republic of Plato has become proverbial as the expression of an imaginary perfection, which can only exist in a disordered brain; and Brucker ridicules the notion that a prince could never govern well unless penetrated by the theory of ideas. But, instead of throwing aside Plato's thought as useless, under the pretext that it is incapable of realization, would it not be better to attempt a development of it, and by renewed efforts draw it from the obscurity in which that excellent genius has left it? The obstacles arise less, perhaps, from the inevitable evils attached to human nature than from a neglect of these veritable ideas in legislation. There can be nothing more unworthy of a philosopher than to appeal to an experience which is acknowledged to be in contradiction to these ideas; for what would have been the experience itself if the institutions in question had been established under happier auspices, conformably to ideas, and if, instead, other ideas, gross and rude, just because they are derived from experience, had not rendered every good design useless? In all that has reference to the principles of morals, and legislation, where ideas alone render experience possible, Plato possesses a merit that is peculiar to him, and which we are prevented from recognising only because we judge according to empirical rules, whose value as principles is as nothing compared with that of ideas. In reference to external nature, experience may, indeed, furnish rules, since, in this case, it is the source of truth; but in reference to morals, experience is the mother of illusion; and it is altogether error to reason from that which is done, or attempt to limit it by laws which have especial reference to that which ought to be done."

> "Powers depart,
> Possessions vanish, and opinions change,
> And passions hold a fluctuating seat:
> But by the storms of circumstance unshaken,
> And subject neither to eclipse nor wave,
> Duty exists; — immutably survive,
> For our support, the measures and the forms
> Which an abstract intelligence supplies,
> Whose kingdom is where time and space are not."

The historical method of inquiry has been recommended by some, as by Schleiermacher, with whom Ethics is an investigation of human nature in its forms and tendencies developing itself in history. It must be conceded that history supplies to Ethics its most valuable illustrations; but as human action is always presented in history as a complex web in which good and evil are mixed together, it is needful to have a test to determine which is the one and which the other. We are thus brought back to the inductive investigation of man's moral constitution as the only method of constructing a scientific Ethics in reference to Jurisprudence.

A most successful illustration of this inductive treatment of moral phenomena will be found in the ethical writings of Butler: — "There are two ways," writes Butler, "in which the subject of morals may be treated. One begins from inquiring into the abstract relations of things; the other from a matter of fact, namely, what the particular nature of man is, its several parts, their economy or constitution; from whence it proceeds to determine what course of life it is which is correspondent to this whole nature. In the former method the conclusion is expressed thus — that vice is contrary to the nature and reason of things; in the latter, that it is a violation or breaking in upon our own nature." Of the former method, the system of Clarke, that virtue is a conformity with the relations of things; and that of Wollaston — that virtue consisted in acting according to truth, are the most eminent examples. These systems which were recommended by the intellectual spirit of the age in which they were produced, when the splendid discoveries of Descartes, of Leibnitz, and of Newton had so dazzled the mind of Europe, have now become obsolete. The latter procedure was universally employed by the ancient moralists; and Butler systematically applying it, "occupying the unassailable ground of an appeal to consciousness," has established, by reasons superfluously conclusive, not merely the existence, but also the authoritative character and the implicit sanction of the moral law. It is as invested with these majestic attributes of eternity, immutability, and universal authority that the greatest masters of philosophy and eloquence, both in ancient and in modern times, have loved to contemplate and depict the Moral Faculty. Thus Cicero says: — Right reason is itself a law congenial to the feelings of nature, diffused among all men, uniform, eternal, calling us imperiously to our duty, and peremptorily prohibiting every violation of it. Nor does it speak one language at Rome and another at Athens, varying from place to place, or from time to time; but it addresses itself to all nations, and to all ages, deriving its authority from the common sovereign of the universe, and carrying home its sanctions to every breast by the inevitable punishment which it inflicts on transgressors. Seneca says —There is a holy spirit throned within us, of our good and evil deeds the Guardian and the Observer. As He is treated by us, even so He treats us. Fenelon says — Le Maitre interieur et universel dit toujours et par tout les mêmes verités. Under the same aspect the moral law is presented by Kant, when he calls it the Categorical Imperative whose absolute rule is — Act according to a maxim which would admit of being regarded as a general law for all acting beings. And Lord Brougham says — There is a law above all the enactments of human codes — the same throughout the world — the same in all times — it is the law written by the finger of God upon the heart of man.

# *CHAPTER III*
# *POLITICAL ECONOMY*

Political Economy is the Science of Exchanges.

The bountiful earth, under the varying influences of soil and climate, produces different things useful and agreeable to man. In tropical climates nature turns every field into a garden; there trees of beautiful form bear rich fruits; there grow the shrubs from which we obtain our spices, and variegated flowers bloom in wanton profusion. The organic richness and abundant fertility belonging to such districts enable them to produce the luxuries of civilized life. Countries more temperate afford vines and wheat. Some places abound in iron and coal; others in gold and silver. All civilized nations require to exchange some of their own productions for those of others; and upon such exchanges does the very existence of civilized life depend.

Between one country and another obstacles exist — seas, mountains, rivers, forests. These things throw difficulties in the way of transit; and to facilitate the operations of commerce the ingenuity of man invents speedy and safe modes of conveyance. Canals are made, harbours widened, rivers deepened, navigation improved. Rapid steamers triumph against the winds; railways pierce mountains and cross seas. Here, Political Economy shows how absurd and inconsistent it is that states should undergo the greatest expense, by building magnificent railways to facilitate intercourse, and at the same time should check intercourse by commercial restrictions and taxes which artificially raise prices.

All the phenomena which occur in the free interchanges of the productions of one place for those of another, the rise and fall of prices, and the reasons for the respective values of commodities, all the questions connected with capital and labour — every thing relating to exchanges, it is the province of Political Economy to investigate. No subjects can be more important; and the investigation of them upon sound principles, now proceeding in most of the civilized nations of Europe, must eventually produce important results on the commerce, the prosperity, the progress of the world.

At first, when this science began to be extensively cultivated, objections were made to it, on the grounds that wealth is not a proper subject for our study, for with it increase also corruption and vice. Persons have derived ideas of this kind from the early study of the Greek and Roman writers; the minds of classical students retain through life the ideas of Cincinnatus nobly poor, and the black broth upon which Leonidas and his Spartans lived. The Roman writers praised sumptuary laws, and declaimed with all the strength of their powerful language against the degeneracy of their fellow-citizens from the old Republican times, ere they knew the refined arts of Greece, or enjoyed the plundered riches of the East.

But no fatal union necessarily exists between national wealth and national corruption. Greece at the time of her greatest material prosperity flourished most in eloquence, in arts, and arms. The Netherlands, in the time of Charles V., were the most industrious and, for their amount of territory, the wealthiest nation in the world — they exhibited no want of devoted heroism, no want of fiery independence. France in modern times has obtained from a union of wealth with the national taste polished manners and refined luxury; but they have not been found to damp her heroism or enervate the national spirit. And although England, like ancient Tyre, has her merchants who are princes, her traffickers who are the honourable of the earth, she still sits very glorious in the middle of the seas, and enriches the kings of the earth with the multitude of her riches and her merchandize. We may banish, then, the idea that the abundant returns of industry, the fruits of genius, the boundless extent of commerce, the exuberance of wealth, and the cultivation of the liberal arts, are enervating to the national spirit, or dangerous to the national liberty. Liberty depends upon the structure of the government, the administration of justice, and the intelligence of the people. It has little to do with wealth, or poverty, or soil, or climate.

The science of Political Economy is of recent origin.

In the first stages of society, wealth, in the present popular meaning, can scarcely be said to exist. The wandering tribes of savages live by hunting and fishing; their habitations are formed of the bark of trees; their wealth consists of the skins which they wear, their weapons of the chase, and their canoes. We see this phase of society exemplified at the present day among the American Indians.

In the progress of society, the next step to this is the pastoral state, in which tribes of men united under the patriarchal system of government, have flocks and live upon their produce. This state is now exemplified among the Tartars of Central Asia.

From this the transition to the agricultural state is easy, in which there are more opportunities for accumulating wealth, and in which civilization rapidly progresses. Next in history arise the civilized nations of antiquity of which we have authentic record.

In Egypt and many other oriental nations there was great wealth; but they laboured under the oppressive despotisms which exist there to the present day. The bulk of the population was in slavery. The government, owning all the land of the country, was enabled to compel the cultivators to labour, and then to deprive them of the produce. The Pyramids of Egypt have often been mentioned with wonder, as evidences of the greatness of that civilization which was able to leave such great memorials. To me, on the other hand, reflecting that they were raised by forced unpaid labour of thousands of miserable beings perishing at the task, they have always seemed to exhibit only proofs of the senseless vanity of tyrants, who dragged so many of their subjects together, and forced them unpaid to raise useless heaps of stones, when those unhappy persons would have been better employed in building comfortable though perishable houses for themselves, and living there with their families.

In Egypt, the sacerdotal caste alone attended to intellectual affairs, whilst the rest of the population was sunk in ignorance. The entire system of castes was strictly enforced. These castes still prevail throughout the East; and the system this moment may be seen in full vigour in parts of India, where Brahmins and their children's children must be priests for ever — where the descendants of soldiers must always be soldiers — where none of the natives who live strictly according to the tenets of their religion can leave the trade or business which their fathers followed — where the miserable Sudras must be slaves for ever. This system in India originated in the worst of despotisms. Brutal oppression characterized the governing classes, grovelling superstition debased the rest. Let us trust that the civilization of the Western Islands may yet abolish the castes of India.

In modern civilized societies there are many examples of men of humble birth raising themselves to the highest position and the greatest fortunes. Under the ancient tyrannies it was impossible for the phenomena attending the free competition of capital and labour to arise — it was impossible for the principles of taxation to be discussed, since taxes were nothing but plunder taken by the powerful from the humble.

In these old times the universal reign of rapine prevented the study of the social sciences from flourishing; notwithstanding that some nations successfully cultivated Literature and the Arts. Things now only practised by the outcasts, were then the pursuits of the leaders of society. Thus, Homer introduces Nestor asking Telemachus whether he and his friends were pirates or merchants: —

> "Say, what the cause — why, traversing the main,
> Steer you from port to port in quest of gain?
> Or to and fro, like roving pirates stray,
> Who, injuring others, cast their lives away?"
>
> — Odyssey, Book III.

The writer evidently did not consider that profession dishonourable which now is punished by the rope, and for the destruction of which civilized nations now offer head-money for slain pirates.

Athens, in the time of Pericles, flourished in wealth; her poets and orators hold still a foremost place amongst the intellect of the world; her architecture is still a model for us; her art is still contemplated by all succeeding time with admiring despair. Rome, under the later Republic, and in the time of the Emperors, accumulated such wealth as London now can scarcely rival, and in Taste and Art surpassed the Paris of the Napoleons. Why, then, did not these countries cultivate the science which treats of the operations that bring the produce of one climate to another, and enable the inhabitants of any district enjoying a fair share of wealth to possess the luxuries of the most remote zones, without the discomforts attending their production? One reason was, the utter contempt with which trade was regarded by the classic times. The citizens of the ancient States, even those enjoying the highest degree of freedom, all despised trade. Those branches of commercial and manufacturing industry which have raised our modern civilization to so great a height, and without which it would at once disappear, were scorned by the warlike citizens of Greece and Rome. Plato excluded tradesmen from his Republic. Cicero, although in most respects so far in advance of his age, thought commerce only not very despicable — "haud admodum vituperanda." He says also, "I do not wish the same people to be the ruler and the carrier of the world," — "Nolo eundem populum imperatorem, et portitorem esse terrarum." Yet it has been the boast of Venice, Holland, and England in succession to be the carrier of the world — portitor terrarum. The Romans prohibited commerce to persons of birth, rank, and fortune, and no senator was allowed a vessel larger than a boat sufficient to carry his wine, corn, and fruits. The military aristocracy of Rome, without trade or commerce, sought wealth in the only manner which can take the place of production — plunder. The wealth of Rome was plunder taken openly from the countries successively overrun by the victorious Roman armies; the principal taxes by which in latter times the Roman government subsisted were tributes drawn from conquered provinces.

The very sense in which the word tributum came to be used, shows how unfair was this — one of the earliest taxes in Rome. It was called tributum, being paid by the thirty plebeian tribes instituted as has been supposed by Servius Tullius. It derived its subsequent meaning from being a partial tax, not paid by the patricians, and a badge of servitude upon the plebeians. I am aware that it is a moot-point amongst historians whether these tribes included the patricians or not; but I consider that the sense in which the word tributum came to be used finally is upon this question decisive.

The wealth of Rome was principally plunder drawn from conquered countries. As each partly civilized nation in turn yielded to the terror of the Roman armies, its wealth accumulated for centuries, was transferred to Rome and spent in a season. Whilst nations thus afforded plunder, Italy flourished in wealth, and was covered with the most magnificent public and private edifices. But when no more new countries could be overcome, and when the tributes could no longer be exacted from the inhabitants of the provinces, the resources of Italy were not sufficient to keep those magnificent edifices from mouldering to decay. The ancient world had within it the fatal principles of decay — the despotism of the government, the tyranny of the governing races, the slavery and ignorance of the masses of the people. The old civilization fell to pieces upon the invasion of the hardy barbarians of the North, and the dark ages for a time covered Europe with a cloud.

When Learning began again to be cultivated, and when the European Universities were founded, the old prejudice against trade and commerce still survived. The Feudal System flourished. The principle of the Feudal System was, that a dominant race tyrannized over a subjected one. The feudal lords extorted from the serfs their property, and insisted on their labour without paying them for it. No man could possess the absolute property of the land. The greatest contempt was manifested for trade. Warriors, in the early ages, contemned the rights of property in all unable to protect themselves by arms. The very name of warrior signifies a robber in its origin; no nobleman or gentleman in the feudal times would sully himself by embracing any profession except that of arms — or the Church. As a proof of the great contempt for trade which once existed in England, now the first commercial nation upon the earth, the most lucrative and flourishing branches of trade there were permitted to fall into the hands of despised strangers, the Jews and Lombards. The Jews invented bills of exchange, without which or some similar documents the vast mercantile operations now based upon credit could not be conducted. The Lombards invented shipping insurances. In this state of society none of the phenomena could prominently appear which arise from the free distribution of property, and from the unrestrained competition of capital and labour. None would consider about the cheapest and best mode of taxation whilst taxes were the property of governing races, who consumed them all for their own benefit, and were careless about the welfare of the producers. War was then the great business of nations, and the attention of government in matters of taxation was directed merely to the most effectual means of raising the supplies to meet the expenses of continual warfare. The best statesman was he who raised most taxes with least trouble from the oppressed common people.

The great discoveries of the fifteenth century began to destroy Feudalism. The invention of gunpowder caused the castles and armour of the barons to be useless, by means of which they had been enabled so long to prevent and defy any general law of the realm, and to live upon the plunder of the poor. It was found that a regiment of labourers, disciplined for six months, and armed with the weapons introduced by this wonderful discovery were superior in the battle-field to the bravest knights, mounted on splendid horses, and clad in costly armour. But the new weapons were expensive; there, again, the wealth of the towns was of more use than the chivalry of the castles. The great invention of Printing diffused knowledge amongst all. The great geographical discoveries gave a new impetus to commerce, which, from its wealth and extended operations, began no longer to be despised. Slavery by degrees vanished from the whole of Western Europe. Thus, with the decline of the Feudal System arose that commercial and manufacturing spirit which is now beginning to be the great moving power of the world.

Once, therefore, that the settled conditions of modern society began to arise in Western Europe, the serfs, emancipated from the feudal system, were enabled to dispose of their labour at the price which they considered sufficiently remunerative for them; merchants, under the protection of the law, no longer feared that their property would be taken from them at the will of some baron; wealth rapidly accumulated; and some men, instead of working with their own capital, began to live upon the profits of their capital lent to others. In consequence, all the nice and complicated questions connected with capital, labour, wages, taxation, and the like, began to attract the attention of learned men, and from their studies and writings upon these important subjects has arisen the modern science of Political Economy. The origin of this science is cotemporaneous with the spread of modern civilization, the increase of commerce, the rise of public liberty.

And briefly reviewing the history of Western Europe, we may see that the march of civilization has been steady and progressive. First, the serfs are emancipated, then trade becomes honourable, and from these conditions, combined with some others, has arisen the great middle class, displaying the highest social activity, and cultivating the greatest spirit of industry ever witnessed in the world. Having accomplished so much, the spirit of progress now directs its efforts to solve the social difficulties of society; and in this, one of its chief aids is the science of Political Economy.

Some have despaired of continual progress, and assuredly all over the earth we behold the ruins of lost civilizations. In Central America, amidst forests a thousand years of age, the traveller beholds ruins of statues and temples that rival the beauty of Athenian art, and themassiveness of Egyptian architecture. They lie, broken and defaced, memorials of great and civilized nations, whose very names ages ago perished from human memory. Babylon, Nineveh, Carthage, once were great cities, and now are either heaps of ruins or effaced from the earth. Still we may anticipate that progress shall have a long career; for though sometimes for centuries it has been interrupted, yet since the dawn of history there is evidence of its continuance. We behold upon the earth places like the impassable morasses of the Amazon, breathing forth devastating epidemics, and affording to the few creatures in human form that linger there the means of dragging on but a dull and joyless existence, without usefulness or dignity. Comparatively recent history informs us that when the Athenian civilization flourished, the greater part of Europe, and now its most flourishing and civilized part, bore the same character. When Pericles lived his glorious existence, those countries which, under the names of France and Germany are covered with rich corn-fields and beautiful vineyards and have produced so many great and good men were disfigured with rocks and marshes, and were inhabited by savages inferior to the present New Zealanders. The rivers, which then formed noisome swamps, have been taught to keep their channels, and are covered with steamers; the rocks are built into libraries and cathedrals; and the descendants of the savages who dwelt there have been brought under the dominion of Law, and into the habits of peaceful life. So also, in the North and South Americas, Australia, and the islands of the Pacific and Southern Oceans, savage life is everywhere being replaced by civilization.

It thus appears that there is a natural tendency in mankind to rise from barbarism to civilization; and it is gratifying to see that the means of subsistence are pro-portionably more abundant in a civilized than in a savage state. "Knowledge, security of property, freedom of internal and external exchange, are the principal causes which at the same time promote the increase of subsistence, and elevate the character of the people; restrictions on exchange and commerce, artificial barriers excluding the great majority of the community from the chance of social eminence, and above all, ignorance and insecurity of person and property, are the general causes which produce improvidence and misery."[9]

In the popular liberty, which has enabled so many men of humble birth in modern times to raise themselves to the high positions which they have adorned, we see the best proofs of the high character of our modern civilization. In the development of society civilized nations have arrived at that stage where commerce is free, where industry is honoured. The fruits of labour are protected by the law, its exertions are respected, and the contempt which its industrious energy received at the hands of the rude soldiers of ancient times, is now reserved for the idle.

The study of the social sciences has aided to produce these sentiments beginning to pervade the heart of modern society. I have always considered that the study of the social sciences, such as Jurisprudence and Political Economy, should form a part of the general education of all, the poorest as well as the richest in the land. The sciences may be placed in two divisions. Some of necessity need to be known only to those who practise them professionally. We all can enjoy the fullest benefit of the mechanical sciences notwithstanding our ignorance of them. Few are acquainted with the mechanism of the steam-engine, yet millions enjoy the benefits of railway travelling. But sciences, like morality, jurisprudence, medicine, and political economy, derive their efficacy, not from the knowledge concentrated in particular professions, but from the general correct knowledge of them diffused through the public; and these sciences have this striking peculiarity, that no one confesses his absolute ignorance of them. Every one every day practises morality, jurisprudence, medicine, and political economy, let them be good or bad — and they are often very bad. Hence arises the importance of general education upon these subjects. And as regards political economy, I may say there are no subjects more interesting than those about which this science is conversant. They are those which concern every individual in the community; they are those upon which, in a very

[9] Senior.

great measure, individual and national prosperity depend. There is no one who does not buy and sell, who does not pay taxes, who does not employ labour or is employed. And there cannot be upon earth a study of more extended dignity and usefulness, more becoming to philanthropy and patriotism, than the requisite and practical reform of the social institutions of the country — the solution of the social difficulties of the day. It is right to cultivate this social knowledge. By the study of these liberal sciences we shall the more assist the diffusion of the sentiments now spreading throughout the world and by means of which all enlightened men regard the human race, without distinction, as one family aspiring to one common aim — the development of the faculties with which they have been endowed. The Social Sciences are of no one country, they belong to the entire world. Those who cultivate them, though separated by distance and by language, yet understand one another. Fellow-countrymen in thought they form one vast intellectual society of citizens of the world, pursuing the same end, the discovery of universal truth, — animated by one feeling, the patriotism of Civilization.[10]

I now proceed to give the definitions of the terms used in these pages, and which are at present generally received in Economical Science. They are taken principally from the works of J. S. Mill and Senior, and are the result of the labours of modern economists.

Wealth comprehends all those things which are transferable, limited in supply, and possess utility.

The constituents of wealth are Utility, Limitation in supply, and Transferableness.

Limitation in supply is the most important of all the constituents of Wealth, and has the greatest effect upon Value.

Value is the quality in any thing which fits it to be given and received in Exchange.

The intrinsic causes of the value of a commodity are those which give to it utility and limit it in supply. The extrinsic causes are those which limit the supply, and occasion the utility of the commodities for which it is to be exchanged.

Steadiness in value depends on the permanence of the in-

---

[10] Mignet.

trinsic causes of value.

Senior states four elementary propositions of the science of Political Economy: —

1. That every man desires to obtain additional wealth with as little sacrifice as possible:

2. That the population of the world, or, in other words, the number of persons inhabiting it, is limited only by moral and physical evil, or by fear of a deficiency of those articles of wealth which the habits of the individuals of each class of its inhabitants lead them to require:

3. That the powers of Labour and of the other instruments which produce wealth may be indefinitely increased by using their products as the means of further production:

4. That Agricultural skill remaining the same, additional labour employed on the land within a given district produces in general a less proportionate return, or in other words, that though, with every increase of the labour bestowed, the aggregate return is increased, the increase of the return is not in proportion to the increase of the labour.

Production is the occasioning an alteration in the condition of the existing particles of matter, for the occasioning of which alteration, or for the things thence resulting, something may be obtained in Exchange. This alteration is a product.

Products are divided into services and commodities. A Service is the act of occasioning the above mentioned alteration. A Commodity is the thing as altered. The real limits to Production are the limited quantity and limited productiveness of land.

Consumption is the making use of a thing.

Productive Consumption is that use of a product which occasions an ulterior product. Unproductive Consumption is that use which occasions no ulterior product.

The instruments of production are Land, Labour, and Capital.

Labour is the voluntary exertion of bodily or mental faculties for the purpose of production.

Productive Labour is that which produces utility fixed and embodied in material objects. All other labour, however useful, is classed as unproductive.

Capital is wealth applied to reproductive employment.

The fundamental propositions as to capital are: — 1st, Industry is limited by capital; 2nd, Capital is the result of saving; 3rd, All Capital is consumed; 4th, Capital is kept up, not by preservation, but by perpetual reproduction.

The advantages derived from the use of Capital are the use of implements, and the division of Labour.

The whole annual produce of the country is divided into rent, profit, and wages. So Society is divided into the three classes, Labourers, Capitalists, and Landlords, each class having a different instrument, a different conduct, and a different remuneration. Production takes place either under a monopoly or not under a monopoly.

Monopolies are divided into four kinds: —

1. A monopoly under which the monopolist has not the exclusive power of producing but exclusive facilities as a producer, which may be employed indefinitely with equal or increasing advantage. The illustration of this is a patent for manufactures.

2. A monopoly under which the monopolist is the only producer, and cannot increase the amount of his produce. The illustration of this is a vineyard, *e. g.*, Johannisberg.

3. A monopoly under which the monopolist is the only producer, and can increase indefinitely with equal or increasing advantage the amount of his produce. The illustration of this is copyright in books.

4. A monopoly under which the monopolist is not the only producer, but has peculiar facilities which diminish and ultimately disappear as he increases the amount of his produce.

The last is the great monopoly of land.

Wages are the reward of Labour.

The promixate cause deciding the rate of wages is the extent of the fund for the maintenance of Labourers, compared with the number of Labourers to be maintained.

The causes on which the extent of the fund for the maintenance of Labourers really depends are — 1. The productiveness of Labour in the direct or indirect production of the Commodities used by the Labourers:

2. The number of persons directly or indirectly employed in the production of things for the use of Labourers compared with the whole number of labouring families.

The causes on which the productiveness of Labour depends are — 1. The Corporeal intellectual and moral qualities of the

Labourer: 2. The assistance of natural Agents: 3. The assistance of capital: 4. The existence or the absence of Government interference.

The causes which divert Labour from the production of commodities for the use of labouring families are Rent, Taxation, and Profit.

Profit consists of the difference between the value of the advance made by the Capitalist and the value of the return. It is divided into three portions — Interest, Insurance, and the wages of Superintendence.

The facts which decide in what proportion the Capitalists and Labourers share the fund after the deduction of rent and taxation are two — first, the general rate of profit in the country on the advance of capital for a given period, and, secondly, the period which in each particular case has elapsed between the advance of the capital and the receipt of the profit.

The cause regulating the rate of profit is the proportion which the supply of capital employed in providing wages bears to the supply of Labourers.

The causes of variation in the amount of wages, and the rate of profits in different employments of Labour and Capital are assigned by Adam Smith: — 1. Agreeableness; 2. Facility of learning the business; 3. Constancy of employment; 4. Trustworthiness; 5. Probability of success.

Money is the medium of Exchange, and is the measure of Value.

# *CHAPTER IV*
# *JURISPRUDENCE*

## 1. Jurisprudence

The term Jurisprudence has been used in very different senses. Originally it meant the science of Right. Afterwards it was used to mean knowledge of the principles of law, or skill in its practice. In the Institutes of Justinian Jurisprudence is defined to be the knowledge of what is just and unjust. Upon the revival of learning in Europe in the sixteenth century, Jurisprudence was used to signify knowledge of the Roman Law. The term has also been used in a sense borrowed from the French to imply a collection of the principles belonging to particular branches of law — thus, Equity Jurisprudence, Maritime Jurisprudence. The term has also been used to signify the whole body of the law of a State — thus, the Jurisprudence of England.

The philological meanings of legal terms best illustrate legal history. There are three phases in the development of law — the religious, technical, and scientific. In the origin of society, every disputed question in law is referred to the decision of God. In all languages the legal terms of pleading causes originally imply the idea of prayer. Trials are by ordeal and by battle amongst all nations in an early state of civilization.

In the second phase of law, nations, by means of preappointed evidence and forms of a minute and cumulative nature, endeavour to attain certainty. Seven Roman Citizens were originally necessary to attest a Roman will. Under the English law, Twelve Jurors must unanimously find a prisoner guilty before he can receive punishment. Justice under such a system becomes minute and technical. The Judges often knowingly do what is unjust in carrying out the letter of the law. The maxim of this second phase is — let justice be done though the Heavens should fall — *fiat justitia, ruat cœlum.* Justice and the corresponding terms in this phase of law mean equality of division in all languages.

Finally, men begin to perceive that there are natural principles of Right and Wrong; and, in the third phase of law, endeavour to attain Truth and Justice by the aid of Reason and Experience.

Whilst the first and second phases prevail amongst a nation, Law cannot be scientifically cultivated. In the third phase the possibility is admitted of arriving at a complete Science of Law or Science of Right. In other words, the possibility is admitted of collecting and arranging in methodical order the fundamental principles which explain the origin of laws and their development towards perfection. Some term is necessary to denote the Science of Law, and I shall so employ the word Jurisprudence. No science can be possibly developed without method, nomenclature, and classification.

*"Nomina si pereant, perit et cognitio rerum."*

Method facilitates comprehension, abridges labour, assists the memory, and trains the intellect to accurate judgment. In every species of knowledge, disorder in language is at once the effect and the cause of ignorance and error. Nomenclature can only be perfected in proportion as truth is discovered. The classification of laws has never yet been adopted upon the grand scale demanded by Jurisprudence. If a system of law were correctly framed, and if codes of laws were drafted on one true principle by all civilized nations, the language of each race would serve as a glossary by which all systems of positive law might be explained; whilst the matter in each code would afford a test and standard by which all might be tried. Thus classified and illustrated, the practice of every nation might be a lesson to every other, and mankind might carry on a mutual intercourse of experiences and improvements as easily in Law as in every other domain of Art and Science.

By Law is here understood Positive Law — that is, the law existing by position, or, the law of human enactment. Jurisprudence is the Science of Positive Laws, and, as such, is the theory of those duties which are capable of being enforced by the public authority. Jurisprudence, so treated, may take its place as one of those inductive sciences in which, by the observation of facts and the use of reason, systems of doctrine have been established which are universally received as truths among thoughtful men.

But Jurisprudence in its investigation of the origin, principles, and development of law, obviously furnishes rules which teach men to acknowledge and select good laws, to shun evil laws, and to practise the existing laws and apply them skilfully. Hence, Jurisprudence is not only the Science of Positive Laws but is also the Art of Legislation and the Practice of Advocacy. A Jurist may state principles of law in his study, enact laws in the senate, or advocate rights in the forum.

A Science is a collection of Truths: an Art is a collection of Rules for Conduct.

The end of Science is Truth. The end of Art is Work.

Since Science is conversant about speculative knowledge only, and Art is the application of knowledge to practice, Jurisprudence, when applied to practice, whether in making of laws as in Legislation, or in the actual working of the law as in Advocacy, is an art; but Jurisprudence, when confined to the theory of law, is strictly a science.

The same term may be strictly applied to both the science

and its corresponding art, as Logic is not only the Science of Thought but is also the Art of Reasoning. So, that I may give an example taken from the practice of the law: Conveyancing is the Science and also the Art of Alienation. If by an investigation of the laws of property we elicit and systematize the principles which govern its disposition, we are then forming the science. If we apply this knowledge in the alienation of property, we are skilful in the art.

The art may exist without the corresponding science having arrived at any degree of cultivation. If the knowledge applied to practice be merely accumulated experience, it is empirical; but if it be illustrated by history and philosophy, and brought under general principles, it becomes a science. Thus, Sir Edward Coke was an empirical lawyer; his writings are a chaos of ill-digested learning. Judge Story was a scientific jurist of a high class, who in his works rises from rules of practice to the principles of eternal justice.

In every age and country different laws produce different results, the same laws generally produce the same results. Observing, then, the actions of mankind differing in the different grades of civilization, it is possible to estimate what rules for human conduct in civil society produce the most beneficial effects. If the physical sciences regard what is, and the mental sciences both what is and what ought to be; so the jurist, in the investigation of the Science of Right, should strive to make the actual law approach the Ideal of Legal Perfection.

## 2. Distinction between Ethics and Jurisprudence

Thus, Jurisprudence as an art, or Legislation, has the same ratio to Jurisprudence as a science which the rules of practical morality bear to the science of Ethics.

Bentham has correctly defined the limits between the provinces of Ethics and Jurisprudence. Ethics exhibit the rules of three classes of human actions; Prudence, Probity, and Beneficence. Legislation interferes directly by means of Punishment only. Punishment should not be applied when it is groundless, inefficacious, unprofitable, or needless.

The cases where the punishment would be unprofitable constitute the great field for the exclusive interference of Ethics.

Punishment as applied to Guilt may be unprofitable in both or either of two ways — by the expense to which it would amount even supposing it to be confined altogether to delinquency — or, by the danger there may be of involving the innocent in the fate designed for the guilty.

Of the rules of moral duty those which stand least in need of the assistance of the legislator are the rules of Prudence. If one err in respect of Prudence, it must arise either from some inadvertence or misapprehension with regard to the circumstances on which his happiness depends. The rules of Probity are those which, in point of expediency, stand moat in need of legislative assistance.

The idea of Right is the bond between Ethics and Jurisprudence. Practical Morality has been defined to be the art of directing the actions of individual men to the production of the greatest possible quantity of happiness by means of such motives as offer themselves. The Art of Legislation teaches how a multitude of men composing a community may be disposed to pursue that course which is most conducive to the happiness of the entire community by means of motives which are àpplied by the Legislator. Ethics and Jurisprudence differ in the means which they employ. They coincide in one general ultimate end, the happiness of mankind by the regulation of human action.

The distinction between Ethics or the science of Moral Duties, and Jurisprudence, or the science of Positive Laws, is compulsion by public authority.

And thus discussing positive laws upon the inductive method — examining the different legislative systems of different nations, and their results upon the happiness of mankind — comparing slavery with freedom, ignorance with knowledge — accordingly as these have been checked or developed by the great forces which have swayed human destinies, we, by the observation of facts and the use of reason, selecting the good, eloigning the bad, may gradually arrive at that system of law which is most in conformity with natural justice.

But the duties of the jurist and the legislator are perfectly distinct. The business of the jurist is merely to state those general principles which are true in all times and under all circumstances. The legislator must regard the historical development of the people. And it cannot be too often repeated that all actual legislation must be a compromise between history and philosophy. No two nations ever existed having precisely the same standard of morality embodied in their laws. In no nation is the moral standard the same at different periods of its development. The law is always below the moral standard of the best citizens, and above that of the worst. The legislator must take heed that his legislation coincides with the public opinion of the mass, or the enforcement of a law becomes impossible. Thus duelling where the issue was fatal, was murder punished with death by the common law of England, but the law could not be enforced until late in the nineteenth century.

There is not in the whole compass of human affairs so noble a spectacle as that which is displayed in the progress of Jurisprudence, where we may contemplate the cautious and unwearied exertions of a succession of wise men through a long course of ages, withdrawing every case as it arises from the dangerous power of discretion, and subjecting it to inflexible rules of positive law.[11]

What can be more instructive than to search out the first obscure and scanty fountains of that Jurisprudence, which now waters and enriches whole nations with so abundant and copious a flood — to observe the first principles of right springing up involved in superstition and polluted by violence, until by length of time and favourable circumstances it has worked itself into clearness — to view the laws, sometimes lost and trodden down in the confusion of wars and tumults, and sometimes overruled by the hand of power — then victorious over tyranny, growing stronger and more decisive by the violence they have suffered; enriched even by those foreign conquests which threaten their entire destruction — softened and mellowed by peace and religion, and improved and exalted by commerce, by social intercourse, and that great opener of the mind, ingenuous science.[12]

## 3. Limits of Jurisprudence

Justice alone of the virtues can be enforced by the public authority. Jurisprudence considers what range of human actions may come within the cognizance of justice, and what rights are

---

[11] Mackintosh.

[12] Edmund Burke.

capable of being protected by the positive law. Gratitude and benevolence are virtues, but incapable of being enforced by legal means, whereas, if one citizen take the property of another, there is compensation or punishment, or both.

The true objects of the science of Jurisprudence are the knowledge of the legal relations which ought to be established by the Positive Law, and the ascertainment of the best means to enforce such relations.

These true principles of Jurisprudence are at the very base of the science of Politics; and the due ascertainment of the province of government is perhaps the most important question of modern times. But the province of government is solely concerned with those human actions which are capable of being enforced by the public authority. It is idle for a government to try to enforce those duties which are incapable of being enforced by it. Duties such as these are not easy of definition, but an idea of them may be obtained by an exhaustive process of reasoning.

There are certain virtues of exalted character which can be attained only by persons of the most splendid moral and physical organization, placed in circumstances where these innate qualities have been developed to the highest pitch of excellence. When Leonidas died for liberty and civilization in the pass of Thermopylæ, he performed a duty to mankind; but what law could enforce the self-devotion of which we read the famous examples in ancient history?

That I may take a recent example: During the battle of Paris in 1848, when the Archbishop of Paris advanced with the crucifix in his hand to meet the terrible Faubourgs St. Antoine and Marceau, careless about death provided he brought peace, he was performing a duty, but a duty incapable of enforcement. The most exalted virtues, exemplified in the great actions which ennoble humanity, are attainable by few, and are beyond legislation.

There is another class of virtues manifested in external action impossible to be enforced by legislative authority. Virtues such as these are less difficult to attain, and are more generally diffused, but still are abhorrent of compulsion.

Such is the virtue of benevolence.

Vincent de Paul devoted his life to the comfort of the afflicted. Las Casas toiled for years in the cause of the oppressed

Indians. Howard visited all Europe, not to survey the sumptuousness of palaces or the stateliness of temples; not to make accurate measurements of the remains of ancient grandeur, nor to form a scale of the curiosity of modern art; not to collect medals, nor to collate manuscripts; but to dive into the depths of dungeons, to plunge into the infections of hospitals, to survey the mansions of sorrow and of pain, to take the gauge and dimensions of misery, depression, and contempt, to remember the forgotten, to attend to the neglected, to visit the forsaken, and to compare and collate the distresses of all men in all countries.[13]

Nor is this exalted benevolence confined to such eminent persons. In our own time Florence Nightingale organized a band of Sisters of Charity, who braved pestilence in the distant hospitals of Scutari, that they might afford relief to the agony of our wounded soldiers. A name in the page of History, and the public thanks of a nation are great rewards for such services. But many abandon the splendour of a patrician life, the ties of family and home, and the luxuries of the civilization of the nineteenth century, in order, living an obscure existence, to console misery in the abodes of the poor. Benevolence, like friendship and gratitude, is beyond legislation.

Again, that we may proceed from the virtues which are shown in relations with other persons to those virtues which chiefly concern the individual — the law cannot enforce prudence, caution, self-control from vice, or a proper disposition in the expenditure of money. Within recent memory, in England, one gentleman spends £100,000 in supporting the Italian Opera for two seasons; another lavishes £300,000 on the Turf in a few years. But the State cannot assume with success the guardianship of fortune. Next to the Crown lands the worst managed property possessed by the English community is under the Receivers of the Court of Chancery. The law cannot enforce wisdom in managing one's own, or beneficence in dealings with others; such things must be left to the discretion of individuals, to the progress of education, and. to the results of an enlightened public opinion.

So, Positive Law appears to be powerless against the vice of intoxication, and can only punish the wretched drunkard who

---

[13] Edmund Burke.

publicly offends against Decency and Order. The vice of drunkenness depends upon the will. In recent times two great aids have been discovered to assist the drunkard's will — the use of a limited period in abstinence, and sympathy or fellow-feeling in abstinence. The greatest drunkards can abstain from drink if the time of abstinence be definitely fixed so that they can look forward to a period when they can use their liberty again. Next comes the aid of sympathy. Men can do together and in company what they cannot do by themselves. Any thing that is difficult to do, any exertion of resolution, any kind of self-denial, is made easier by the aid of sympathy, by knowing that other persons are feeling and doing the same thing. Father Mathew and other leaders of the recent temperance movement in England and Ireland well understood this principle of human nature, when they organized the votaries of temperance into an army with medals, bands, and banners. But no law has ever been successful in preventing the vice of drunkenness.

Now, if it be impossible to enforce by public authority, first, the most exalted virtues; secondly, disposition stewards others, such as benevolence and friendship; thirdly, virtues belonging to the class of prudence and self-control, how much more impossible must it be to force the individual sentiments of the mind into the particular form ordained by any human law. Yet, in this last particular, how many governments have erred.

But the individual acts of the mind are independent. And belief of any thing rests upon the amount of evidence offered in respect of the fact to be proved and the natural capacity of the mind for judgment. Belief is independent of the will.

At present, by the universal consent of civilization, what is involuntary deserves neither reward nor punishment at the hands of the magistrate; but through the history of all nations, in the examples of religious persecution is seen the fearful amount of misery caused by persons invested with the supreme power attempting to enforce belief — a thing incapable of being enforced. And this alone is sufficient to show the importance of ascertaining the province of Government — the importance of the science of Jurisprudence.

## 4. Development of Sympathy

The end of Government is the Security of Rights. The natural rights of man are Life, Liberty, and Property. To protect these rights has been the professed and real object of all the systems of civil polity that ever illumined the world with a ray of freedom. These rights, in the first beginnings of civilization, are not only practically insecure, but, even in theory, are imperfectly acknowledged. Where slavery still exists these rights are imperfect. The aggressive wars of our own times show that the rights of strangers to their lives and property are not yet perfectly admitted by the civilized states in the world.

The theory of Hobbes is not wholly wrong, that, agreeably to the lowest law of Nature, man aims at the injury of his neighbour when a stranger to him. To savages all strangers are enemies; every thing unknown is an object of fear — Omne ignotum pro horribili. In all languages the same word originally signifies both stranger and enemy. But the more persons know one another, they generally love one another the more.

> "Les hommes ne se hairont plus,
> Quand ils s'entendent tous."

During the progress of civilization the sympathy of man for his fellow creatures extends in an ever-widening circle. At first, none but immediate relatives are held entitled even to the common rights of life and property. Slaves are without rights. But in the advanced nations a poor law provides for even the outcasts of society; and humane legislation prevents cruelty to animals.

The first nucleus of society must have been the family, although nowhere in savage life has an isolated family been discovered unconnected with others by language or kindred. The existence of language proves that everywhere men exist in intellectual communities.

The family develops into the tribe. Men, whilst in the stage of the tribe, fanatically regard its interests beyond any thing else. They do not yet recognise the positive rights of other men belonging to other tribes, to their lives, liberties, and properties. They do not hesitate to rob and murder persons even belonging to neighbouring tribes, speaking the same language, and having the same national origin.

Thus the Arabian tribes were engaged in mutual war before Mahomet for a time united them. The native chiefs of Ireland never ceased from their efforts at mutual destruction. The right of private war between the feudal barons was one of the most difficult to be abolished. The clans of the Scottish Highlands, up to the time of their disorganization, maintained the right of private war. The Indian tribes of North America still massacre one another when opportunity may offer. The petty nations of Northern Africa still are engaged in deadly mutual strife, scarcely interrupted by their common danger from the superior arms and civilization of the French.

Yet during this phase the tribes of the same race in process of time regard one another with less animosity than they regard persons belonging to other races. The Berbers of Northern Africa are sometimes mutually at peace, but towards Christians they entertain perpetual hostility. They rob and murder Christians whenever an opportunity may offer; nor do they perceive that they violate any natural right, or transgress any natural duty.

Sympathy develops from the tribe to the nation, and thence to the race. The word *δήμος* originally means parish; Democracy now means the government by a people. In ancient Greece, though piracy at first was not a dishonourable profession, the rights of all Hellenes were finally recognised; but the rest of mankind were still considered barbarians, perpetual enemies without natural rights to life, liberty, or property. The Roman Citizen united many nations, but warred upon the rest of the ancient world. The Proconsul in the Roman Theatre applauded the sentiment — "Homo sum, humani nil a me alienum puto," but he disregarded it in the foreign province. Still the acknowledgment of the rights of humanity, and the consequent fusion of races, unceasingly proceed. In modern Europe the different States of France, once independent, have coalesced into one. The old kingdoms of Spain are now under one government. The British Islands, in which have existed such diversities of races and languages, are now a United Kingdom. Most of the Sclavonic races have coalesced under the empire of Russia. Whilst in present Continental politics the schemes of a German Empire — a United Italy — a Pansclavonic Confederation — are agitated by many ardent politicians.

Such is the development of Sympathy proceeding upon the more ancient idea of the bond of Union existing between family, tribe, nation, and race, both for aggressive and defensive purposes.

Another development of Sympathy, more based on Reason,

arises from the recognition of the equal rights of all men as citizens of the world to share in the gifts of Providence. Commerce and Emigration are the two great agents by which in modern times the clannish distinctions of nation or race are obliterated.

Amongst the races of men whilst in an imperfect state of development, the tie of country is so strong that nothing but the most positive evils of war, pestilence, and famine, will compel them to abandon their native land. I take an illustration from my own time and country. The famine of 1846 loosened the hold of the Irish peasant upon the soil. From 1847 to 1855, yearly a greater Celtic emigration left Ireland than from Gaul one Brennus led to Rome, or the other to Greece. Yearly a greater multitude abandoned Ireland than in old tunes sufficed for a crusade. This flight of the Irish people surpassed any thing previously known and recorded of the migrations of the human family. It was caused by the failure of the potato and the repeal of the Corn Laws. The failure of the potato caused the famine. The repeal of the Corn Laws rendered the price of grain crops less at home, and increased the price of grain crops in the fertile virgin soils of North America.

No more deplorable condition could be imagined than that of the Irish-speaking peasantry who, by their ignorance of the English tongue, were cut off from civilization. They were worse lodged, clothed, and fed than the peasantry of any other civilized country, or even than the savage and heathen races in Central Africa. Their life was stagnant and hopeless misery. Their cabins were inferior to the habitations of any other human beings. Families slept in the same narrow chamber — at once a cause of disease, and an offence against good manners. The damp, the filth, the vitiated and corrupted vapours arising from want of drainage and ventilation, in periods of epidemics, caused a terrible mortality. In such pestilential abodes, the most robust constitutions were weakened; natures more delicate succumbed; generations were decimated, and the survivors languished through life enerved. The roofless walls of these miserable hovels are now seen all through Ireland, and I trust they will never again be roofed for human beings.

Emigration has, since 1847, emancipated two millions of these Celts from a state of pauperism in which they scarcely possessed the rights of men.

In civilized countries the poor may be divided into three principal classes. The first and least numerous is composed of those wretched beings who, from organic deformity, whether manifested in mind or body, are unable to earn their bread; with them may be comprised the aged and infirm. The next class is composed of the wicked and idle, who refuse to labour for their subsistence, and who, not possessing realized property of their own, are supported by the labour and charity of their friends. The third and most numerous class consists of the great masses of mankind, descendants of savages, who as yet have scarce emerged from primitive barbarism, and who, through ignorance of the methods of life, linger always upon the verge of starvation.

The last division includes the great majority of the poor in every country. In Ireland it is principally formed of the Irish-speaking peasantry, who for ages have subsisted in the same state. Nor can it be said with certainty that the ancestors of these poor persons, in all their migrations from Irania through Europe to Ireland, during so many thousand years, were ever in a positively better condition.

Ignorance has been the great check to prevent the poor from emigration. Men rather bear the ills they have than fly to others they know not of. But the National Schools have dissipated much of old prejudice. Their friends in America, by transmitting £1,500,000 per annum to Ireland, have informed the Irish poor that beyond the Atlantic exists a continent where the same laws are better and more cheaply administered, and where there is plenty of good land to be had at a low rate. The more go, the more will go, until the rate of wages and the rent of land be the same in Illinois and Connemara.

It is difficult, perhaps not desirable, for one writing on a general theme to avoid the illustrations nearest to his own point of view. But the beneficial effects of the Celtic Exodus can scarcely be overrated by me. Through this emigration two millions emerged from primitive barbarism into the position of citizens. The next great advantage to the human family must spring from the fusion of races in America. The more the population is mixed the more prosperous will be the country. This result arises from the principle of the division of labour. Individual races excel in some qualities, and are deficient in others. The French,

Italians, Germans, Sclaves, and English of the present day, each have their different qualities in which they severally surpass the rest; and if they were fused into one community of United States, would each apply themselves solely to those departments of human skill and industry in which they are superior. This principle has long since been perceived, and termed the territorial division of labour. But it never can be completely developed whilst men remaining under different governments are separated by international tariffs, custom-houses, and wars.

In effect, pure races, like the Turks, languish and become etiolated. The most flourishing communities, like the city of Romulus, have sprung *ex colluvione gentium.* In the mythical story of the foundation of Rome, Livy tells us that the founder opened an asylum for fugitives — the political refugees of the neighbouring petty states of Etruria and Latium. All the young men for whom Society in those states provided no employment, and who became its enemies in consequence, as naturally as the sparks fly upwards, fled to the protection of the seven hills of Rome. England has owed much of her greatness to being a similar asylum. Hither have fled the artisans of the Netherlands and France from the terror of the Duke of Alva and Louis XIV., whilst the modern Englishman is the result of the Celt, the Roman, the Saxon, and the Norman.

In thus mentioning different races I do not insist upon the intrinsic superiority of one race over another; nor do I use the term race to denote difference of origin. At the present time, certain aggregations of individuals have developed peculiar mental and physical qualities, and use different languages. So they are termed races. Some are at the height of prosperity; others in the lowest depths of degradation. The primitive causes of these things we know no more than the causes which have sunk Atlantic continents into the seas, and raised the Alps from the bottomless abysses of some primæval ocean. But St. Paul said at Athens, "God hath made of one blood all mankind to dwell upon the face of the earth." In the lowest Australian savage exists the germ of the intellect of Socrates, of Cæsar, of Bacon, of Napoleon. From the most unsightly Esquimaux at the Pole, or negroes of the Tropics, may, in the process of centuries be developed forms of god-like strength and beauty, like the living models of the Athenian sculptor. Even in recent memory, the splendid

Magyar aristocrat came from Asia — a deformed Tartar savage — his language and origin the same with those of the Laplanders and Ostiaks. The Daco-Romans of Transylvania are the descendants of the Roman legionaries who conquered and colonized the ancient world. But a thousand years of prosperity have changed the Magyar into one of nature's finest types of man; a thousand years of oppression have changed the Roumans into serfs, like those of the Hebrides, or of Kerry.

These two developments of Sympathy received an immense acceleration from the Russian war (1854-5). For the polished Athenian, for the Roman citizen, for the Feudal Lord, sympathy with mankind did not exist. But the inhabitants of England and France were not merely united by self-interest with the barbarians of Bulgaria, Armenia, and Circassia; they sympathized with them, and, for the sake of aliens in language and religion, sacrificed their blood and treasure, although the power of the Czar need not be feared by the Civilization of the West. This war against Russia was the first war undertaken by civilized nations ostensibly in defence of Abstract Right, where their own interests were not immediately concerned.

The stage of civilization at which no nation has yet arrived — to which all nations have a slow but certain tendency, is that in which men shall entertain the same sympathy towards all mankind which has been felt by them for family, tribe, nation, race — in which the crime of killing a stranger in aggressive war shall be regarded as murder is now regarded; — in which the liberty of the individual shall be completely developed, — and in which the absolute power of individual governments disappearing, men, true citizens of the world, shall possess over the earth their rights, and by the Law the means of enforcing them.

> "Self-love but serves the virtuous mind to wake,
> As the small pebble stirs the peaceful lake;
> The centre moved, a circle straight succeeds;
> Another still, and still another spreads.
> Friend, parent, neighbour, first it will embrace,
> His country next, and next all human race.
> "Wide and more wide the o'erflowings of the mind
> Take every creature in of every kind;"[14]

[14] Pope.

The word patriotism now expresses the highest idea of sympathy which men can entertain. A patriot is honoured; a national feeling is applauded. But the time will come when the word national will be used as the word provincial is now used, to designate a narrowness of thought incompatible with a true appreciation of the destinies of mankind.

Still, although all human races upon the earth are in a state of progress tending towards the same legal civilization, there need be no apprehension that the nations of the world will so fall into one sink of level avarice. The gifts of nature are variously scattered amongst the children of great national families, and the brilliant variety of genius, taste, and imagination in races constitutes the splendour of mankind. The types of nationalities disappear with difficulty, and there is in nature one uniform variety. Grandeur and beauty would vanish from the earth if it were smoothed into level plainness. As the soldiers of all civilized nations use the same arms, the rifle and the bayonet, so once that the laws shall be discovered under which we best may live in happiness, all nations in a similar state of civilization will adopt them. But the glorious diversity of mankind must ever still proceed.

## 5. Definitions in Jurisprudence

Jurisprudence embraces a great portion of what has been considered by various writers under the heads of Ethics, Polity, Political Philosophy, and Political Economy. Writers on political economy, in particular Adam Smith and John Stuart Mill, have discussed in their economical works many of the subjects of Jurisprudence. But Political Economy is only the science of exchanges. It has developed the great principle that exchanges should be free. Political Economy, starting from this principle, teaches as its corollaries that the permanent and regular increase of human comfort is grounded upon the absence, so far as depends on law, of all favoured classes, professions, and pursuits; in the equal protection afforded by the law to every citizen, and the unrestricted liberty of spending as he pleases his honest earnings. It teaches that the machinery of trade and commerce should be left free; that every system of restrictions or prohibitions on commercial intercourse cuts off the foreign market, diminishes the number of our buyers and the demand for our produce, and so checks production. It teaches that all men should be permitted, without the interference of their government, to produce whatever they consider it most to their interest to produce; that they should not by laws be prevented from producing one thing, or by laws be bribed to produce another; that they should, so far as is consistent with public morality, be left alone, and allowed to follow their own interests as they please.

But Law has been only recently illustrated by its kindred sciences, — very recently the existence of a science of Society has been suspected, — but recently has Political Economy or Jurisprudence been taught in the universities of the United Kingdom of Great Britain and Ireland. However, the general progress of society has told upon the progress of Jurisprudence in the British Islands. Our Criminal Law has made wise and merciful progress from the time when trial by ordeal and battle existed, — from the time when mute prisoners were pressed to death, — from the time when Sir Edward Coke prosecuted Sir Walter Raleigh, — from the time of Chief Justice Jeffrey's bloody western assize, — from the time when prisoners were not allowed counsel to speak in their defence. So from the period when Lord Mansfield presided in the King's Bench, the doctrine and practice of our Commercial Law have been rapidly extended and improved. From the reign of William IV. the Law of Real Property in England is undergoing a process of wise and beneficial reform. Independently of legal science, the progress of the nation in wealth and the arts introduces new species of property, and necessitates cheap and expeditious forms of procedure.

Still science aids the progress of society, and a know. ledge of law is incomplete without the knowledge of what Bacon terms the laws of laws — leges legum. As Sir Edward Coke says, the reason of the law is the life of the law — for although a man can tell the law, if he knows not the reason thereof he shall soon forget his own superficial knowledge. But when he finds the right reason of the law and so brings it to his natural reason that he comprehends it as his own, this will not only serve him for the understanding of that particular case, but of many others. The knowledge of law is complicated. To know is properly to understand a thing by reason, and through its causes: — Cognitio legis est copulata et complicata. Scire autem est proprie rem ratione et per causam cognoscere.

It has been maintained by many that politics and laws cannot be reduced into a science: the ancient sophists were of opinion that there were no such things as Right and Wrong by nature, but only by convention. That which appears just and honourable for each city is so for that city so long as the opinion is entertained, was one of their maxims. The opinions of the sophists may have been exaggerated by their great opponent Plato, still I believe they did protest energetically against the possibility of metaphysical science, whilst Plato against them maintained in the doctrine which Pope has poetically translated: —

> "All nature is but art unknown to thee;
> All chance, direction which thou can't not see;
> All discord, harmony not understood;
> All partial evil, universal good;
> And spite of pride, in erring reason's spite,
> One truth is clear — whatever is, is right."

The possibility of metaphysical science, and, in particular, of the complete development of a science of law and government, is now admitted. The great system of Jurisprudence, says Sir William Jones, like that of the universe, consists of many subordinate systems all of which are connected by nice links and beautiful dependencies, and each of which is reducible to a few plain elements. If law be a science, and really deserves so sublime a name, it must be grounded upon principle, and claim an exalted rank in the empire of reason; but if it be merely an unconnected series of decrees and ordinances, its use may remain, though its dignity may be lessened; and he will become the greatest lawyer who has the greatest natural or artificial memory.

So Edmund Burke has said that we are all born in subjection — all born equally, high and low, governors and governed — in subjection to one great immutable and predestined law prior to all our devices, and prior to all our contrivances, paramount to all our ideas and all our sensations, antecedent to our very existence, by which we are knit and connected with the eternal frame of the universe out of which we cannot stir. And he has described the science of Jurisprudence as the pride of the intellect, the collected wisdom of ages, combining the principles of original justice with the infinite variety of human concerns.

So also Vico considered that the development of society, like the heart of man, was subject to one constant, universal, and divine law; the variable application and progress of which depended upon the uncertain will and erring nature of man; and he hence conceived the hope of discovering the eternal principles of the natural law.

In Jurisprudence, a law properly so called, is a rule of conduct addressed to creatures capable of feeling an obligation by means of reason; or a law may be defined as a general command given by one intelligent being to another.

St. Thomas Aquinas defined law as a certain rule and measure according to which any agent is led to act or restrained from acting: — Lex est quædam regula et mensura, secundum quam inducitur aliquis ad agendum, vel ab agendo retrahitur. This definition is plainly too indefinite and extensive. Suarez gives another description, and says, a law is a certain measure of moral acts of such a kind that by conformity to it they are morally right; by discordance with it morally wrong: — Lex est mensura quædam actuum moralium, ita ut per conformitatem ad illam rectitudinem moralem habeant, et si ab illa discordent obliqui sunt.

Up to the present time four great divisions of Law have been enumerated by jurists: — Divine Law, Natural Law, International Law, and Positive Law.

With the pagan philosophers, following Plato, the divine law was the sovereign reason existing in the mind of God.

The doctors of the middle ages termed this principle of nature the Eternal Law. The Divine Law, with Plato, is the governing reason existing in the mind of the Universal Deity, which Theologians also acknowledge, but call the eternal law. Lex ergo divina apud Platonem est ratio gubernatrix universi in Dei mente existens, quam legem etiam Theologi agnoscunt sed legem æternam appellant.

The Positive Divine Law is that which has been immediately promulgated by God. Lex positiva divina dicitur, quæ ab ipso Deo immediate lata est et toti legi naturali addita. Our duty as to the Divine Law is simply to know it and obey it.

The Natural Law, according to Grotius, consists in certain principles of rectitude of reason which enable us to know whether an action is morally right or wrong according to its congruity with a reasonable and social nature. Jus naturale est dictatum rectæ rationis indicans actui alicui, ex ejus convenientia vel disconvenientia cum ipsâ naturâ rationali, inesse moralem turpitudinem aut necessitatem moralem, et consequenter ab auctore naturæ ipso deo talem actum aut vetari aut præcipi. The Natural Law is thus considered under two aspects first, its nature and essential qualities; secondly, its obligatory force.

Grotius compiled this definition from the previous authorities. But in Jurisprudence it can scarcely be adopted as correct. This definition of Natural Law embraces the whole sphere of both moral and legal duty. In Jurisprudence, however, Natural Law cannot include so wide a circle. It only includes the rights and duties capable of being enforced by the power of the State.

It is most important in legislation to avoid intermeddling with the peculiar province of Ethics or Divinity. The Divine Law is the province of the Theologian, Ethics of the Moral Philosopher. Neither uses the compulsion which it is the province of the Legislator to employ.

Natural Law may accordingly be correctly defined as the theory of that part of our duties which, in reason and equity, is capable of being exacted.

On the other hand, if Jurisprudence be viewed as only one branch of the Social Science whose object is to ascertain the great natural law of the progress and development of society, and according to what laws men may best live in happiness — then Jurisprudence maybe held to include the entire domain of the rights and duties which come within the province of Positive Law, Ethics, and Theology. The definition of St. Chrysostom might then be adopted that natural law is the instinctive knowledge of good and evil, *αὐτοδίδακτος ἡ γνῶσις τῶν καλῶν, και τῶν οὐ τοιούτων*. As civilization proceeds, Jurisprudence continually encroaches upon the kindred sciences, and embraces an ever-widening range of social rights and obligations. I repeat an illustration. In the early ages of society human slaves have no rights. In modern times animals are recognised as having a right to good treatment, and cruelty is punished by the Positive Law.

The purposes of laws were distinguished by Modestinus: — to command, to forbid, to permit, or to punish.

The laws rendered effectual by rewards were defined to be of two species: first, those the object of which is to induce men to do something which all men are unable to do, such as those which offer a reward for scientific inventions; secondly, those laws the object of which is to make men more vigilant in the performance of legal duties, or in the enforcing of other laws, — such as laws offering rewards for the detection of offenders.

The civilians attempted to point out the laws made by States not conformably to the Law of Nature; thus, slavery was described as an institution of the Law of Nations contrary to the Law of Nature. Domat, following the civilians, has divided all laws into immutable, and mutable, or arbitrary. The former are defined as those which, being principles of the Law of Nature, cannot be changed without violating those natural obligations upon which the order of society is founded; the latter are defined as those which are not principles of natural law, and which, as they are not essential to the obligations in which society is founded, may be changed without violating those obligations.

These definitions are erroneous. In one stage of society slavery is as natural as freedom in another stage. In barbarous countries order cannot be maintained without a despotism impossible in free countries. Tyranny is equally the result of the natural law of one stage of society as Liberty is of another. The Problem of Society is to combine Order with Freedom. According to a natural law, society appears to progress from barbarism to civilization; and to assist that progress the social sciences contribute their aid by ascertaining under what positive laws men in their present stage of civilization best may live in happiness.

There have been thus two principal definitions of natural law. The Institutes define natural law as that which Nature has taught to animals; for this law belongs, not to the human race alone, but to all animated beings which are produced in the heaven, the earth, or the sea. This is erroneous, because in Jurisprudence nothing can be properly called a law, except a rule of conduct addressed to, and binding on, creatures capable of feeling an obligation by means of reason. Cicero, on the other hand, says — Ex qua illa lex quam Dei humano generi dederunt recte est laudata; est enim ratio mensque sapientis ad jubendum et ad deterrendum idonea.

The definition of Justinian is not a legal definition, but one which might be placed as an axiom for any science. But, again I repeat, Natural Law, legally defined as a subject of Jurisprudence, is the theory of those duties capable of being enforced.

The fundamental principle and starting point of natural law is the natural equality of the rights of all men. But in society this theoretical equality is speedily destroyed by the diversity of their respective and reciprocal duties and rights, as members of families, as reasonable beings living under the social state, and as having voluntarily entered into and contracted obligations with one another by express or tacit consent.

The Natural Law includes all the principles of Right common to just men living in civilization. And the doctors of the middle ages, accordingly, have defined Natural Law as the principle in the human mind by which the just is discerned from the unjust. Thus, Suarez says: — The Natural Law which pertains to moral philosophy and theology, is that which is seated in the human mind to distinguish good from bad. — Lex ergo naturalis propria quæ ad moralem doctrinam et theologiam pertinet, est illa quæ humanæ menti insidet ad discernendum honestum a turpi.

Positive Law is the law of human enactment. It is called Positive as existing by position. For hence it is called Positive as it were added to Natural Law not necessarily flowing from it. Whence by some it is called fixed law. — Inde enim positiva dicta est quasi addita naturali legi non ex illa necessario manans. Unde ab aliquibus jus positum vocatur. With former jurists end before the importance of International Law was recognised, Positive Law was held to mean the law enacted by the sovereign government of an independent political society. It must now be taken to include also International Law, so far as the latter is capable of being ascertained and enforced. The element of compulsion to obedience through the public force, distinguishes the Positive Law from all others enumerated by jurists or moralists.

Sir William Blackstone and others have termed this species of law Municipal Law. But the term is inappropriate. Derivatively, the word municipal refers to a corporate town. Blackstone defines Municipal Law — or, as it should be termed, Positive Law — as a rule of civil conduct prescribed by the supreme power in a State, commanding what is right and prohibiting what is wrong.

Now, the error of this definition is, that a law prescribed by the supreme power in a State is still a law, even though it does not correspond with the latter part of this definition, and command what is right and prohibit what is wrong. The essence of a positive law is compulsion by the public authority; and provided the force of a State be employed to compel obedience to any rule of civil conduct, such rule is a law. A bad law is that which imposes an obligation without doing any service. There have been evil laws in all ages, yet they have not the less been laws.

Internal Positive Law is, therefore, a rule of civil conduct prescribed by the supreme power in a State.

It is defined as a rule, in order to distinguish it from any thing in the nature of a sudden command, a request from an inferior, an advice from a friend, or a compact between equals.

It is termed a rule of civil conduct, that it may be distinguished from the rules of moral conduct with which as such the public law does not interfere. The criminal branch of Positive Law does not punish vices, only crimes. The civil branch of Positive Law is concerned with the maintenance and enforcement of private rights, where the violation of them has not affected directly the public security. Individual wickedness is not punished directly by the law except where it interferes with the happiness of others in a manner of which the laws can take cognizance. The prodigal may squander his fortune in dissipation: the fool may waste it by reckless mismanagement; the miser may bury it from his friends and the world; but the law is unable to enforce prudence in dealing with one's own, or benevolence towards others. Such things must be left to the progress of knowledge and education. For Justice alone of all the virtues can be enforced by the public authority.

Again, the rule of law is prescribed — that is, promulgated by the official power of the State, and, in the last resort, enforced. Laws, to be obeyed, must be known. Yet ignorance of the law must never be permitted to be urged as an excuse for any accountable citizen. *Ignorantia juris neminem exeusat.* It would be absurd to permit any man to profit by his ignorance of the law, so as to place himself in a more advantageous position than another, who did not neglect to make himself acquainted with those rules to which every member of the society ought to conform.

In the Institutes of Justinian the subjects of Law are divided into persons, things, and actions. This arrangement has been followed in modern times, in the code Frederic, the code Napoleon, and by Sir William Blackstone, in his Commentaries upon the Laws of England. It is a most unscientific division, and has checked the progress of the Science of Jurisprudence in Germany, France, and England.

Leibnitz first pointed out that the Roman arrangement confounds fact with law, and assumes as the objects of law persons and things, which are no more the objects of human law, than they are the objects of the greater number of the Arts and Sciences. Such a division is founded, not upon matters of law, or differences in the component parts of law, but upon matters of fact or differences in substances mental and material, tending to indefinite repetitions. The Roman division of things into corporeal and incorporeal, is equally wrong. The term, incorporeal things, was a mere fiction to hide the confusion of ideas. All these incorporeal things are only rights to the services of men.

The compilers of the Roman code set out with a wrong division into two parts which are not exclusive with regard to each other — rights of persons — rights of things. They were led to this division by a species of grammatical symmetry. But there is no correspondence between the two terms except as to form. There is none as to sense. The term, rights of persons, is clear. It means rights conferred by the law on persons, rights which persons may enjoy. But if this explanation be transferred to the term, rights of things, it leads to an absurdity. Things can have no rights belonging to them. The law confers no rights on things. The law does not favour things. Instead of rights of things the expression ought to be rights of persons over things. The change appears slight. But it overthrows the nomenclature — the division of rights, the pretended arrangement of the Roman lawyers adopted by Blackstone, and according to which he has classified the objects of law.

Such have been the views of some most eminent jurists in their department of knowledge. I propose a more convenient division and nomenclature of Jurisprudence and Positive Law. In the present state of the science the following classification of its departments appears correct. Some of the definitions already given are repeated.

Jurisprudence is the Science of Positive Laws, the Art of Legislation, and the Practice of Law.

A Positive Law is a rule of civil conduct prescribed and enforced by a State.

In the Positive Law of every nation there are two elements — the philosophical and the historical. The first element to be acknowledged is the philosophical. The absolute ideas of Justice and Truth constitute its essence. But these ideas assume different forms in different states. Prejudices, manners, and passions, change and deform them. And in Law History becomes associated with Philosophy. From this union the Positive Law of every state arises. And Positive Law becomes an association of universal principles and of national maxims, of rational axioms and of political adages.

The end of Jurisprudence is utility or the happiness of mankind. Nor is this principle peculiar to Jurisprudence. But it has been the professed and real end of all the sciences and arts. The greatest happiness of the greatest number is the true object of Legislation.

All the sciences and arts have for their end and aim utility, civilization, and the happiness of mankind.

Civilization is the highest development of the physical and intellectual faculties of mankind.

Jurisprudence, like every other mental science in the discussion of subjects within the domain of the will, considers not only what the law is, but what it ought to be.

The virtue of justice is the disposition to give every man his right.

Justice alone of all the virtues can be enforced by the public authority.

Legal relations are those which arise from the natural constitution of mankind, and which give individuals a right to the use of force as necessary to society.

The subjects of Jurisprudence are rights and their correlative duties.

Rights are defined by Jurisprudence.

Legal duties are enforced by the Positive Law.

The three natural rights of man are Life, Liberty, and Property.

Rights arise between persons concerning either persons or things.

Actions or forms of legal procedure are the means by which the performance of rights is insured, or their violation redressed.

An action is the legal demand of a Right.

Actions include both a civil action or the legal demand of a right by an individual, in which the end is compensation, and a state prosecution, in which the end is punishment.

If the different rights and duties incident to man in society be analyzed, they naturally divide themselves into four classes: —

Those which arise between individuals in such a manner that the community is not immediately concerned with them: —

Those which arise between individuals in such a manner that the community is directly concerned, and directly suffers by the violation of the right: —

Those which arise between individuals and their government: —

Those which arise between different states, or the subjects of different states.

Rights and duties arise between individuals in such a manner that the community is not immediately concerned with them. For example, in a civilized country, if a merchant do not deliver corn to a purchaser according to the contract of sale, the violation of the right of property does not immediately cause any injury to the rest of the community.

Rights and duties arise between individuals in such a manner that the community is immediately concerned, and immediately suffers by the infringement. If a burglar break into a house at night, or if a highway robber assault and murder a traveller, independently of the parties immediately wronged, the rest of the community is directly injured. Persons in the neighbourhood of the burglary are put to the expense of protecting their houses by additional safeguards. Perhaps they are obliged to pay additional taxes for police. Terror is diffused. A sense of wrong is therefore sustained by the community, and vents itself in the punishment of the offender with an intensity proportioned to the degree of injury caused by him, and the degree of suffering felt by the people.

Revenge is the origin of punishment. In the early stages of society punishment is severe according to the hatred against the offender, and the indignation which his neighbours feel towards him. The accumulated rage of a community against an individual murderer demands his death. Finally, in the more advanced stage of society, the reformation of the criminal is attempted, and punishment is used only as an example and a means for the prevention of crime, that the punishment may reach a few, the fear, all; — ut pœna ad paucos, metus ad omnes perveniat.

The branch of Positive Law which gives individuals compensation for a violation of their rights is termed the Civil Law; that branch of Positive Law which punishes offences is termed Criminal Law. If damages completely satisfy the loss, and if the public security is not weakened by the injury, the matter may safely be left to the Civil Law. But whenever the public security is endangered, compensation is insufficient to vindicate Justice, and punishment must be added.

A crime is that violation of a right for which the State provides punishment.

The chief end of the Civil Law is compensation, the chief end of the Criminal Law is punishment; but in many cases both have a concurrent jurisdiction.

In the law of England crimes are divided into three classes — treason, felony, and misdemeanour. The offences against a right designated by the first two classes cannot be the subject of a civil action. Some misdemeanours may come within the province of the Civil Law, and may be redressed by the award of damages against the offender, to be paid to the sufferer.

If we desire to ascertain whether a violation of the natural rights of man — life, liberty, and property — come within the province of the Civil or of the Criminal Law, we have only to ascertain whether such violation concern the individual immediately, and the community remotely, or whether the interest of the community be not thereby directly affected.

Rights and duties arise between individuals and their governments.

The procedure to redress the violation of a right is in all the rode stages of society vague, violent, and uncertain. The savage, who has been wronged, waylays and assassinates the enemy, or else, in the struggle, falls — the victim of superior strength. In time the authority of the law assumes the place of uncertain strife; and the process by which mankind submit their disputes to the cognizance of legal tribunals is perpetually developed further.

At first only the rights arising between subjects are determined and protected by the law, whilst the Sovereign remains above the law. Under barbaric despotisms the Sovereign acknowledges no legal rule binding upon him in his conduct towards his subjects.

But in time the relations between the government and the people become subjected to certain positive laws. And the body of law determining the relations between individuals and their governments is generally termed Constitutional Law, or Political Law — the latter term is preferable.

The things of the world must be appropriated, whenever that appropriation is necessary for the purpose of rendering them as beneficial and valuable as their nature admits of their being made.

The business of government is to promote the happiness of mankind, by means of rewards and punishments. The rewards, however, in most cases, are given indirectly to the energetic and able men who carry on the business of society.

Government is a necessity. If all men were cultivated, virtuous, and talented, they would discharge towards others all the duties of life better than any government could enforce them. A community of such persons would be a law unto themselves, needing no coercion; and each individual would be urged by the spontaneous impulses of his own nature to do right. Rivers, in the comedy of *False Delicacy,* well says: "Laws were never made for men of honour; they want no law but the rectitude of their own sentiments; and laws are of no use but to bind the villains of society."

However, laws are of use to bind others besides villains; and the object of every good government is, by means of laws, to strive to bring all its subjects up to that standard of duty which the wisest and best of themselves attain.

If this, then, be the necessity for government, we have to consider what right a government has to coerce and punish its subjects upon occasion.

It is necessary to define the three natural rights of men — Life, Liberty, and Property.

Natural Liberty is the individual's right of not being obliged by any judgment or will with which his own judgment and will do not coincide. But, scientifically defined in Jurisprudence, Liberty is freedom of action, controlled only by laws tending to promote the greatest happiness of the greatest number.

Slavery is obligation of service unlimited in extent or time.

Property is the right of Using.

The right of property is founded upon its subserviency to the subsistence and well-being of mankind. The institution of property is necessary for social order. The exclusive appropriation of things is essential for the full enjoyment of them. The sense of property is bestowed upon mankind for the purpose of rousing them to action. It is the principal foundation of social improvement. It leads to the cultivation of the earth, the institution of government, the establishment of Justice.

In the Right of Property, Bentham includes four things: —

1. The right of occupation: —

2. The right of excluding others: —

3. The right of disposition, or the right of transfer to others: —

4. The right of transmission, in virtue of which the integral right is transmitted after the death of the proprietor, without any disposition on his part, to those in whose possession he would desire to place it.

All modern civilized life rests upon the two institutions of Property and Marriage.

The original titles to property are Occupancy and Labour. Finders are keepers by common consent where there has been no previous appropriation. What a man has produced by Labour is his own.

The secondary titles to property are Consent and Inheritance.

Consent includes Gift, Sale, and Exchange.

The right of Inheritance by children of the property of their parents depends on three principles. The children may have contributed by their labour to the formation of the property. Naturally they expect to receive it, and the State's gift to them of the property prevents disappointment. Lastly, by the receipt they are prevented from becoming a burthen to the people. From the inheritance by children to the inheritance by relations the transition was easy and obvious.

Some jurists and publicists have proposed that by law the discretion of the testator should be limited to this, that a certain fixed portion of the property should be distributed amongst the immediate descendants in a ratio suitable to the property and position of the testator. Where persons die without kindred and intestate, the State must succeed to their property. In avoid contention an ultimate heir — *ultimus hæres* — must be appointed.

## 6. Political Jurisprudence

The great questions of Political Jurisprudence, the right of government to the use of force, the province of government, its duties as the machine of police and order, and as the guide to progress, demand a more lengthened investigation.

The right of Society to enforce the law by punishment, may be judged from the following considerations: —

When man enters into Society he naturally intrusts the three rights of Life, Liberty, and Property, to the guardianship of his rulers.

As every man in his independent state has by nature the disposal of his property, he can convey the disposal thereof to society as amply and absolutely as he was by separate right entitled thereto.

It is the right, perhaps the duty, of every man to defend his life, liberty, and property. It is his right to kill or bind those who would grievously wrong him. — This right he can convey.

Upon such conveyance it becomes the right and duty of the trustees of the Society to put to death, or imprison, or inflict any punishment suitable for the prevention of crime upon all who take away, or attempt to take away, the life, liberty, or property of its members.

In the infancy of civilization the private disputes of individuals appear to be decided by arbitrators, chosen and paid by the litigants. Afterwards the State is naturally resorted to as the decider of disputes, because it is the only impartial third party possessing the requisite compulsory force. The whole people, in its collective capacity, is incapable of exercising legal power correctly; for such power ought to be exercised with intelligence and impartiality; and from the tribunal must be excluded the aggressor, the injured party, and their friends. Where the judicial body is very numerous, and where the responsibility is much divided, an honest decision in important cases appears impossible. Historical exam-plea of this are the Athenian Courts in political trials, and the decisions of the English House of Commons as to contested elections when the entire House voted, before the

Grenville Act was passed, which referred such matters to a select committee.

The three functions of Government are the Judicial, Legislative, and Executive.

In the infancy of society all political powers are united. They are all held in the hand of the Sovereign, and obey his arbitrary will. But, according to the natural law of the division of labour, a separation of these powers takes place. The Sovereign sinks under the weight of duties which surpass his strength, and which cannot be neglected without exposing himself to complaints, disagreeable even to despotism. To dissipate alarm, and prevent resistance, the protection of a special authority is given to what citizens hold most dear — their property their personal liberty, their life. The judicial order is founded. By the establishment of tribunals, nations enter into the path of regular institutions.

In point of time the Judicial power is prior to the Legislative, as disputes must have arisen and have been decided before the State thought of enacting a law to regulate future controversy. The duty of Courts of Justice is to apply the Law. But, if the Law be arbitrary, the security which tribunals accomplish is illusory and incomplete. As a consequence of the Judicial establishment Law must be rendered certain. The right of legislation, then, ceases to belong to the Sovereign power, and is transferred to assemblies which represent the nation.

Two powers, the Judicial and the Legislative, are thus detached, and acquire a separate existence. To the Sovereign is reserved only the Executive power.

The Executive power is divided into two branches — the political, that is to say, the direction of the general interests of the nation, and the administrative, which consists in the accomplishment of the public service.

Under constitutional government, political power passes to the legislative assemblies representing the people. The more parliamentary power increases, the more it invades the domain of politics. It conducts the policy of a nation by laws, by financial votes. Arrived at its extreme development, it leaves to the executive power only the accomplishment of that which it has previously determined.

Similarly in the advanced nations the institution of Police

takes the power of punishment from the hands of the central government, and, except in the instances of great crimes, confides it to local administration.

Police is a system of precaution for the prevention of crimes and calamities.

It is a step in the progress of society, and in the development of the liberty of the individual, where order is maintained under a system of police, not under soldiers devoted to the central authority and isolated from the citizens.

The private law of a State is divided — as to its sources into common or statute law — as to its subject matter into rights and obligations — and as to the mode of ascertaining and enforcing them into civil and criminal Law. Procedure is the course taken for the execution of the Laws. It is the means for attaining an end. It is the method of employing the instrument called Law.

The Laws of Procedure are termed adjective, because they assist the enforcing of the substantive laws. The business of a Court of Justice is to examine and ascertain, by legal evidence, the facts; to apply the law to those facts; to pronounce judgment that such is the law, and that certain consequences will follow to individuals, or their property, if the law be not obeyed.

The Political Law of a nation is the whole of the legal relations existing between the governors and the governed. It determines the organization of the legislative, executive, and judicial powers.

Political Jurisprudence embraces a wide range of study — the constitutional history of the Oriental nations — of Greece, of Rome, of the Italian Republics, of France, of England, of the United States, in a word, of all the nations that have developed important political systems. In the progress and development of Society, the most intricate questions arise as to the separation of the judicial, legislative, and executive powers of government, and with respect to taxation and colonization.

In Jurisprudence the term constitution of a State embraces the body of the written and unwritten fundamental laws which regulate the rights and privileges of magistrates and subjects.

Union in Society is the destiny of man. This does not arise from the social compact of which the philosophers of the eighteenth century dreamed; it is progressively worked out by the interior development of the family, and the aggregation of other families. The sense of property is amongst the earliest of our ideas. The child knows he owns his toy as well as the peer knows he owns his land.

Civil government arises from the desire of men to protect their property and combine order and freedom in their intercourse with one another. The interposition of the State is required to redress wrongs, to determine disputes, to enforce obligations. Without government no property could be secure, no liberty certain, no civilization completely developed. At first, order is the main purpose of government, whilst personal liberty and individual security for property are not so much regarded by those in power. Yet, the despotisms of Asia are preferable to anarchy. Men prove this by living and trading under such systems. In effect, where undeveloped and partially civilized communities exist, absolute monarchy appears to be the natural form of government — as children learn to obey others before they learn to act for themselves.

The tendency of civilization, as developed in the most advanced countries, is to diminish the great power which the Central Government possesses in the early stages of society, whilst in modern times, the entire force of a country can be more directly used for external purposes.

With the progress of knowledge the despotical restraint becomes intolerable; it is no longer necessary, and it disappears. Then the liberty of the individual subject is perfect. The importance of the individual governor ceases. Government becomes the mere machine of police and order. In the more advanced and Republican nations, the individual becomes emancipated from any permanent bond of allegiance. He can transfer his person and property to whatever soil he pleases, secure of equal protection in England or the United States, provided he obey the law. The secret of organized liberty is willing obedience to limited power.

The forms of government diner in various countries, and from causes hitherto by politicians termed accidents. Yet, even politics in time may be reduced into a science; and from Political History may be derived certain general principles which will hold true at all times and under all circumstances.

The different forms of government, the distribution in each state of the power by which the people is governed, the influence of such diversities upon the prosperity of the several nations subject to them, — these are facts from which must be drawn the principles which constitute the science of Political Jurisprudence.

Two systems of government now contend for superiority in the civilized world. One is the system of Freedom of popular institutions, and of representative government as exemplified in England and the United States of North America. The other is the system of centralized Despotism now existing in Russia, Austria, and France. The principal political disadvantage of Despotism is that it rarely opens a career to the talents of the people. Austria has been a grand despotic state for five hundred years. The suppression of knowledge and the extinction of independence appear the conditions of her existence. Consequently Austria has never produced a single great name in arts or letters — has never produced a great artist, painter, orator, historian, or poet. The main advantage of the system of Freedom is that it opens a career to talents. Nor does it appear now possible to govern enlightened populations by the iron despotic rule of former times. A despotism to be cheerfully obeyed must be that of greatness of intellect and knowledge over ignorance and incapacity. Whenever a great man has been a successful despot, he has succeeded by his power of organizing obedience to himself, and by procuring the talent and energy of his fellows to work in the same direction.

Alexander by his greatness of soul and power of organization swept the soldiers of Greece over the barbaric empires of the day. He was cheerfully obeyed. All the clever men of Greece were proud to be captains under him; but when he died they aspired to be kings, they quarrelled with one another, and the rule of Greece over Asia ceased. So, Cæsar, Mahomet, Cromwell, Napoleon, were in their spheres organizers of great political revolutions. But in order now to acquire the power of Caesar, one must of necessity be in intellect and power as far superior to the country gentlemen, lawyers, professors, merchants, editors, artists, tradesmen, and students, that swarm through modern society, and through clubs, universities, Mechanics' Institutes, reviews, and newspapers develop, criticize, and influence the life in which we live, as these latter are in knowledge, political capacity, power of critical perception, and practical ability, superior to the senators, knights, and plebeians of the last days of

Republican Rome.

Napoleon, whilst he held power, in many respects used it well. The public works which his administrative genius constructed; the code of laws which owes its origin to him; the destruction of the Feudal abominations effected by him; — these things show what may be done by a despotism. But the fall even of Napoleon was hastened by men like Lafayette and others who insisted on a share in the public government, and were not content with the Emperor's promotion of solely military talents. Yet men like Cæsar and Napoleon arise but once in a thousand years. So far as we have record there were not five other such in all history. And the rules of politics, law, and government, must be made with a view to the ordinary capacities of mankind, and not with the hope of a perpetual succession of men like Napoleon and Cæsar in every State.

The middle classes never had a career more open to talent than now in England. Competitive examination permits all to enter the great Civil Services. A great political career alone is difficult of attainment for those who are unaided by wealth and aristocracy. In England it is almost impossible for persons not connected with the aristocracy to arrive at the high places in a political career. But many fortunate circumstances have developed English liberty. Many centuries have moulded our political organization. Many races have formed our modern character. The reckless courage and plastic spirit of the Celt, the genius of the Roman for law and government, the working earnestness of the Saxon, the chivalry of the Norman — these things, aided by that zeal for knowledge which consults the wisdom of all languages and ages, aided by those mechanical inventions which circulate the thoughts of the great men of all time through the enlightened populations of these realms — all form the constituent elements of the modern civilization of England; and that civilization will never brook a despotism however beneficent, until it verges to its fall.

We live in uncertain times. The populations of Europe demand a career open to talent. And the prizes of revolution, the governments of the realms are perpetually before the ambition of the crowds of youthful, ardent, cultivated minds, produced by modern civilization. If these are not employed by the old governments, they seek to overturn them.

All over Europe the revolt of the over-governed populations in 1848 and 1849 showed that Despotism could be maintained only by cannon at the street corners, and by turning drawing-rooms into barracks for barbarian soldiery. The oppressed populations are for a time again enslaved. Italy under the Romans the mistress of the world, during the middle ages the cradle of public liberty, the seat of commerce, the school of art, writhes in vain under the insolence of foreign armies. But Milan, Venice, and Florence cannot forget their former splendour, when self-governed and free they rose Republics upon the ruins of imperial power or feudal barbarism. They cannot now be drilled into prosperity. Still in vain has despotism with musketry and cannon these two hundred years cut down the ranks of the people; the voids are filled up, new generations grow up full of hope and ardour, remembering the sorrows and the triumphs of their fathers, and the battle re-commences on every side.

## 7. Province of Government: Taxation

Security is the principal advantage possessed by modern society beyond every previous stage of man's social existence. Security does not now exist only for privileged races or classes, but, in most civilized countries, is for all. By this protection of the law the public liberty exists; so far as liberty is security against the aggression of the powerful members of society. When we analyze the means by which this modern security is obtained for the manner of levying taxes. The word *tax* is probably derived from the same root as the verb to take, and literally means something taken or lifted. In Latin we meet the words *taxare, taxatio* — in German, *taeckse* — in French, *taxer* — in Italian, *tassare.* In English the word *task* seems originally to have been synonymous with *tax.* Thus, in the old statute, the *confirmatio chartarum* (25th Edward I.) we meet the expression "aids, tasks, and prises."

Almost all that is now comprehended under the term taxation comes within the definition which I have given above, with the exception of the rates levied for purely local purposes and all rates which are paid for other purposes than those of public security. The taxes in all civilized countries are devoted to almost the same objects. It is necessary to maintain an army and navy to guard our properties and liberties against the ambition of foreign states; part of our taxation is devoted to this purpose. In all civilized societies the proper administration of justice, and the punishment of criminals, is essential to the well-being, indeed to the existence of the community; part of our taxation is devoted to the business of justice and police. In all governments it is necessary to pay the officers at a high rate in order that able men may be obtained to fill such offices; part of our taxation is devoted to the payment of those who carry on the transactions of government. In all countries it is necessary to support in proper affluence and dignity the head of the nation; and every country accordingly pays something to maintain the head of the nation, whether that head be the chief of a barbarous tribe or as in civilized countries called emperor, king, or president. Part of the taxation of all the old countries of the world that maintain their credit, defrays the interest of the national debt contracted in former years, when the taxes raised were not sufficient to meet the expenditure.

It has been made a question with some jurists, although seldom in modern times, whether the support of paupers should be provided for at the public expense. Paupers have no absolute right to support founded on the institution of society. It cannot be said that those who possess property are, on account of the possession of that property, bound to feed those who do not possess it, and are unable to maintain themselves. The latter are not in a worse condition than they would have been had society and property never existed. But in relation to civil society, the right of paupers to subsistence may be said to be founded on the obedience to the law which society exacts from them. For breaking the law as regards property they would be punished, but not in modern times starved, or otherwise put to death. If one breaking the law should steal a loaf to satisfy his hunger, he would be imprisoned, but during that imprisonment fed. Would it not then be absurd to support the criminal, and allow the pauper who obeyed the law to starve? The support of the poor, once that their right to support, so qualified, is acknowledged, should not be left to voluntary contributions. These are uncertain, according to the fortune and ability of the benevolent. If they be deficient, starvation ensues. If they be superabundant, they offer a reward to laziness. Again, it would be most unjust to leave the support of the poor only to the benevolent, as this would be an exclusive tax upon the best members of society. Besides, under the voluntary system of relief, a just distribution is almost impossible. The most importunate will obtain the greatest quantity of alms; whilst silent poverty will be left unnoticed. And we are to remember that in times of famine the support of the poor by private benevolence would be impossible. The principal reason, therefore, for the support of the poor by a rate is, that it is unsafe for society to leave them without bread. Hunger is a foe to social security. But these juridical reasons for raising a provision to support the poor by compulsory taxes, are quite apart from the charitable duties enjoined by Christianity.

As regards the poor who are too far advanced in life to receive education, no provision should be made for them beyond the necessaries of life, otherwise the poor's rate becomes a provision and a premium for the idle, and industry is taxed for the support of laziness. But unquestionably the children who are on the rates should be educated and taught some trade, in order that they may in after-life be able to support themselves, and that they may not be a burthen to the community. If all were well educated, and possessed of those prudent, industrious, and virtuous habits which a good education engenders, none would be cast on the rates except the aged and infirm.

It has often excited surprise that, with the advance of nations in the wealth, liberty, and general prosperity which compose our modern civilization, poverty at the same time increases, and able-bodied men are unable to support themselves by their labour. The causes of poverty are to be found in the greater amount of labour required as the society advances in civilization. Labour increases in intensity with the progress of society. The same amount of labour which in an imperfectly organized and thinly inhabited community would be sufficient to maintain a person in tolerable comfort, will, in a more advanced community, scarcely keep him from starvation. This principle has been well exemplified by Mr. Burton, in his "Political and Social Economy." The further that the community has made industrial progress from the original unproductive habits of the savage, the more does it tax the energies of each individual member, and the less will any one who is indolent, or capable only of the lowest species of labour, be able to keep pace with the march of society. A Hindoo must practise more productive industry than a New Hollander — a Chinese than a Hindoo — a Russian than a Chinese; — a merchant in a metropolis must work harder than a merchant in a provincial town, and, generally speaking, the inhabitants of London exercise more skill and untiring industry, and require to exercise more than the inhabitants of any other place upon the earth. It, therefore, is natural and inevitable, that, with the progress of society, a greater amount of a superior kind of labour is required from us; and, consequently, if unaided, a greater number will continually be left behind in the race of social progress, and will be unable to provide themselves with the necessaries of life. The only means of counteracting this downward tendency is by education, which, to speak economically, enables the poor to employ skilful labour, instead of unskilled. A man able to read and write is, in plain terms, a more valuable member of society than he who is unable to read and write; and unless the poor be well educated, in the progress of civilized nations the numbers thrown on the poor-rates must increase. Juridical science has discovered the true causes of the evil, and points out the remedy — the industrial education of the people. The cheapest and best way for the rich to guard against heavy poor-rates, is to give a good education gratuitously to the children of the poor. Let the best masters and the best systems be provided for them. It is the cheapest policy in the end. Those who otherwise would be paupers and criminals, become useful members of society. How different would the state of Ireland this moment be, if the able-bodied who are in our poorhouses had been well educated and brought up to trades, and were now by industry increasing, instead of, as they are, consuming the national wealth. It follows that the education of the poor, meaning by that term all unable to pay for it, is a proper subject to be provided by the State out of the public general taxes. The economic reason for this is, that if the poor be well educated, the probability of their being unable to support themselves is greatly diminished; and the rates for their support may consequently be expected to be lower. We are also to consider, that where the population is well instructed, and early trained to moral, peaceable, and virtuous habits, less expense is required for the police regulations of society. For almost true it is —

> "Were half the power that fills the world with terror,
> Were half the wealth bestowed on camps and courts,
> Given to redeem the human mind from error,

There were no need of arsenals and forts." —
LONGFELLOW.

And so, the education of the poor may be considered as an auxiliary measure of security.

The duties of Government, in return for which the public taxes are paid, are the defence of the country, the administration of justice, and the preservation of order, all which may be included under the term public protection or security, which latter phrase I shall for the future employ. And a brief mode to express this is to say, taxes are paid in exchange for security. All the taxes paid for the support and maintenance of the executive Government, for the purposes of Justice, Police, the Army and Navy, and the Poor, are all paid in order to obtain security.

## 8. Direct Taxation

Speaking economically there are no other purposes for which taxes ought to be raised, except those connected directly with public security. The education of the poor is directly connected with security — otherwise, they could not obtain education. But it is at least doubtful whether provision should be made from the public taxes for the education of those who are able to pay for it. No person ought to be supported from the public taxes who does not, by his present services, directly contribute to the public security. It should constantly be present to the minds of all statesmen in representative Governments, that taxes are paid in exchange for security, and ought in rare instances to be applied in any other way. This principle appears very obvious, yet it has been much disregarded. It follows, also, from this principle, that all applications of the public money such as loans to capitalists to increase their trade are improper and mischievous. Some States have lent money to agricultural capitalists for the purposes of drainage, and other similar improvements; other States have lent money to manufacturing capitalists for their business. But all the treasure of Government arises only from taxes — taxes levied by constraint upon the community. For a Government to take from one portion of its subjects in order to benefit another, is merely to do a certain evil for an uncertain good. Even if the taxes were repaid to the State, still the injustice would continue for the time during which they remained unrepaid. But all public loans, grants, and advances, have a natural tendency to be jobbed, misemployed, wasted, and stolen. This is borne out by all history. The capital so lent will always be employed upon branches of industry less productive than those towards which it would have naturally directed itself. The very individuals who borrow the Government money at a low rate of interest, and employ it in drainage or manufactures, would not employ their own capital similarly, or could not borrow money at the ordinary rate for such investments. Why, then, should the Government tax its subjects for these purposes, when individuals consulting their own interests will not meddle with them?

All citizens are interested in having public protection for their private property, therefore all are bound to pay taxes to maintain those persons without whom this public protection would not exist. All are interested in having this public protection in proportion to the value of their property. But in levying taxation, the principle should be kept in view that all departments of the public service which do not come under the head of security, should be made to defray their own expenses. Their accounts should be kept separate, and their cost defrayed, not from the public general taxation, but from the moneys raised in the individual services. For example, the Post Office should defray its own expenses. The rate of postage ought to be lowered, whenever the receipts from that source exceed the expenditure, because a tax upon commercial intercourse is an improper source of revenue. All other expenses which do not come under the head of public security should be defrayed by local rates.

Political science cultivated in free countries, has now demonstrated that all taxation should be for the public good, and is justified by necessity alone; whilst in oriental despotisms, like Russia or Turkey, taxation is regarded as an engine to take property from the people for the purpose of enriching the governing classes, and maintaining the standing armies essential to support their supremacy. In England, such opinions have long been exploded. Our armies are no longer as in feudal times the masters, hut have become the servants of the State; and taxes are shown by political science to be not the property of governing races, but to be wages paid by the people to certain of their own number in exchange for the public services which are necessary to the existence of public liberty and security.

It is a very common sophism to say we are burdened with

taxes; the country groans beneath the weight of taxes. It is quite true that in most of the old countries of the world the rate of taxation is very high. We pay a great sum for justice and police; but then we have justice and police, the security which they afford us — the time which they save us, and it is very probable that production is neither active nor easy amongst people where each takes the law into his own hands.

For example: In some countries the judges are very indifferently paid, and are chosen almost solely from political motives, without regard to their knowledge or ability. The consequence in the first instance is that they take bribes and give their decisions according to the will of the highest bidder. The consequence in the second instance is that the merchants of those countries give no credit, from the great difficulty and uncertainty in recovering their debts. Thus trade and commerce are paralysed. Without credit our modern system of trade could not proceed. The manufacturer gets his bill of exchange discounted by a banker, or some other capitalist, thereby obtaining an advance of money to enable him to pay wages to his labourers who work up the raw material into manufactures. He sells these goods to the wholesale merchant; the latter, however, is unable to pay for them until he has received remittances from the retailers; and the manufacturer, aware of his solvency, is contented to receive in payment another bill of exchange due at some future period. The merchant hopes by the time the bill will have arrived at maturity to have disposed of the goods to the retailer, to be able to meet the bill, and to have made some profit to support himself in the meantime. Thus, goods pass from hand to hand, and from one country to another. However, only for the system of credit, and the advance of money made by the capitalist in the first instance, to maintain the labourers and others employed in the production of the goods until these were fit to be sold, the probability is, the goods would not be produced. And no man would advance his capital to another, unless there were an easy and secure mode of recovering it by legal process, in case the debtor proved unwilling to pay at the proper time.

Taxation, therefore, is an incident of society. Public order, public liberty, and public justice, are as essential to the complete development of the resources of a country, in the production of wealth, as each of the great agents of production, capital, labour, and the land. No one would till the stubborn earth, or sow it with seed, if he were not certain that the fruit of the harvest would be reaped by himself. The triumphs of mechanical science used as an agent of production in modern times would never have existed if the products had not been secured for the benefit of the producer. The gigantic system of credit now prevalent in commercial countries could not have arisen, if the people had not been willing in the first instance to remunerate and place in an honourable position those members of their own body who discharge the public functions of Justice and Order.

The natural advantages of soil and climate avail very little, unless use be made of them by the energy, honesty, and ability which are required to lay the foundations of civilization. There are countries where the bread-tree grows spontaneous; where fruits and spices hang upon every shrub; where the larger kinds of corn grow with but little labour. Yet, such favoured regions, illumined by a cloudless sun, with valleys cooled by mountain streams — every field a garden of variegated flowers, coloured with hues unknown to colder climates — are inhabited by listless savages, who sometimes perish from starvation. These magnificent regions are uncultivated and savage, because they never have been inhabited by an energetic and laborious race capable of originating free institutions. Whilst knowledge, capital, and industrious labour, fostered by security, raised Venice and Holland from the seas, and made them both the seats of flourishing communities, powerful in government and war. The barren wolds of Lancashire have been changed into mines of prosperous wealth worth all Golconda, or Peru — to show us that of all the gifts with which the earth has been blessed, and those who inhabit it, the greatest is that prolific mind, that untiring energy with which Providence has endowed man.

In considering the entire question of Taxation, it is most essential to bear in mind the difference between the Western European States of the present day, and the feudal monarchies from which they sprung, and whose forms are still in part retained by them. France, Germany, Spain, and England, during and subsequent to the dismemberment of the Roman empire, were occupied by bands of successful barbarians, who parcelled out the lands of the conquered amongst themselves, and established military aristocracies. The king was their general in war, but had little power in time of peace over his military companions. The word count, which was extensively used over Europe as the name of the feudal chieftains, literally means companion, and is the same with the Latin word *comes*. The mode of taxation in all the countries where the feudal system prevailed was simply this: The descendants of the conquering tribes held their land by military tenure. These military tenants were bound to serve in war at their own expense in their own country, whenever it was necessary to do so, but were originally exempted from all other state burthens. Those who cultivated the land under them were mere serfs. Trade in those days was contemptible, and traders were plundered openly of their property by the feudal lords. To lend money at interest was almost unlawful for Christians; and the principal part of that business fell into the hands of the Jews, who were persecuted and plundered openly. The taxes, whether levied on the agricultural serfs or on the burghers of the town, were considered to be the property of the governing races, and aided in purchasing the arms and equipping the retainers, by which they maintained their power. Countries ruled under the feudal system by governing races were taxed to the utmost for the benefit of those who governed; and the tax consumers were careless about the cheapest or best mode of collecting taxes, since an extravagant and expensive mode of collection was to them only an increased source of profit and patronage. The lowest class of those subject to the feudal laws suffered more from the individual oppression of the barons than from the taxation imposed by the government. And when we contemplate these feudal oppressions, we are not surprised at Wat Tyler's or Jack Cade's insurrection, or the Jacquerie in France. Even down to the first revolution in France, there existed feudal rights, a number of burthensome privileges, having for their origin not a contract freely entered into, but an usurpation of force over weakness. It was necessary for the feudal tenant to bake his bread at the oven of his landlord; it was necessary for him to grind his corn at his mill, to buy exclusively the goods and merchandise which his feudal Lord could sell him. It was compulsory on the feudal tenant to allow his grain to be devoured by his landlord's game. The feudal rights were given up by the French nobility, as it is well known, on the night of the celebrated 4th of August, when the other privileged classes also surrendered their privileges.[15] Fortunately for most civilized countries now, they have not to discuss such sweeping reforms. Most civilized countries now tax themselves; they pay their taxes as wages to the public servants in return for the protection and security afforded by their services; and it is the interest of the people everywhere to have their taxes collected in the cheapest possible manner, and also to have them collected in the proportion most just to every individual in the community.

Adam Smith, in his "Wealth of Nations," has laid down the four following maxims on taxation, and since they were published they have received the concurrence of every sound writer on Jurisprudence.

The subjects of every state ought to contribute to the support of the government as nearly as possible in proportion to their respective abilities — that is, in proportion to the revenue which they respectively enjoy under the protection of the state. The expense of government to the individuals of a great nation is like the expense of management to the joint tenants of a great estate, who are all obliged to contribute in proportion to their respective interests in the estate. In the observation or neglect of this maxim consists what is called the equality or inequality of taxation. Every tax, it must be observed, once for all, which falls finally upon one only of the three sorts of revenues — namely, *rent, profit,* and *wages,* from one or other of which the private revenue of all individuals must be derived, — is necessarily unequal in so far as it does not affect the other two.

Secondly — The tax which each individual is bound to pay ought to be certain and not arbitrary. The time of payment, the manner of payment, the quantity to be paid, ought all to be clear and plain to the contributor, and to every other person. Where it is otherwise, every person subject to the tax is put more or less in the power of the tax-gatherer, who can either aggravate the tax upon any obnoxious contributor, or extort, by the terror of such aggravation, some present or perquisite for himself. The uncertainty of taxation encourages the insolence of tax-gatherers, the corruption of an order of men who are naturally unpopular —

[15] Thiers' "Droit du Proprietè."

even where they are neither insolent nor corrupt. The certainty of what each individual ought to pay is, in taxation, a matter of so great importance, that a very considerable degree of in. equality, it appears from the experience of all nations, is not nearly so great an evil as a very small degree of uncertainty.

Thirdly — Every tax ought to be levied at the time.or in the manner in which it is most likely to be convenient for the contributor to pay it.

Fourthly — Every tax ought to be contrived so as both to take out and keep out of the pockets of the people as little as possible over and above what it brings into the public treasury of the State. A tax may either take out or keep out of the pockets of the people a great deal more than it brings into the public treasury in the following way: — 1st, the levying of it may require a great number of officers, whose salaries may eat up the greater part of the produce of the tax, and whose perquisites may impose another additional burthen on the people. — 2ndly, it may obstruct the industry of the people, and discourage them from applying to certain branches of business which might give maintenance and employment to great multitudes. While it obliges the people to pay, it may thus diminish or destroy some of the funds which might enable them more easily to do so. — 3rdly, by the forfeitures and other penalties which those unfortunate individuals incur who attempt unsuccessfully to evade the tax, it may frequently ruin them, and thereby put an end to the benefit which the community might have received from the employment of their capital. An in-judicious tax offers a great temptation to smuggling; but the penalties of smuggling must rise in proportion to the temptation. The law, contrary to all the ordinary principles of justice, first creates the temptation, and then punishes those who yield to it; and it commonly enhances the punishment, too, in proportion to the very circumstances which ought certainly to alleviate it — the temptation to commit the crime. — 4thly, by subjecting the people to the frequent visits and the odious examination of the tax-gatherers, it may expose them to much unnecessary trouble, vexation, and oppression; and though vexation is not, strictly speaking, expense, it is certainly equivalent to the expense at which every man would be willing to redeem himself from it.

Thus, the fundamental maxims on the subject of Taxation

are — first, that the subjects of a state should pay taxes according to their ability; secondly, that the tax should be certain, not arbitrary; thirdly, levied at a convenient time, and in a convenient manner; fourthly, collected at the cheapest rate.

The statesmen of all civilized countries, in arranging the financial systems of each, and in levying the taxes necessary to carry on the government, all agree that every tax should combine the last three principles — namely, that the tax should be certain, levied at a convenient time and in a convenient manner, and should take and keep out of the pockets of the people as little as possible, or, in other words, be collected at the cheapest possible rate. But the first maxim, namely, that all subjects should pay according to their abilities, is controverted by almost the entire system of taxation all over the world. In fact, most of the taxes levied seem to be based upon exactly the opposite principles. Equality ought to be the rule in matters of taxation, because it ought to be so in all affairs of government. A government ought to give to no one subject more than to another, so it ought to take from no one subject more proportionally than another. As a government ought to make no distinction of persons or classes in the strength of their claims upon it, whatever sacrifices it requires from them should be made to bear as nearly as possible with the same pressure upon all. And thus, least sacrifice is occasioned on the whole. If any one bear less than his fair share of the burthen, some other person must suffer more than his share, and the alleviation to the one is not, other things remaining the same, so great a good to him as the increased pressure upon the other is an evil. Equality of taxation, therefore, as a maxim of politics, means equality of sacrifice. It means apportioning the contribution of each person towards the expenses of government, so that he shall feel neither more nor less inconvenience from his share of the payment than every other person experiences from his.

Such ought to be the rule in matters of taxation. Now, all taxes are either direct or indirect. A direct tax is demanded from the very person who is intended absolutely to pay it. An indirect tax is one which is demanded from one person in the expectation and intention that he should remunerate himself at the expense of another. In practice, direct taxes are generally levied in the first instance upon capital or income. Indirect taxes are levied upon articles of consumption, or paid for permission to enjoy certain privileges. Taxes of this nature were formerly levied upon articles of home produce, when they were exported to foreign countries. But this system has been almost entirely abandoned by every country. A third species of taxation may be said to arise where a portion of the land of a country, or of the rent of the land, is set apart for the payment of a particular class of the public servants. These, however, are never to be considered as proprietors. In the words of Sir James Mackintosh, they are salaried for the performance of certain duties. The mode of this payment is indifferent. It is generally, in rude ages, by land; in cultivated ages, by money; but a territorial pension is no more a property than a pecuniary one. All the taxes in Great Britain and Ireland are indirect, with the exception of the income-tax, and the land-tax in England and Scotland; and throughout the most of Europe the principal taxes are indirect. The principal sources of revenue in the United Kingdom of Great Britain and Ireland are the Customs, Excise, and Stamp Duties — all indirect taxes.

Customs are the duties levied at the frontier upon foreign articles entered for home consumption. One principal objection to taxes of a nature similar to the custom duties has been, that they have enabled government to interfere with the natural operations of trade, by levying taxes for the purposes of protection or prohibition. It cannot be too often repeated that all taxation should be solely for the purpose of raising a revenue to pay the public servants, that all taxation ought to be solely for the purpose of paying for security. The different countries of the earth, favoured by nature with differences of soil and climate, produce different articles suitable for the taste of man, and we only deprive ourselves of additional sources of enjoyment when, by taxes, we prevent from coming to our own country articles which otherwise would have been consumed by us.

The customs duties have the following economic effects: on the one hand, their large amount is a proof of the extent of trade, and the ease with which a wealthy and powerful people can bear such heavy burdens; on the other they prevent the importation of foreign goods, and the production of home manufactures to the amount of the tax levied.

Excise duties are the taxes levied upon articles of consumption produced within the country. Most of these articles are consumed within the district where they are produced. The price of them to the consumer is raised by the excise duties. The consumption is consequently diminished, and individuals are deprived of that portion of happiness which consisted in the use of these particular articles of enjoyment.

There are other results different from economic results arising from the imposition of excise duties.

A tax on soap is a direct discouragement to cleanliness. Numbers of benevolent gentlemen by means of large subscriptions erect model baths and washing-houses for the poor in several great towns. They would accomplish more of their benevolent purposes if they used their efforts with success for the purpose of removing the tax on cleanliness. It is better to abolish the tax on soap, and educate the people generally, than to give them special instruction how to wash themselves.

A considerable portion of the public general taxation is raised in many countries by taxes upon the instruments for the communication of knowledge. Thus paper is taxed. The tax on paper is indefensible. It is now admitted by all reasonable men, that the poorer classes of the community ought to be educated. And, accordingly, the education of the people is increasing every day among the nations furthest advanced in civilization — the United States, England, France, Prussia, Belgium. It was once the fashion to discuss whether Education ought to be extended to the People — whether the poor had capacity to be safe elements in institutions.

> "Once we thought that education
> Was a luxury for the few;
> That to give it to the many,
> Was to give it scope undue;
> That 'twas foolish to imagine
> It could be as free as air —
> Common as the glorious sunshine
> To the child of want and care:
> That the poor man, educated,
> Quarrelled with his toil anon;
> Old opinions, rags and tatters,
> Get you gone! — get you gone!"
>
> — MACKAY.

Happily for the progress of mankind, and the peace of the days wherein we live, such sentiments have almost vanished in these countries. The Universities of England and Ireland have been gorgeously endowed, and the middle classes of society principally enjoy their benefits. The magnificent educational charities in England ennoble the country and character of Englishmen. We may reckon these amongst the public endowments for education, although many, if not most of them are of private foundation. They arose from fortunes acquired in trade and bequeathed by private citizens, with that desire to do good, that noble liberality and zeal for knowledge, which form some of the most prominent and best features in the English character. Of late years vast sums are annually voted by the English parliament for the purposes of National Education. At the same time the traces of former barbarism in matters of legislation remain. There are still heavy taxes upon the instruments which circulate knowledge amongst the people. How absurd it is that the supreme legislative council of a free and enlightened nation should at the same time vote money for education — and tax paper!

The taxes upon knowledge fall in a very slight degree upon expensive books. They bear with most pressing severity upon newspapers and all cheap publications, inasmuch as these consume comparatively a greater quantity of paper. And nearly two-thirds of the duty on paper used in printing are paid by newspapers and the cheap weekly publications unstamped.

The vast benefits which newspapers enjoying liberty of the press diffuse, cannot be too highly appreciated. The liberty of the press happily exists in these countries. Why do the taxes on knowledge remain? If newspapers did not exist, how ignorant should we not be of the affairs not merely of foreign nations, but of an adjoining county. The mutual ignorance of nations is one of the most prominent causes of national jealousies and wars. The mutual ignorance of local districts fosters paltry local animosities. These evils the newspaper helps to remove. It is now one of the most prominent aids to civilization; the more we cheapen it, the more we aid the advancement of the people. Taxes on the newspaper impede the social progress of the nation, prevent the diffusion of sound political knowledge, and impede peaceful reforms. Nor need there exist any apprehension of the people becoming dangerously devoted to politics if the printing of news be cheapened. With the generality of persons the most important part of the newspaper is the news. The only politics from which any true danger can be apprehended are the politics of ignorance, which lead to misery and beggary, and Jacqueries and Socialism. The politics of knowledge lead to prosperity, and wealth, and peaceful progress. Representatives of very opposite opinions in this country have lately agreed that the study of the daily events which befall the human race — the forming of the mind upon those questions which affect the destiny of the nation, and the destiny of the world — is a necessary duty for every free citizen; and that to read that page of contemporaneous history, the daily paper, is a worthy avocation for the working man, engaged in business however humble.

"Experience has shown, contrary to the general expectation, that newspapers are one of the best means of directing opinion — of quieting feverish movements — of causing the lies and artificial rumours by which the enemies of the State may attempt to carry on their evil designs, to vanish. In these public papers instruction may descend from the government to the people, or ascend from the people to the government; the greater the freedom allowed, the more correctly may a judgment be formed upon the cause of opinion — with so much the more certainty will it act."

The function of the newspaper is to diffuse a knowledge of cotemporaneous history — to disseminate the ideas of the present time — to translate into popular and easy language the opinions of the scholars of the age — and, by all these, to correct old bigotries and prejudices. Newspapers create and maintain that habit and freedom of public discussion — that interest in public affairs which characterizes free nations; they assist to form and express the public mind. Under despotic governments they are not permitted to exist free from the censorship of the press: for newspapers have essentially a liberal tendency, even though conducted upon principles the most adverse to liberty. Discussion in the long run elicits the truth. Absolutism is only most formidable when it has strength to be silent and not to need defenders. Under despotic governments newspapers do not exist; but free countries adopt the despotic policy, when, by taxes, they obstruct the circulation of newspapers.

And as in the case of the tax on soap, benevolent persons subscribe for wash-houses, without thinking of removing the tax, so in the case of the taxes on knowledge, benevolent persons eloquently commiserate, and liberally assist men of letters in distress, without reflecting that the taxes on knowledge are among the causes of that distress.

Patronage, as a support for literary men, is now at an end. In ancient times men of letters, who enjoyed no private fortunes, looked for their support to patronage alone. Horace and Virgil had Mæcenas and Augustus; and, until the art of printing and the diffusion of knowledge had created a sufficient number of readers to remunerate authors by the sale of their writings, it is evident that thus alone could genius be rewarded. But "those who labour for mankind should be rewarded by mankind — by the many, not by the few." Government may sometimes sparingly exercise a judicious patronage — it may sometimes be a duty to relieve genius in distress — but any regular system of government patronage for literary men is attended with obvious evils. Indeed government patronage and interference appear to be peculiarly inapplicable and injurious in the case of literary men. Authors, above all, should be recompensed solely by the value of their productions, and should not look for reward to the recompense of flattery, or a price for the advocacy of party.

All distress claims sympathy. But there is something peculiarly heart-rending in the poverty of a man of genius. That very same sensibility which had inspired him to eloquence or poetry, serves but to aggravate his calamities in destitution. Numbers of authors must, like the majority of the professional classes and all who labour, be men originally of indifferent circumstances. The chains of wealth fasten men to indolence, and rarely will those bound in their thraldom exert themselves to conquer the difficulties which meet the aspirant to fame at the threshold of every department of professional, literary, and scientific labour. I do not say that in consequence literary men should be supported by taxes from the rest of the community; but those mechanical agents which circulate thought throughout mankind ought to be exempted from taxation.

If it be desirable to have men of letters in the state, and to endow universities for them, why tax the paper upon which they write, and which printed with their thoughts enlightens the public, and whose sale furnishes their just remuneration? The advancement of Knowledge, the welfare of the People, all Art, Civilization, Happiness, rest most of all upon the strenuous efforts of intellect. All systems of legislation, therefore, which provide for men of letters the full rewards of their genius and labour, in the highest degree contribute to human Progress.

In the course of Time, — that greatest innovator, I trust that a liberal policy will yet abolish the taxes on knowledge. I now resume the general consideration of taxes upon articles of home consumption.

The great objection to the excise duties is their inquisitorial interference with industrious pursuits. The manufacturer, whose productions are subjected to the excise duties, is constantly watched by the officers appointed to gather the taxes; and the necessary interference of the excise-officers during the process of manufacture is even more injurious to the manufacturing interest than the amount of the tax levied. The control of the excise-officers ties the manufacturer to certain rules and processes preventing him from applying the most recent scientific and chemical discoveries, and so retards improvement. And it is certainly a strong objection against these duties, that the security of the revenue is held to be incompatible with the freedom of the manufacturer. Another great objection to the excise duties is the facility which they offer for the commission of frauds against the revenue. In the seventeenth report of the commissioners appointed to inquire into the management and collection of the excise revenue, it was stated, as a striking proof of the extent to which frauds are committed by manufacturers of soap, that "there are in England fifty that take out licences, for which they pay £4 per annum, each of which makes or rather brings to charge less than one ton of soap per annum, from which it is obvious that as the profits of such a sale would not pay for the licence, the entry is made in order to cover smuggling." These, then, are the principal objections to the excise duties; first, the direct discouragement to home manufactures, by far more than the amount of the tax levied; second, the indirect but far greater discouragement caused by the necessarily vexatious control exercised by the excise officers over the processes of the manufacturer; and thirdly, the temptations to and the facilities for fraud.

Again, keeping in our recollection that the first maxim of taxation is that the subjects of every state ought to contribute to the support of their government as nearly as possible in proportion to their respective abilities, we at once perceive the inequality of the system of taxation upon expenditure. It can never be levied upon individuals in proportion to their incomes. Indirect taxation, in order to be productive, must be levied chiefly or only upon articles of necessity, and these are consumed proportionately in larger quantities by the poor than by the rich. It is useless and almost impossible to tax articles of luxury. The moment a tax is levied upon any article of luxury, ingenuity immediately finds an untaxed substitute, or else the use of the article is dispensed with altogether. Thus, in the celebrated case of hair-powder, Mr. Pitt laid a tax upon it, and the article in a very short time almost ceased to be used. Therefore, the indirect taxes upon articles of consumption must be laid upon articles almost of the first necessity. The poorer a man is the more of his income is laid out upon articles of necessity. One with an income of £150 a-year, consumes the same amount of mere necessaries, in the year as a man with £10,000 a-year. It is a mere trifle to the latter, it is some portion of the income of the former. Even assuming persons with large incomes to consume about the same quantity of taxable articles as persons with small incomes, the latter pay the same amount of taxation as the former, instead of contributing to the support of the Government in proportion to their respective abilities as they ought to do according to the first maxim of Adam Smith.

Another great portion of the public taxation in civilized countries is raised by taxes on contracts. They have been imposed in various forms. One expedient is that of taxing the legal instrument which serves in a court of justice as evidence of a contract, a sale, or a receipt of money, and which, commonly, is the only evidence legally admissible. In these countries, few contracts are binding unless executed on stamped paper, which has paid a tax to Government. Stamps are impressions made upon paper or parchment, by the Government or its officers, for the purposes of revenue. Stamp duties were first levied in Holland. The great con. test with Spain had exhausted the resources of the Republic; and a reward was offered to any one who should devise the best new tax. Amongst others, the *vectigal chartæ,* or stamp-duty, was suggested, and introduced in 1624. Stamp duties were first introduced into England by the 5 Wm. and Mary, c. 21 (1694), but for a temporary period. Other statutes have followed, enlarged them, and made them perpetual. Different

Acts of Parliament in Great Britain and Ireland make a variety of unstamped instruments invalid; and in order to increase the revenue they multiply the number of stamped instruments necessary to authenticate transactions. Thus the Stamp Acts have given rise to many questions in courts of law, as to the amount of the stamp required for particular instruments — the nature of these stamps, the effect which the insufficiency or erroneous nature of the stamp may produce upon the instrument, and the use which may be made in a court of justice of a paper not stamped, but nevertheless unquestionably recording a particular fact.

Of taxes on contracts, the most important are those on the transfer of property, chiefly on purchases and sales. Taxes on the purchase and transfer of land are amongst the most objectionable of all taxes. Landed property in old countries is seldom parted with, except from reduced circumstances, or some urgent need. The seller, therefore, must take what he can get, while the buyer, whose object is an investment, makes his calculations on the interest which he can obtain for his money in other ways, and will not give the seller any greater sum, because he is charged with a Government tax on the transaction. The seller, therefore, is the person by whom such taxes, unless under peculiar circumstances, will be borne. The tax accordingly falls upon a man at the period of his distress.

But there is a more important and general reason for condemning such taxes upon sales. Such sales tend to make the property of both seller and buyer more productive. A man sells lands either because he is so reduced in general circumstances that he has no longer the available capital to pay the labour which may render the land productive; or if he be not embarrassed, he hopes with the money obtained by the sale to realize larger profits in some other pursuit than in that of agriculture. The buyer in every case is not ordinarily a poor man, and he wishes to invest his money in land, because he hopes to realize greater profits by so doing. Therefore, all taxes, and all difficulties and expenses annexed to such contracts, are detrimental, especially in the case of land, the source of subsistence, and the original production of all wealth, on the improvement of which, therefore, so much depends.

Similarly all buyers and sellers exchange their property, because they expect the subjects of the respective exchanges will be more valuable to them than the objects which they formerly possessed. If, then, those who wish to sell and those who wish. to buy be able forthwith to effect an exchange, the general income will be increased provided they be successful in their new undertaking, by the respective profits which they will make, in addition to what they realized before.

On the other hand, if the taxes be so exorbitant as to prevent or delay the exchange, they are an obstacle to the increase in the general income. The more facility is given to the exchange of property, the more likely is all property to find its way to the hands of those who will make it most productive.

Amongst others of the objectionable stamp duties in many countries, may be mentioned the taxes on medicine, and the taxes on insurances. By the former, bodily injury may be inflicted upon all unable to afford the payment of the tax; by the latter, provision against accidental calamity is lessened, and the number involved in such calamities is increased.

Taxes on Justice are unjust and indefensible upon the sound principles of juridical science.

The duty of protecting property by means of just laws, promptly, uniformly, and impartially administered, is one of the strongest and most interesting of obligations on the part of government. Mr. Hume looked upon the whole apparatus of government as having ultimately no other object but the distribution of justice. Lord Brougham has graphically expressed the same idea, when he said, that the end of the whole paraphernalia of king, lords, commons, army, and navy, was to place twelve honest men in a jury-box. The passion to acquire property is incessantly busy and active. Every man is striving to better his condition. Constant struggles and jealous collisions take place between men of property and no property — the one to acquire, the other to preserve; and between debtor and creditor, the one to exact, the other to postpone payment. We pay taxes in return for the security afforded by government to our properties and liberties, and it is worse than absurd to discourage by a tax the very means by which an injured subject seeks redress from the laws of the realm.

It was perhaps natural, in the early stages of society, that the sovereign of a petty state should receive fees from his subjects, upon the arbitration of their private disputes. His revenue derived from his private lands, or from tributary exactions, was not sufficient to pay the expenses of judicature, in addition to the other expenses of government. Even if it were sufficient, the imposition of judicial fees upon suitors was an easy method of raising additional taxes. Thus, the plan of imposing taxes upon suitors who wished the decision of the authorized courts of law upon their private disputes, was originally adopted by every state. The judges even, in every country, were originally paid by fees exclusively; and they accordingly derived an additional source of income from the business in their courts, and were thus interested in the abundance and protraction of litigation. The judges are now paid in most countries by fixed salaries. However, some of the expenses of justice are still defrayed by suitors. This should not continue. Courts of justice should be provided at the general expense of the country in the same way as the army and navy are paid for out of the public general taxation; and suitors ought not to be compelled to undergo any expense, except that which is naturally incurred by providing legal assistance in order to conduct the particular case. In effect, a tax upon the administration of justice is a direct reward offered for injustice. What can be more absurd than that the same legislators should at the same time give rewards for informers, and impose taxes on justice? By giving the bounty they acknowledge that it is right to encourage persons to come forward, and to further the ends of justice; by imposing the tax they throw difficulties in the way of the legal redress for wrongs. It was natural that, in early times, the expenses of justice should be defrayed by suitors. To those rude reasoners it appeared certain that he who obtained a judgment in his favour reaped the principal advantage to be obtained, and, therefore, that it was but right he should bear the expense incurred. But the parties who are compelled to have recourse to legal process, in order to obtain redress of their wrongs, are precisely those who have obtained least benefit from the general law of the realm. They, at the expense of time, care, and money, have purchased that protection which others enjoy, only paying the ordinary amount of taxation.

Another grievous objection to taxes on law proceedings, is, that they fall upon a man at the period of his distress. At the very moment when something of a man's property is taken from him, and he applies for redress to the public law of the state whereof he is a subject, this is the time chosen to call on him for an additional contribution to the support of the State. To the poor this effects almost a denial of justice. But public justice is a part of the general system of public protection which governments in civilized societies afford in return for the taxes which they receive from the people. By the system of courts of law, that is, the public arbitration of private disputes, and supported in the last resort by the military power, the rights of all are protected. And every contested case which at great cost decides a right, assists in protecting the rights and liberties of all. Therefore, the parties who suffer some injury to their rights ought not to defray the expense of the public justice by which they are redressed. They are the persons least benefited by the law and its administration. As Bentham says, the protection which the law affords them is not complete, since they have been obliged to resort to a court of justice to execute their rights and maintain their rights against infringement, whilst the remainder of the public have enjoyed the immunity from injury conferred by the law and its tribunals without the inconveniences of an appeal to them. A precisely parallel case is aggression by a foreign state upon part of our community, and a war in consequence for their redress, and to protect them from further molestation. The parties aggrieved are not compelled to pay the expense of the war. In fact, if it were possible to have private rights settled entirely at the public expense, it would be desirable. But this is impossible; for those whose business it is to manage legal proceedings, could never be expected to have the same zeal in individual cases, if they were paid public officers, and assigned accordingly. The best system of providing for the expense of public justice appears to be, that the-public machinery of the law should be paid for entirely out of the public treasury, whilst suitors should be put to no expense, beyond what the advocacy of their individual cases may demand.

The subject of law taxes may be concluded by a quotation from Bentham: — "The statesman who contributes to put justice out of reach — the financier who comes into the house with a law-tax in his hand, is an accessory after the fact to every crime: every villain may hail him brother — every neighbour may boast of him as an accomplice. To apply this to intentions would be calumny and extravagance; but as far as consequences only are concerned, clear of criminal consciousness, it is incontrovertible and naked truth."

I have now pointed out the economic evils arising from the system of indirect taxation. The duties levied upon articles of consumption produced abroad discourage the importation upon such goods, and prevent the production of home manufactures to be sent abroad in exchange. The duties levied upon articles produced at home discourage home manufactures by more than the amount of the tax levied; and by the necessary and vexatious interference of the officers employed to collect the revenue the most injurious effects result upon production. The duties on contracts are most injurious, particularly those on the transfer of land. Where one sells property, it is either because he cannot make an advantageous use of it, or because he hopes to lay out more productively the money which he will procure by the sale. When one buys property, it is because he hopes to derive an increase of profit from such investment of his capital. If any taxes or difficulties prevent these parties from seeking this transfer, the country loses the increase of profit which each of them in all probability would have made by the exchange. In addition to these objections to particular taxes belonging to the indirect system, there is the general and insuperable objection to indirect taxation, and that is its inequality. Indirect taxation can never be levied upon individuals in proportion to their means. On the contrary, since, in order to be productive, indirect taxes must be laid upon articles of necessity, which are consumed in as large, if not larger quantities by the poor than by the rich, the poor are taxed at a higher rate in proportion to their income than the rich. A country curate, or schoolmaster, in all probability consumes personally as much tea in the year as a nobleman, yet each pays the same tax; an author writing a single work, consumes as much paper as a nobleman in his lifetime, yet the tax upon a ream of paper is the same for each. We deservedly blame those in France who advocated a progressive Income Tax, increasing in proportion to the amount of the tax, and the consequent ability of the taxed to pay. But under the present system of indirect taxation, the proportionate amount levied in taxation increases with the person's inability to pay. Independent of the amount of taxation, the mode of collecting a tax is of the greatest importance. By adopting a correct mode of taxation, and effecting a saving in the expense of collection, the gross sum levied may be materially diminished. Taxes which in themselves produce but little, may by the manner of collection become the most oppressive. On the other hand, even those taxes which are the principal source of revenue may be collected in a manner so as scarcely to be felt by a wealthy and prosperous community.

The rate of taxation in different countries is now a matter of the first importance. Since steam navigation has bridged the Atlantic and Southern Oceans, it is easy to remove from the old countries to the new. Heavy taxation drives both capital and labour from the countries where it exists. Poor men go to that country where their labour is of equal or greater value, and where they have less to pay in supporting the machinery of government. Rich men emigrate because in the new countries the rate of profit is higher, their capital is of more value, and because they escape at the same time their former burthens. They thus increase their income in two ways. However, we have to consider that the countries of Europe have not only incurred a vast debt by means of the wars in which they were formerly engaged, but also, that even the reforms proposed in late years require additional and great expenditures of the public moneys. If we require our paupers to be tolerably supported and fairly educated, it requires a considerable sum of our taxation. If we provide national education for our agricultural and manufacturing classes, it demands an increased public outlay. Some able and enlightened reformers require that the resources of our empire abroad should be developed, and the sources of industry at home relieved by an extensive system of emigration and colonization. But if we attempted any thing of the kind, it would necessarily cause a great addition to the public taxation. So, if we seek to provide more efficient and humane treatment for our criminals; if we multiply courts of law for the convenience of parties; if we maintain a good system of police for the protection of property in our cities — all these salutary reforms demand an additional sum of the public money, and entail additional taxation. Hence is the vast importance of the method of taxation, since in all civilized countries the necessity for taxation will increase with the progress of society, and an additional amount of taxes will require to be levied.

The fundamental maxim of taxation is, that the subjects of every state ought to contribute to the support of the Government as nearly as possible in proportion to their respective abilities. Dovunque vi è societa, vi deve essere un corpo che la governi nell' interno, e che la difenda al di fuori. Questa doppia cura esige delle spese che debbono esser pagate dalla societa che ne profitta. — Wherever there is society there must be a political body to govern it internally and defend it externally. This double care occasions expense, and it is just that the society which profits by it should pay that expense. This is simply a question of justice, and, as Burke says, "justice is the great standing policy of civil society, and any eminent departure from it under any circumstances, lies under the suspicion of being no policy at all." In considering the general question of taxation, it is of course of the utmost importance to remember this maxim of Adam Smith, and at the same time to remember that taxes are no longer, as in the time of ancient Rome, principally tributes from plundered provinces, or, as in the feudal world, levies upon the poor, but wages paid by the people to the public servants.

Where the pressure of taxation exists upon raw materials, on manufactures, on food, and on the profits of capital, industry is checked — capital and labour are transferred to other countries. It ought to be a general maxim in taxation, that taxes should not be laid in the first instance upon production, but rather upon accumulation. Taxes laid in the first instance upon capital and labour, immediately discourage production; but taxes laid, for example, upon the existing rent of land, do not discourage industry nor accumulation, if there be security that no further tax will be imposed.

The existing land tax in England is an example of this kind. It is a tax of four shillings in the pound, according to an old valuation. At present it cannot, in most instances, be said to be paid from the income of any person, although undoubtedly it is a deduction from the income which the landlord otherwise would have. When it was first laid on it amounted to a confiscation to the amount of the tax, of the landed property of the existing proprietors. The tenant paid no higher rent in consequence of the tax having been laid on his landlord. It was immaterial to him whether the sum which he paid upon stated gale-days went entirely into his landlord's pocket, or partly into the coffers of the state. So the proprietor, when he sold this property, lost a fifth part of the purchase-money, which he would otherwise have obtained; but the purchaser of the property suffered nothing by the tax. He, when buying, made his calculations accordingly, remembering that he would have to pay this tax, and in consequence offering a less sum; and the tax cannot now be said to be paid by any one. The unredeemed part of it may be treated as a fee-farm rent on the land liable to it. It does not deprive the present landowners of any thing they ever possessed, and they have no right to be exempted from it.

Thus it appears that a fixed tax on rent, in the process of time, would absolutely injure no person; and the rule is similar with regard to a tax on such sources of income as dividends on stocks, and other funds of the same nature. Industry is not injured by such taxes, and the country may go on paying them without the same impediment to her becoming richer and richer which exists where taxes are laid in the first instance upon production. In all new countries, therefore, which have waste lands at their disposal, an advantageous method of taxation is to reserve out of those lands, when disposed of to subjects, a fixed annual rent. The state, of course, cannot compete with private individuals in agricultural or other undertakings, as the management of crown-lands in most countries shows. But the reservation of a fixed portion of the rent of public lands can injure no individual subject.

Again, where production increases, facilitated by new inventions and discoveries, and relieved from excessive burthens of taxation, accumulation goes rapidly on; and even greater taxes may be laid upon accumulated capital, with scarcely any additional burthen on the people. But where taxes are laid upon production, they directly check it and consequently prevent accumulation. The condition of the artizan, the mechanic, and the agricultural labourer, is of the first importance to modern civilized communities, all whose greatness depends upon their agricultural and manufacturing prosperity. The morals, habits, and education of all labourers are of the dearest interest to every nation, and, to aid their development, the systems of taxation all over the civilized world must be revised, if the word progress for the future is to be synonymous with improvement.

## 9. Duties of Government: Education

Taxes fall either on Capital or Income. It is plain, if the

taxes are paid from capital — that is, if they be so excessive that they cannot be defrayed from the income of the country — they will impair the sum which otherwise would be allotted to productive consumption, and to that extent lessen the national resources. If this continue for any time, and be not met by increased productive energy on the part of the people, their wealth will diminish; the fund from which the taxes are to be paid will gradually cease to exist — disasters and ruin will follow. Taxes do not necessarily fall on capital, because they may happen in terms to be imposed on it; nor do taxes necessarily fall on income, because they are laid on income. Suppose a tax of ten per cent. to be laid on income, a man with a present income of £1,000 per annum is required to pay £100. Now this really will be a tax upon his income if, after the tax be imposed, he continues to expend £900; but will be a tax upon his capital if he continues to spend £1,000 per annum.

The capital from which the individual's in come is derived may be £10,000; a tax of one per cent. per annum on this would be £100; but, again, if he spends only £900 instead of £1,000 per annum, it is drawn from income only.

As most men are possessed of a fair share of prudence with respect to themselves, and a desire to provide for their families, they guard against paying taxes from their capital, and pay them, no matter in what form levied, out of their annual income; that is, the receipts from all sources during the year. Therefore, if we recognise the first maxim of Adam Smith, that subjects should pay according to their ability, we see that the justest mode in which to make them do so is, to raise the annual sum required for the public expenses by an annual tax on income. Taxes, whether direct or indirect, are ultimately paid from income, and, upon the first principles of justice, they should be levied upon that income according to its amount. In the present system of taxation in Europe no reform upon so large a scale is possible to be accomplished. Laws can only be effective when they suit the general expectation, the temper, wishes, and education of the people; and the people in most countries require a much superior juridical education before they can perceive the cheapness and justice of an income-tax. Large bodies move slowly, and existing interests and liabilities must be regarded. For these reasons it would not now be possible to introduce a direct tax upon income in exchange for the present system of indirect taxation.

Besides, it is always expedient to keep in view, that it is easy and unobjectionable to raise as large a revenue as conveniently may be from those classes of luxuries which have most connexion with vanity, and least with positive enjoyment— such as the most costly varieties of all kinds of personal equipment and amusement. It is also easy and unobjectionable to raise a considerable sum by taxes upon stimulants, such as spirituous liquors and tobacco, provided the tax be not so large as to encourage smuggling. These stimulants are scarcely required as necessaries by any. And the fiscal is crowned with amoral use when such taxes diminish the consumption of an article like ardent spirits, the excessive drinking of which is pregnant with future misery. Wherever smuggling prevails a useful hint is given to the financier that the tax is too high; and once a heavy system of taxation causes smuggling, and the government tries to prevent it by forcible means, there is hardly any limit to the evil; for the collection of the taxes requires an immense number of officers, comptrollers, overseers, and soldiers. The public freedom even of honest individuals, is laid under restraint, and a great part of the revenue is exhausted by the expense of collection.

The reasons which I have given above merely show that the most equitable system of taxation is a direct tax upon income; and it therefore might at once be substituted for the taxes on knowledge, the taxes on justice, and other taxes, when they shall be removed in the progress of civilization.

The great objection to an income-tax has been the supposed difficulty of ascertaining the incomes of individuals who would be inclined to evade it. Incomes arising from the rent of land and houses, mortgages, funded property, may generally be known with almost mathematical accuracy. The persons, therefore, to whom an objection of this class could possibly apply, are professional men, merchants, manufacturers, and traders. As to these it is perfectly plain that with the progress of society the false returns would be comparatively few. Honesty is the best policy, and not only the best, but the most successful. All, with scarcely an exception, who have succeeded in life, in trading or professional pursuits, have succeeded by the strictest adherence to truth, and their honesty would not desert them in the payment of their taxes. With the general progress of enlightenment, the reluctance to pay taxes will gradually diminish, provided the taxpayers through their representatives possess an efficient and direct control over the public expenditure. In countries where a representative government does not exist, the greatest reluctance to pay taxes is shown, because there the people have no control over the expenditure of the taxes which they pay.

The next great objection to the income-tax is, that it is inquisitorial in ascertaining the exact amount of a man's income. The amount of annual income derived from realized property is generally as well known to a man's neighbours as to himself. The landlord, the tenant, and the mortgagee, all know what they pay and receive; and if any one wish to conceal the amount of his income, it is generally in order that he may live beyond it for some time, and in the end defraud his creditors. An income-tax is certainly not nearly so inquisitorial in its nature as the Excise; the officers of which branch of the public service keep a continual watch over the manufacturer, and know almost every thing concerning his trade, the manner in which he conducts it, his receipts, profits, and expenditure. Persons, besides, who carry on trade, not in a hazardous and too speculative a manner, but prudently, do not dread an exposure of the state of their affairs; and I am certain that publicity in all cases would be beneficial to the public, and would only injure a few fraudulent inidividuals, who by concealment are enabled to carry on their projects somewhat longer, terminating in consequences finally more injurious to themselves and all connected with them. Private convenience must yield to public good. It is essential to all great questions of finance to ascertain exactly what is the taxable income of the community, and what, in cases of national emergency, they could afford to pay. One of the greatest of the social evils of modern life is the custom of attempting to maintain the appearance before the world of a larger income than is really possessed; and it would be better for those who yield to this weakness, if the extent of their means were publicly known, and the temptation removed of expending more than they can afford — stinting real wants to make a false show externally.

Another objection is, that the tax-payers would be unwilling to pay directly so much money as is required in old countries to carry on the expenses of the Government — although paying indirectly at present they have but little objection. This is an objection which will disappear before the progress of education.

But even the reluctance to pay directly appears to me one of the arguments in favour of the income-tax. The public would see with their eyes open the sums which they pay in taxation, and would insist on a proper application of the public moneys. As a means of decreasing the difficulty, the income-tax might be collected in small sums — for example, once a month.

There is another objection urged, which is, however, of small weight — that such a tax has a tendency to diminish the fund which otherwise would be used in employing labour. There is no doubt but that there is such a tendency. However, it only shares this evil in common with all other taxes, and as it is cheaper in the collection, and does not raise the prices of the articles of consumption, it is less open to that charge than any other species of tax.

It must be apparent that the same amount would be collected at a cheaper rate through means of an income-tax than through the customs and excise. There would not be required the same numerous staff of officials watching the different manufactures, nor the police force, the preventive service, the coast-guards, and all the expensive machinery required to prevent smuggling by the laws which hold up a premium for it.

It remains to be considered with respect to an income-tax, whether it should be levied in the same proportion upon all incomes, or whether incomes derived from realized property and permanent sources should be taxed at a higher rate than incomes derived from precarious property — such as the wages of mental or bodily labour, and the profits of trade. It is also to be considered whether small incomes ought to be taxed at the same rate as large incomes. On these two questions various statesmen and economists have at different times proposed various plans. They are of the utmost importance to consider, as the gravest objections to the income-tax arise from the doubts concerning them.

I shall first consider whether large and small incomes ought to be taxed at the same rate. And it is necessary to remember that at present, under the indirect system of taxation upon necessaries wherever it prevails, persons with moderate incomes are taxed at a higher rate than persons with large incomes, because the former consume as much or more of taxable articles than the latter.

In taxation, equality of sacrifice is, if possible, the first thing to be attained. Is this, then, accomplished by making each contribute in proportion to his pecuniary means? It is plain that a tax of £10 taken from a person who has only £100, is a greater burthen than £100 taken from a person who has £1,000. It deprives the former, perhaps, of some of the necessaries, the latter of only a few of the luxuries of life. Therefore, the French school of economists have sometimes advocated "I'impot progressif," that is, a graduated income tax, in which the percentage rises with the amount of the income. This appears to me to be erroneous in principle, as it is a sort of penalty upon wealth, and a direct check upon accumulation. The plan originally suggested by Bentham, and adopted by Mill, appears to be the best — namely, to leave untaxed a certain minimum of income — say £50 per annum — sufficient to provide the necessaries of life for a family. Or if it be considered expedient that all enjoying the protection of the law should pay a small sum by way of contribution towards its expense, let there be a small capitation tax, or a tax per head upon all whose incomes are under £50 per annum; and let incomes exceeding this amount be taxed, not upon the gross amount, but upon the net excess above £50. For example, an income of £60 should be taxed only as a net income of £10.

But the more important question is, whether the profits of trade, salaries, annuities, and the gains of professions, may not justly be taxed at a lower rate than the incomes derived from realized property. Remembering that persons should pay for public protection according to their ability — that is, according to their property, — it would appear at once that those who derive their incomes from uncertain or temporary sources should not pay so much, or at the same rate, as those who derive their incomes from permanent sources. This question has been argued with great ability, and has been made the principal objection to the income-tax in Great Britain and Ireland. But I will illustrate the position by an example. Compare the case of one deriving his income from an annuity of £400 which will perish with him, and one possessing an estate of £400 per annum, the landLord is more interested than the annuitant in the protection afforded by the law, and should pay more; he is better able to pay, and should consequently pay more. Such is the argument advanced.

Again, compare the condition of a professional or mercantile man beginning the world with the condition of a landed proprietor enjoying the same income. In the present day there are many such men, of education and talent, who have to surrender most physical comforts, strain every nerve, and often sacrifice health itself to eke out a scanty income as the stepping-stone to ultimate advancement. In such a case a tax falls upon a man's energies and abilities, which, of all other things, ought to be fostered and protected by the law. Precarious health, daily exertion, the studies of night, ought not to be taxed at the same rate as realized property. This argument, however, is equally strong both against the present system of indirect taxation on expenditure, and an income-tax which would tax at the same rate all incomes, in the usual sense of the term. Nay, the argument is much stronger against the present system of indirect taxation upon expenditure; because, now, the smaller the income which is spent upon taxed articles the heavier in proportion is the tax. And it is very strange that although some eloquently commiserate a professional or mercantile man paying an income tax at the same rate as a landed proprietor, and ingeniously use this as an argument against the income-tax, they do not reflect that, under the present system, all noblemen, landed proprietors, mercantile and professional men, mechanics and farmers, are taxed at the same rate for every shilling spent on taxable articles; and according as the income is less, the rate of the tax proportionably is greater. However, in effect, an even tax on income, as the word is generally understood, might, in certain cases, be more unjust than the present indirect system of taxation. For although a person with a precarious income, under the indirect system, pays as much in taxation as one with a permanent income, still that portion of his income which he saves almost altogether escapes taxation.

The problem to be solved is, how to have these various species of incomes taxed equably — namely, the rent of land, the profits of capital in trade, annuities purchased by the parties enjoying them or by others for them, salaries in situations which may not be permanent salaries in situations which end only with life as in the case of beneficed clergymen and fellows of colleges, and lastly, that class of income which may be termed the gains of professions, the wages of intellectual or bodily labour, paid by those who reap its benefits, and lasting only so long as its recipients are able to serve their fellow men.

Moved by the considerations which I have mentioned above, some have proposed to tax realized property at a different rate from wages, profits, or annuities. The value of landed property averages about thirty years' purchase, in old countries and in prosperous times, whereas the income derived from wages or from the gains of a profession, can never be rated at a higher value than fifteen years' purchase. Again, the profits of trade may be considered as half derived from personal exertion, and half from capital sunk in realized property. It is generally understood that the rate of profit obtained on capital employed in trade, including the wages of superintendence, is double the rate of interest on money lent in the same country. Therefore, if a scheme should be adopted of taxing different species of incomes at different rates, the incomes derived from wages or professional gains, should be taxed at half the rate of the incomes derived from realized property; and one-half of the profits of trade should be taxed at the rate assigned to real property, and the other half according to the rate at which wages and the gains of professions are taxed.

Different other schemes have been proposed in different countries. For example, in the free city of Frankfort the following portions of income are entirely excluded from the taxation: — first, that part of the yearly income which has been employed in the extension and improvement of trade — secondly, that part which, owing to existing taxes, is a charge upon trade, for example, licenses for innkeepers.

But the strictly scientific scheme of taxation is to tax all incomes at the same rate. Where men enjoy a certain amount of income for a certain time under the protection of the law and the government, they should pay for the support of that system of public protection equally in proportion to the amount of their incomes. All should pay to the government at the same rate for the security which enables them to enjoy a unit of income during a unit of time. Such is the scientific principle. But, then, what is income? It appears to me that the difficulties into which economists and statesmen have fallen on this subject, aided by that large class of worthy citizens who are always anxious to shift the burthen from their own shoulders to those of others, have arisen from their not considering what income is. Now, income is, literally, all that comes in to a man in the year — all that he receives as gain during the year over and above his property at the commencement of the year. Therefore, the income-tax should be paid upon all the property which one receives as gain during the year. And this at once solves the difficulty about apportioning the rates of taxation to different incomes; for, if one received property by gift inheritance, or any other means, say to the amount of £20,000, he should pay the income-tax for £20,000 for that year. It is self-evident that this solves the suggested difficulty as to the inequality of taxation upon incomes of the same amount arising from sources essentially different in their nature. The capital, on coming into the hands of a new proprietor, without purchase, is taxed as income for that year. The income from it is taxed every year it lasts.

I include under the income tax the tax on successions, which, in itself, is one of the least objectionable methods of taxation. Mr. Brodie has summed up its advantages. A person, on coming into possession of his property, pays a portion at once more willingly than if he were to be harassed by the periodical visits of the tax-gatherer. Such a tax is levied at the precise time when the owner acquires his fortune, or an increase of it.

It is probable that the laws of inheritance will for some time occupy the attention of jurists and economists. We are evidently on the eve of regulations concerning them, which will have the most serious effect upon the economic conditions of society. Mr. Mill considers that freedom of bequest should be the general rule, but limited by two things; first, that if there are descendants, who, being unable to provide for themselves, would become burthensome to the state, the equivalent of whatever the state would accord to them should be reserved from the property for their benefit; and secondly, that no one should be permitted to acquire by inheritance more than a moderate independence. In case of intestacy, the whole property ought to escheat to the state, which should be bound to make a just and reasonable provision for descendants — that is, such a provision as the parent or ancestor ought to have made. It may, in future times, be considered whether any except descendants, or the nearest relatives in the ascending line, should be permitted by the State to acquire property by succession. It may also be considered whether persons have a right to leave their descendants unprovided for, and whether all descendants should not receive a certain share of the ancestor's estate. Lord Alvanley, when Master of the Rolls, said, in Rawlins *v.* Goldfrap, "If the father had thought fit, he might, I am afraid, by the law of this country, leave his children upon the parish. I am surprised that should be the law of any country; but I am afraid it is the law of this; and I have taken occasion before to say so. Not even the parish, in such a case, can come against the executor." But questions such as these are far in advance of the present state of legal or economic education.

In conclusion, one general argument may be noticed in favour of direct as contra-distinguished from indirect taxation. A direct income or property tax reaches absentees. I have never agreed with those political economists who contend that absenteeism is no evil to a country. It is true, the worst results of absenteeism are seen only in the remote agricultural districts, where no middle class exists. In rich and flourishing cities, if some of the principal proprietors be absent, they are scarcely missed — there are others to discharge the various important duties without them. But in districts where there are only two classes — a poor dependent peasantry and some few great proprietors — the absence of the latter, and the bad administration of the powers which belong to a landlord, cause incalculable injury.

An absentee is one who derives his income from one country and resides in another; but the term is generally applied to landlords only as the most numerous class of absentees. They are the most numerous class of absentees, because from the peculiar powers which the law gives them over those who rent their land, such as the power of distress, it is easier for them to absent themselves from the personal superintendence of their property than it is for any other class of capitalists: if a merchant were an absentee from his office, he would soon be a bankrupt. And the best way to provide against absenteeism is, to leave the land-Lord only the same powers to recover his rent which other creditors have to recovertheir debts — to remove all the legal restrictions which tie up land from being used and enjoyed to the fullest extent, either by the legal proprietors or the tenant cultivators — to make land a marketable commodity, and teach men to regard the possession of large landed estates, not as a source of paramount influence, but as a mercantile speculation.

Absenteeism has the following injurious effects upon the

production and accumulation of wealth in a country.

Accumulation, or the increase of wealth in a country, can only ensue from profits and from savings. All persons who supply the demands of others obtain a profit by the transaction; at least, the obtaining of a profit is the object with which a demand is supplied, and the actual obtaining of a profit is the object without which a demand cannot be supplied. It is in one sense immaterial whether the absentee spends his income productively or not. But no income, whether received in money or in kind, can be spent without indirectly causing profitable production, for every person who supplies the wants of the spender of the income receives a portion of the spender's money, part of which portion is the profit of the supplier. If the income derived from England be spent in France and Belgium, persons in France or in Belgium derive a profit from supplying the absentee, and this profit enables them to accumulate. This profit also is something taken from the profits of those who would otherwise supply the demand of the consumer in England. If all the rich persons who now live in London and require commodious houses, servants, furniture, clothes, fruits, vegetables, and soforth, were to settle at Brussels, the houses which are now built in London for their residences, or for those of the shopkeepers who supply them with luxuries, and the grounds which are employed as gardens round the metropolis, would not exist. All the shopkeepers who supply the persons in London with luxuries would cease to make so great a profit, and would follow the wealthy classes, by whose expenditure they had existed, if distance, language, and other difficulties did not prevent them. Hence there would be no longer occasion to supply those who minister to the wants of the wealthy classes with the corn and meat raised in the country, and the production of England would be diminished. Such are the injurious effects of absenteeism upon the production of wealth.[16] I do not now treat of it otherwise. At the same time I do not propose that any tax should be laid upon absentees, for the purpose of compelling them to reside upon the spot whence they drew their income. Such a principle is adopted by Russian policy; but the only effect it could have, if enforced, would be to diminish the value of certain remote districts. Absentees, besides, are suf-

---

[16] Bohn's "Standard Library Cyclopædia." Title, "Absentee."

ficiently punished by the necessary deterioration which ensues when agricultural property is not under the eye of the owner. However, absentees ought to pay an income-tax for the following strictly juridical reasons. As I have before stated, taxes are paid by the subjects of a Government, as wages to the public servants, for the protection afforded by their services to their properties and liberties, and taxes should be paid in proportion to the individual's ability. One who derives an income from a country should, wherever he resides, contribute a just proportion to the taxation which pays for the public protection and security, without which his income could not be collected. At present, one who derives an income from England or Ireland, and resides in France, has his property still protected for him; but, except under the income-tax, he escapes the taxation, which he should have paid had he resided at home. This is manifestly unjust. It would be considered monstrous if one deriving a large income from a country, and resident in it, were exempt from its taxation. Is it not more unjust that one being out of the country, and not benefiting it by his expenditure, should not contribute to its public burthens? At present, under the indirect system of taxation, an absentee enriches a foreign country by his expenditure, while he wholly escapes the taxation of his own; but if a direct system of taxation were substituted for the present system, by remaining abroad the absentee would be at least under a double set of taxes; and in any event it is just that a person deriving an income from a country should pay proportionately for the protection by which he is enabled to enjoy it.

## 10. Divisions of Jurisprudence

I cannot conclude the subject of government without discussing the important and debated questions which relate to the encouragement of Art, Science, and Education, by endowments from the public moneys. The primary object of government is security; but the question arises — is it advisable for a powerful and wealthy community to make public provision for other purposes? In Great Britain and Ireland, there is less spent by government upon Education, Literature, Art, and Science, than in any other great community.

I have already discussed the question as to the education of the poor by the State. It is a measure of security; and for the poor education should be gratuitous. Nay, places of public amusement, museums, parks, and picture-galleries, open to the public — even these may be considered as auxiliary measures of security, inasmuch as they refine the public taste, create more wide and generous judgments, unfold more ennobling pleasures. The craving for excitement and recreation is natural to us. The wearied and depressed spirits of those who live the crowded life of laborious cities, must in some way be refreshed. When daily labour is performed, when the claims of social duty are fulfilled, moderate and timely amusement claims its place as a want inherent in our nature. The rich have a thousand ways of gratifying this natural desire for excitement and relaxation. In England and Ireland the poor have almost but one — intoxication by the drinking of ardent spirits. It is right to strive to rescue the poor from this dominion of the grovelling and the vile — to give them some idea of the grand achievements of antiquity — the magnificent efforts of the human race — the beauty of Nature and Art. But institutions such as I have alluded to can be supported on a large scale only by public taxation.

To make, also, the education of the people with certainty a measure of security, they ought to be instructed in the principles of law and political science. Under the title of law, the children of the people should be instructed as to the criminality and penal nature of the most prominent offences. It has been remarked that crimes against the person occur more frequently in some districts than others. This is to be attributed not merely to a degree of greater barbarity, but also to a greater ignorance of the law. The danger now to be apprehended from the Socialist sects through Europe, arises from the prevalent ignorance of history, of the true nature of man, and of correct political principles.

But the question arises, should colleges and universities be provided out of the public general taxation to educate those of the middle and upper classes, who may be able to avail themselves of them, Adam Smith entertained a very strong opinion upon the subject. He considered such endowments most injurious to the cause of science and education. He considered that if a man's emoluments be precisely the same, whether he does or does not perform some very laborious duty, it is his interest either to neglect it altogether or perform it in a careless and slovenly manner; and that were there no public institutions for education, no system nor science could be taught for which there was not some demand. A private teacher could never find his account in teaching either an exploded and antiquated system of a science acknowledged to be useful, or a science universally believed to be a mere useless and pedantic heap of sophistry and nonsense. Such systems, such sciences can subsist nowhere but in these incorporated societies for education, whose prosperity and revenue are, in a great measure, independent of their reputation, and altogether independent of their industry.

Such have been the views of this first of economists upon this important subject. I have given his words: they are worthy of the gravest consideration. These are among the most serious dangers against which universities have to guard. Adam Smith argues not merely that it is wrong to tax one part of the community for the sake of endeavouring to give a higher class of knowledge to the other, but that these endowments are positively injurious to science and education. Can this be true? Does independent wealth destroy the desire for knowledge and the zeal to communicate it to others? And is that poverty which we have learned to mourn as the wretched companion of laborious genius, absolutely then the condition by which that genius is forced to labour? In most numerous instances in England, Ireland, and Scotland, it certainly has happened that apparently the most triumphant success in a college career has been the ruin of the fortunate individual, in every point of view except his material comfort. High and varied talent and strenuous industry have often found in these old universities a sudden grave by obtaining a comfortable and idle competency!

And yet few things are greater than a well-conducted National University, wherever it is to be found, or such, at least, as one might be made. A National University — at the same time flinging open its gates to all — embracing amongst its professors the matured intellect of the nation — affording the soundest instruction in the varied branches of that social education becoming the gentleman — and employing that special discipline necessary for individual professions — cultivating Art — elucidating Antiquity — instructing the youth of a nation in the practice of its laws — and with funds for the assistance of penniless young men to educate themselves for the professions of their choice — this is one of the noblest institutions of Civilization;

and wherever it may exist, exercises the most important and beneficial influence.

Can it be said to be injurious for the nation to continue the primary instruction given to the poor up to the highest order — to rescue from the drudgery of manual labour the intellects which occasionally appear amongst that peasantry which has produced such men as Arkwright and Robert Burns? A distinguished publicist understands national education thus: — One grand system of public instruction, given and regulated by the State, commencing from the village school, and proceeding step by step to the College — higher still to the Institute — to the University, — the gates of science opened wide to all the talents, — no parish without a school, no town without a college, no city without a faculty, — one great net-work of intellectual studia, lycea, gymnasia, colleges, chairs, libraries, mingling the radiance of their knowledge over the surface of the country — everywhere arousing capacities and animating vocations; — in a word, the ladder of human knowledge, held firmly by the hand of the State, placed in darkness the most obscure, and ending in the light — the heart of the people put in communication with its brain. — Such a system may yet exist. But the question of taxing the community for the education of certain of the middle and upper classes of society is different.

A University has two functions — one to be a centre for educated intellectual men, to pursue together the investigations of science — the other as a place for superior education, whether general or professional. The success which has attended the old Universities of Europe has arisen principally from their discharging the first function. A college has no magical power to make scholars. The education given by endowed teachers, wholly independent of their pupils, never has been, and never can be, so successful as where a teacher is paid directly for the work which he does. That the portion of collegiate endowments applied for this first purpose has been well-spent money, the names of Sir William Blackstone, Adam Smith, Judge Story, Chancellor Kent, Guizot, Niebuhr, and Savigny prove — all lecturers in colleges, and who, by their genius and research, have advanced to the highest degree of excellence the subjects which they taught. Therefore, taxation for the first purpose is right, as a homage to Science and Art; and in order to provide their votaries with the means, untrammelled by worldly care, to follow their favourite pursuits. But taxation of the entire community for the education of some of the upper and middle classes through means of Universities, cannot be justified with certainty. Still, incidental to the first function of a University is a certain proportion of education. Unquestionably in most branches of science teaching improves the teacher. And to this amount at least, education ought to be cultivated in Universities. At the same time, it ought to be paid for by those who receive it.

The entire question is one of the greatest difficulty, and not to be settled until a very distant period. In the meantime, vast endowments at present exist for the purpose of giving superior education. And it is our duty to render them as available as possible to satisfy the wants of the age, and to aid the progress of society.

The sanitary arrangements of the public are evidently proper subjects to be under the public control, and to be provided at the public expense. If each person were left alone and undirected to make such arrangements as he pleased for the cleansing of his house, the cities of Europe would soon be like Cairo and Smyrna, reeking with filth, and periodically decimated by the plague. The public cleansing and draining of cities may be considered as a measure of security. If through a reckless disregard of the poor, the legislators of society permit owners of land to let to the poor unwholesome dwellings undrained, unventilated — if they neglect to provide for the cleansing of the ways before their houses — neglect to supply them with water — tax their soap — leave them to wallow in filth, which their daily labour leaves no time to remove — the laws of disease punish the wealthy for that neglect; and Death generated in those unwholesome dwellings marches with an equal step to the palaces of the rich. Hence, even leaving benevolence and charity aside, it is incumbent on those who have property to consult for these things, and to raise money for these purposes by public taxation.

The great cities of the modern world, in wealth so far superior to the congregations of human beings who dwelt in the cities of the ancient world, are, in respect to sewerage and the supply of water, in many instances inferior. This blot upon our modern civilization it should be the aim of the public men of all civilized countries to remove. One duty is on us all, to lavish our social energies upon the destruction of misery. No more effectual means can be found than to bring the light of day, the air of heaven, and the water of the streams to those noisome alleys where the poor rot in filth uncared for and unknown.

Some departments of the public service are supplied with funds out of the public general taxation, some by local rates. Whatever directly concerns the public security at large should be provided for out of the public general taxes; whatever institution or department only benefits the district where it is placed should be supported by local rates. Thus, the departments of the executive government, justice, the army and navy, should be supported out of the general taxes. But it is only just by local rates to provide for the police of cities, and the expense of making and repairing roads.

The principle has been adopted under the poor-laws in the United Kingdom of giving the power of taxation and general control in the first instance to local bodies, subject to a central board which provides for the legal discharge of the duties with respect to the relief of the poor, revises the general management of the local guardians, and receives the reports of inspectors appointed by the government unconnected with the local boards. It appears to me an admirable precedent for the management of all departments requiring local taxation; it is a direct precedent for the manner in which sanitary affairs should be conducted. Sanitary guardians might be appointed in a manner similar to the poor law guardians, with power of taxation for sanitary purposes. And their proceedings might be subject to the authority and approval of a central board, constituted like the poor-law commissioners, and like them receiving reports from its own inspectors.

For purposes of the education of the poor also, powers might be given to local boards to raise taxes, subject to the approval of the government, or of a commission appointed by government. In matters of education the control of a central authority is most essential. The same powers ought to be given to local bodies for the purpose of building museums, picture galleries, and libraries — all of course public. Every institution in the country to which the public taxation has ever contributed, or does contribute, ought to be open to the public. All these local rates, in the same manner as the public general taxation, should be raised by a direct tax upon income. All who live in the district are as much interested as the owners of real property, in the security obtained by the legal provision for the poor. And the same principle applies to the other subjects which I have stated as proper for local taxation.

Plenary powers of taxation for local purposes ought to be conferred on boards elected by the ratepayers at large, and to which all ratepayers ought to be eligible. No taxation is paid so cheerfully by the people as that which they see directly expended amongst themselves. The power of managing such public matters also cultivates a municipal spirit and a capacity for public affairs, founds public order upon the widest basis, and gives increased security for public freedom.

Whilst I have commented upon the economical advantages of an income-tax, I do not mean to imply that a general adoption of the income-tax would now be expedient, at least until the tax-paying public are better educated in the principles of political science. The efficiency of laws depends essentially upon their conformity to the general expectation. And unless a tax suit the previous habits and wishes of the people, and unless they be thoroughly convinced that they are not paying too highly for their government, discontent ensues. It is true, that, in reality, the laborious classes of the community, under the indirect system of taxation, absolutely pay more for their government than they would if the income-tax were universally adopted. They consequently suffer for their ignorance and impatience of taxation; and as long as they remain so ignorant, taxes must be collected in the easiest instead of the justest manner.

However, Education is spreading through the masses of the people to prepare them for the social changes that ensue in the progress of society. We are advancing in our social phases from system to system ever nearer to the truths of Political Science. We move slowly, it is true; but there is nothing of which we ought to be so convinced as the slowness of progress. In the scheme of the universe centuries are but seconds — ages produce the diamond. How long did the granite and marble slumber in darkness from the time they were fused in the primeval earth, until the time when the artist's skill wrought them into the Temple of Theseus, the Parthenon, the Colosseum, St. Peter's! So those who in the civilized countries of the world now cultivate the social sciences, are forming the materials from which some future statesman shall rear a Social Fabric, more enlightened, more equal, more just, better fitted for the advancement of Knowledge and the welfare of the People — the Progress of the civilized world.

It is true that in this great age of discoveries, of events, of conquests, of freedom, Progress is moving at an accelerated pace. In all the free civilized countries of the world, merit, unaided by birth or fortune, can now force its way to the very highest positions. Behold what a future of glory, thought, intelligence, this principle has unfolded! "A high ambition entertained independently of social station, expansion and boldness in political thought; desire for intervention in the affairs of the realm; full consciousness of the dignity of man as a human being, and of the extent of his power, if he have capacity to exercise it — these are sentiments and dispositions altogether modern, the proceeds of modern civilization, and the fruits of that glorious and elastic generality which characterizes it." The exertions formerly made only by privileged races or classes are now participated by all. The entire community, instead of a small section only, works for prosperity, for advancement. And, in consequence, the human race has within the last two centuries accomplished more material prosperity than in all the former ages. At the same time we may be assured what a grand career is yet before mankind, when we reflect how minute a portion of the earth is occupied by free civilized men. We are but in the infancy of Civilization. To continue this glorious Progress the first requisite is Social Order — Security.

## 11. Condification

Rights and duties arise between different states or their subjects, and form the province of International Law.

International Law is the rule which civilized independent societies observe towards one another in modern times. So far as it is capable of being enforced, it comes within the province of Positive Law. The term *international* is of recent origin. Dr. Zouch, in 1650, first distinguished *jus inter gentes* from the Roman jus gentium. D'Aguesseau, in 1757, distinguished *le droit entre les nations* from *le droit de nations.* Finally, Bentham, about the year 1790, invented the term international.

A great portion of what is called International Law, cannot

be yet said to come under the denomination of Positive Law; and Political Law is in the same defective condition as International Law. No punishment can be assigned for the offences of the Sovereign. *Quis custodiet ipsos custodes?* All that human wisdom has been able to devise is a system of precautions and indirect means, rather than a system of legislation; so that a treaty between two nations is an obligation which does not possess the same force as a contract between two individuals; and the organization of International Law remains most incomplete. In this department of the science of Jurisprudence there is a great desideratum. The complete recognition of this branch of Jurisprudence will not take place until some international code be adopted by the principal civilized nations, promulgated by their authority, expounded by their international tribunals, and enforced by their combined strength in the last resort. Such a system partially exists in North America, where the States federally united submit to the supreme court of justice those quarrels which, in ancient times, or even now in the greater part of Europe could not be so peaceably arranged.

The happiness of the civilized nations of the human race would be fixed so far as it depends on law, if it were possible now to raise Political and International Laws to the rank of complete and organized sciences.

In accordance with the four-fold division of Positive Law, I divide Jurisprudence into four parts, termed respectively Civil, Criminal, Political, and International.

Civil Jurisprudence is concerned with those rights which are sufficiently protected by awarding compensation to the injured party upon any infringement of them. This compensation is afforded by civil process.

Criminal Jurisprudence punishes the violation of a right on behalf of the community in many cases where no compensation can be awarded. This punishment is effected by criminal process.

Political Jurisprudence embraces the province of government, and its relations to the people.

International Jurisprudence is separated into two divisions, public and private.

Public International Law defines and adjusts the mutual rights and duties of the governments of different states.

Private International Law defines and adjusts the mutual

rights and duties of individual citizens in different states. Within the sphere of International Law are included the greatest social and political problems of the age, amongst them the Right of Intervention — the Liberty of the Individual, his independence of his own Government and his Right to call for protection against wrong.

In point of expression the whole body of the Positive Law of a State has been usually divided into common and statute, or unwritten and written.

The Common Law is the collection of rules of civil conduct recognised by the members of the community without any positive interference of the legislative power.

The Statute Law is the law prescribed and promulgated in writing by the supreme power in the State.

The object of a statute is to fix the nature of a legal relation, by which the existence of that legal relation may be secured against error or caprice.

Both Common and Statute Law fall under the denomination of Positive Law. They both spring from the same authoritative force — the will of the community. — And custom is the sign by which we recognise that Common Law which arises and grows amongst a people as naturally and necessarily as their Language.

The Common Law has been called unwritten law, — *lex non scripta* — because without any interference of a legislative body it is a rule prescribed by the common consent and agreement of the community, as applicable to its different relations, and as capable of preserving the peace good order and harmony of society, — rendering to every man that which of right belongs to him.

The Common Law is not the production of the brain of one legislator, it is the growth of time and circumstance, the offspring of the necessities which the manners, religion, and circumstances of a nation have imposed. Antecedent to all law enacted by the supreme legislative power; antecedent to the existence of the legislative body in a state, its inhabitants are governed by customs, spontaneously arising and binding by the force of public opinion. These ancient customs of the people must be recognised by the Judges, as much as the general expression of their will through their representatives in the Legislature, and must equally with the statutes of a realm be considered as Positive Law.

The sources of the Common Law are in the usages, habits, manners, and customs of a people; its seat is in the breast of the judges, who are its expositors. Every nation must of necessity have its Common Law, and that will be simple or complicated in its details according as the society is simple or complicated in its relations. Some practical rules suffice a wandering horde of savages; laws minute and nice in detail are demanded by the exigencies of a nation which agriculture and commerce have enriched, which civilization and the liberal arts have polished. The Common Law, therefore, is never stationary; but is modified and extended by analogy, construction, and custom, so as to embrace the new relations which spring from a change in the society. In modern times, the new principles which are argued by advocates and determined by judges, are principles of the Common Law, although they are not found in the old books. They are held to be immutable principles, which have slumbered in their repositories, because the occasion which called for their exposition has not arisen.

The Common Law system of England as administered by the judges of the land, consists in applying to new combinations of circumstances those rules of law which are derived from legal principles and judicial precedents. For the sake of attaining uniformity, consistency, and certainty, those rules must be applied by the judges to all cases which arise where they are not plainly unreasonable and inconvenient. And the judges are not at liberty to reject them, and to abandon all analogy to them in those cases to which such rules have not yet been judicially applied, because the expounders of the law may consider that the rules are not so convenient and reasonable as those which they themselves could have devised.

It was important under the early feudal governments that the Judges should have been strictly tied up by precedent; but in the present day, in a free country such as England, with Judges of the independence and integrity attained in modern times in England; with the publicity of justice, and the liberty of the press as security against corruption, it does not seem necessary that the Judges should be so bound by the ancient strict rules of precedent, many of which might usefully be relaxed in the progress of society.

In the English phraseology another division of Law is into Common Law and Equity.

Equity is defined as the correction of strict Law wherever it is deficient owing to its universality. This definition has been adopted by Grotius and Puffendorf. Grotius says, — Equity is properly and simply a virtue of the will, corrective of that wherein the Law is deficient on account of its universality. That is equitable by which the law is corrected. Proprie vero et singulariter æquitas est virtus voluntatis, correctrix ejus, quo lex propter universalitatem deficit. Æquum id est quo lex corrigitur. Thus, that species of law which may be termed unwritten, in the sense of not enacted by legislative authority, and which in England is called Equity, is at first wholly distinct from the Common Law, or that part of the immemorial and recognised custom of the realm which is *stricti juris;* and is always distinct from the Statute Law, except so far as the Statute Law in the progress of society professes to regulate the equitable jurisdiction. In its redress of the evils flowing from an unbending adherence to the rules of Common Law, Equity may be termed according to Schlegel's definition, the law qualified by historical circumstances. In respect of the Statute Law, the necessity for the application of Equity happens either against the design and inclination of the lawgiver, or with his consent. In the former case particular facts may have escaped his knowledge, or facts may arise in the progress of society requiring a less strict application of the law's unbending rule. In the latter case the legislator may be aware of all the facts; but from their number and complicity may be unable or unwilling to recite and provide for them. Cases admit of infinite varieties of circumstances: the law must be conceived in general terms. So Mr. Charles Butler has said that Equity, as distinguished from Law, arises from the inability of human foresight to establish any rule which, however salutary in general, is not, in some particular cases, evidently unjust and oppressive. And in this he has followed the Digest. Neither laws nor decrees of the Senate can be so written that all cases may be embraced wherever and whenever they may happen: but it is sufficient that those be included which most frequently occur. Neque leges neque senatûs consulta ita scribi possunt ut omnes casus quâ quandoque inciderint, comprehendantur: sed sufficit ea quæ plerumque accidunt contineri.

The method of administering law in the early history of every people is technical. The system of pleading in the ancient Roman Law, the system of Common Law pleading in England, the formalities of written instruments required by statutes — all have frequently had the result of deciding cases, not upon the real merits, but upon the most technical subtleties. This arises from general incapacity and ignorance. Judges in the early stages of law in all countries are unable to decide upon conflicting evidence according to what is true and just: they endeavour to attain certainty. But in the progress of society the method of administering justice ceases to be technical, and endeavours to be equitable. Thus, in the history of the ancient Roman Law, the technical system was finally suppressed: and the equitable jurisdiction of the Prætor became paramount. In New York, in the year 1850, the technical system has been, in a great measure, destroyed by the fusion of the Courts of Law and Equity. In England, in 1852, special pleading was abolished pursuant to the report of the Common Law Commissioners. And the union of Law and Equity in the Courts of England and Ireland is a project approved by every enlightened law reformer.

But the technical meaning of Equity, as used in the English Courts of Law, is different from that meaning which has been employed by moralists and jurists. Equity, as understood by English lawyers, is that portion of remedial justice which is exclusively administered by the Court of Chancery as contradistinguished from that portion of remedial justice which is exclusively administered by the Courts of Common Law. The Courts of Common Law in England are Courts of Limited Jurisdiction, able to give relief only in certain prescribed forms of action, to which the party must resort to give him a remedy; and if there be no prescribed form to reach the case, he is at law remediless. But the forms in the Courts of Equity are flexible; and their decrees can be adjusted to all the varieties of circumstances which may arise. Thus, the Courts of Equity have had a two-fold function. They have relieved against the rigour of the Common Law Courts, as, for example, in the cases which they have held to be not within the spirit though within the letter of the Statute of Frauds. And they have also administered justice where it was impossible for the Common Law Courts so to do by reason of their limited jurisdiction and defective machinery. The most precise definition of a Court of Equity, as understood in England, Ireland, and the United States, is, that it is a Court having jurisdiction in the case of rights recognised and protected by the Positive Law of the country, where a plain, adequate, and complete remedy cannot be had in the Courts of Common Law.

It is to be hoped that the division of the administration of justice between the Courts of Law and Equity will be abolished in England and Ireland, after the example of New York in 1850; and that every Court, as to the decision of rights, will be made a Court of unlimited jurisdiction; although different processes may be adopted to enforce such rights; and some Courts may decide questions of larger pecuniary importance than others.

## 12. The Study of Jurisprudence

Historically, Law thus arises amongst a people. First the Common Law, like their language, springs from their common consciousness. That primitive customary law is antecedent to all formal legislation. Next the Statute Law in its origin in every state embraces public law and defines the constitution. In the development of society law becomes two-fold. Its primitive fundamental principles still continue to live in the common consciousness of the people. Its more accurate formation and application to particular cases become the particular vocation of the class of lawyers. Finally, the Statute Law is busied with details. It corrects the errors and supplies the deficiencies of the Common Law in private matters,

In the last stage of Legislation in a State, the principle of Codification appears. It appears to be a natural law that whilst a nation is rapidly progressing in Wealth, Knowledge, and Civilization, it is impossible to codify the Laws. Whilst the necessary preparation for a Digest is taking place, already has the natural progress outstripped the legislators. When a complete code of Laws is possible for a nation, its progress must have been arrested; it must already have reached that maturity in which further development becomes difficult if not impossible. Historical examples are the code Justinian and the code Napoleon. From the consolidation of the Roman Law under Justinian, the development of the Roman Law ceased: the development of the Roman civilization had already ceased. France now appears stationary in wealth and population.

Codification is attended with many dangers. There is the risk of error in definitions. There is the risk of perpetuity being given to those errors by the legislative enactment, so as to preclude their correction upon discovery, as under the present mode of administering the Common Law in England. Definitions in a statute may be useful, when they contain a command or a prohibition, when their object is to determine acts, which individuals are bound to perform, or to abstain from; but when they have no other object than to make known the nature of things, they are useless and dangerous, and should be left to science. In codification there is also the danger of cramping the development of the scientific principles of the Common Law, and of retarding the adoption of advanced rules of justice more consistent with the public welfare and the progress of society.

It is impossible to codify the laws of a nation in such a manner as that no change will be necessary. The rights of the different classes of society are continually changing, and the narrowness of human wisdom cannot foresee the cases which time discloses.

Nor does the conversion of Common Law into Statute Law render it absolutely certain. It is still exposed to the risks of ambiguous construction arising from the natural imperfection of language as the representative of thought and from the imperfect use of language.

But by arrangement and classification the disadvantages of the accumulations of books and of the judgments of the courts may be diminished.

The Statute Law may be improved by a more scientific method of enactment and the skilful use of appropriate language. The carelessness of former legislation may be remedied by a strict definition of terms, and by a strict adherence to the judicial phraseology as having a fixed and generally recognised if not technical meaning.

The wants of society are so varied, the communication of men so active, their interests so multiplied, and their relations so extended, that it is impossible for the legislator to foresee all. In the materials which particularly fix his attention, there is a crowd of details which escape him, or which are too contradictory or fleeting to become the object, of a legal test. It is impossible to chain the action of time, to oppose the course of events, or prevent the insensible change of manners. It is impossible to calculate in advance what experience alone can reveal. A code, however complete it may appear, is no sooner finished than a thousand unexpected questions present themselves to the magistrate. Laws once digested remain as they have been written. Men, on the contrary, never repose — they always act; and this movement which never stops, and the effects of which are differently modified by different circumstances produce at each instant some new-combination, some new fact, some new result. Many things are then necessarily abandoned to the empire of custom, to the discussion of learned men, and to the arbitrament of the judges. The duty of the Law is to fix, with enlarged views, the general maxims of Right, to establish principles fertile in their consequences, and not to descend into the detail of the questions which may arise upon each matter. It is for the magistrate and the lawyer, penetrated with the spirit of the laws, to direct the application of them. Hence amongst all polished nations, in addition to the laws made by the legislature, a store of maxims, decisions and doctrines is daily promulgated by practice and by judicial duties. The Professors of the Law are reproached with having multiplied subtleties, compilations, and commentaries. This reproach may be well founded. But what art, what science does not deserve it? Must a particular class of men be accused of what is only the general tendency of the human mind. There are times when we are condemned to ignorance because we have not books; there are others where instruction is difficult because we have too many. Excess in commentary, discussion, and authorship is to be pardoned above all in Jurisprudence. We cannot hesitate to believe this if we reflect on the innumerable ties which bind citizens. There is a constant development and a successive progression of the objects with which the magistrate and the jurisconsult are obliged to busy themselves. The course of events modifies in a thousand ways the social relations. He who blames subtleties and commentaries becomes, in an individual cause, the subtle, fastidious commentator. It would be without doubt desirable that all matters should be regulated by laws. But in default of a precise text on each matter, an ancient usage, constant and well established, an uninterrupted current of similar decisions, an opinion or a received maxim, holds the place of law. When we are directed by nothing that is established or known; when we treat of an absolutely novel fact, we ascend to the principles of natural justice.

Bentham enumerates four conditions which ought to belong to a code of Laws, and which ought to be regarded in its Division.

The first condition of the code should be the greatest happiness of the greatest number.

It should have for its end the general interest; and if this condition has been satisfied in the political code, that is, in the code which establishes the different powers of the state, it will be easy to follow it up in all the other branches of legislation.

The second condition is *integrality;* that is to say, it ought to be complete, or, in other words, embrace all the legal obligations to which a citizen should be subjected.

The third condition is imperfectly expressed by the word *method.* Bentham means by this, not only precision of language and clearness of style, but such an arrangement as would allow all those interested in it easily to acquire a knowledge of the law. All that is included under this comprehensive head is expressed by the word *cognoscibility;* that is to say, the law should have a great *aptitude to be known.*

There is no one word which can express the fourth condition to be satisfied by a body of laws. The meaning must be conveyed by a periphrasis. Each law should be accompanied by a commentary or exposition of the grounds on which the law is founded, showing what relation it bears to general utility. This commentary is, as it were, a justification of the law; *justifiability* of the law would, perhaps, be the proper word to express this characteristic of good laws; since those only are good for which we can give good reasons.

A code of Laws is like a vast forest; the more it is divided the better it is known.

The first principle of division in a code consists in separating laws of universal interest from those of special or individual interest.

There are some laws with which every man should always be acquainted, and there are others which are only required on certain occasions; in other words, there are laws of a permanent, and others of a temporary and occasional interest.

The penal code is the first in importance; all human actions which are the object of law are necessarily included in it. What is called the civil law is only a collection of explanations, or, in other words, an exposition of what is contained in the penal code. Thus, the penal code prohibits from taking an article of property to which the taker has no right; the civil code explains the different circumstances which give such right, or make any thing property. The penal code forbids adultery; the civil treats of all that concerns the marriage state, and the reciprocal obligations of man and wife.

13. The development of Jurisprudence has arisen in two ways, — from the individual labours of learned men, and from the natural progress of society. Thus, one important branch of law has sprung in modern times from the necessities of commercial intercourse. International Law is entirely the offspring of modern civilization; and is the latest important discovery in political science. Communities which anciently admitted of no political superior upon the earth, — no law to guide them in their intercourse with foreigners, except the dictates of capricious ambition, — are now willing to regard themselves as subject to certain rules, the observance of which is expedient for the interests of all. In ancient times International Law had no existence. But from the number of civilized states in Modern Europe, — of nearly equal power, of similar political and ecclesiastical institutions, and united in the friendly ties of commerce, — a set of rules has been adopted in diplomatic intercourse and the settlement of international disputes. International Law, however, is only Positive Law, in so far as it will be supported by an appeal to arms in the last resort. And although the appeal to arms may not be resorted to in every case, yet the fear of incurring general hostility operates upon nations, keeping them within the rules of national comity. The term law of nations, is used by Vattel to designate the science which teaches the rights subsisting between nations and states, and the obligations correspondent to those rights. The Law of Nations teaches the rule which ought to be observed. International Law is the rule observed. The origin and progress of International Law is in itself a remarkable step in the march of civilization. Nations now begin to acknowledge their subjection to laws in conformity with natural justice and reason, as in the very origin of society individuals acknowledge themselves so bound. And the development of International Law will

proceed amongst the civilized nations of the earth until citizens can enjoy, in foreign countries, all the rights which they enjoy in their own. There is no good reason that a malefactor, by changing his domicile, should evade justice. There is no good reason that a debt incurred in one civilized country should not be recovered with the same facilities in all others.

The great desideratum in International Law is a code adopted by the civilized nations of the earth, and to be enforced by their combined strength in the last resort. The practicability of such a scheme is exemplified on a small scale in the recent enactment of the law on bills of exchange for all Germany, to replace the numerous laws which had previously existed in all the several independent States. Prussia, Hungary, Austria, Baden, Bavaria, Saxony, and all the minor States of Germany, had their distinct laws of bills of exchange. But at a Congress held at Leipsic in 1848, consisting of bankers and lawyers from all parts of Germany and some of the Austrian provinces, a general law of bills of exchange was established, which came into operation in 1849. This example must in time be followed, and upon a more extensive scale.

The complete development of International Law can only take place from the influence of commerce, which unites the human family by the strongest tie, — the desire of supplying mutual wants. Commerce demands an international code for the civilized nations of the earth; so that the law of partnership, insurance, bills of exchange, shipping, and bankruptcy should be uniform. Commerce demands that there should be throughout the civilized world a uniform standard of the precious metals, and a uniform system of coinage. Commerce demands a uniform system of taxation, so long at least as the indirect system of taxation may be retained. Commerce demands that debts should be recovered with equal facility in every country, irrespective of the place of contract. Literature demands that the property in its works should be secured by international copyright. Art demands that the property in its inventions should be secured by an international law of patents. If ever there shall exist a common coinage and uniform taxation for the civilized world, with international courts of justice whose jurisdiction shall extend over continents, civilization will owe these advantages to the origin and progress of International Law. Then, to use the words of Cicero: — There shall not be one law at Rome, another at Athens; one now, another hereafter; but one and the same law shall obtain at all places and times; — Non erit alia lex Romæ, alia Athenis; alia nunc alia posthac; sed et apud omnes gentes, et omnia tempora una eademque lex obtinebit.

The study of Jurisprudence will aid in the most important degree the development of International Law; and will assist the progress of law reform at home. Certainly, if there were ever an age in which it was important for gentlemen to be acquainted with the principles of Jurisprudence it is the age in which we live. In matters of law and government *stare super antiquas vias* is no longer held to be the leading maxim. In England almost the whole legal world is toiling in the paths of law reform. And the labours of other countries are no longer unknown and despised. Laing and Kay travel Europe, and inform us how the feudal system of real property, and many of its attendant institutions, are abolished in some of the seats of the oldest civilizations. Certainly the experiment of agriculture in the hands of freemen, in farms of moderate extent belonging to themselves, is now being tried upon the most extensive scale in Continental Europe. And it is at least worthy of our attention to study on scientific principles these great phenomena, with the view of introducing into the English real property reforms the best portions of the new landed system of modern Europe.

Next to the real property reforms the new systems of national education attract our notice. It is from the combination of natural powers that man derives his civilization. Having acquired a certain amount of knowledge, it is partly optional with him whether he will make use of the powers of nature, or obstinately struggle against them. And so availing themselves of their natural capabilities, some races of superior energy have arrived at a partially developed civilization. But the cultivated energy of human thought shall yet develop greater results. Now, in almost every civilized country there exists a vast number of paupers, for whom civilization has been in vain, to whom it has scarcely brought any benefit. Yet these are not permitted to rage with their original barbarity. The Law provides for offenders, police, judges, the prison, the scourge, and the gallows. Some States, a little further advanced in social knowledge, try also the effects of national education. They act thus upon the soundest principles of political science. In moral and physical nature alike over the earth we see the results of cultivation. In physical nature, a large extent of country left as a marsh or swampy forest in its original rudeness shelters beasts of prey, herds noxious vermin, and from its baleful precincts spreads pestilence over the adjacent country. Time advances, and with it the steps of civilized man. He fells the trees which kept the sunlight from drying the ground. He drains the marshes, which speedily bear the abundant harvests. The wild beasts, deprived of shelter, perish from the place no longer fit for their habitation; the dry and cultivated ground no longer breeds fevers and agues. This spectacle, either in its progress or in its fruits, is witnessed over the entire earth. In moral nature we now see the minds of the lowest class in society left stagnant and disfigured by moral pollution and ignorance. As the earth left to itself becomes waste and tangled, — the pestilential abode of reptiles and wild beasts, so the mind uncultivated produces crime and pollution. But in both cases, if we would perform our duty to ourselves and society, we must cultivate; we must cultivate the savage earth, we must cultivate the ignorant minds of the poor. If we wish the earth to be wholesome and fruitful, it must be drained and cultivated. So, too, with the wholesome crop of knowledge we must banish the bitter thorns of ignorance. If we wish the poor to take their places as citizens in society, we must educate them, and, by means of laws in conformity with natural justice and reason, place the poor in a condition wherein they may use that education, and earn their bread. There can be no more gratifying proof of human progress than the teach-in o-of modern political science, that the true way to provide for the general happiness is to give all citizens an interest in the prosperity of the nation, to leave trade and labour free, and to give the humblest a good education. And the countries which have emancipated and given independence and education to the lower classes, have not only given liberty to them, but security to all.

Science is often abused, as not being practical; but it will not be denied that such questions as these are practical.

So also, since the arts of Sculpture and Painting have been united with Manufactures, and aid in their development, is it important to consider on what principle the Laws of civilized nations now refuse to the inventor the complete property in his works. Schools of Design are endowed and encouraged by patrons of the Fine Arts. Yet in the British Islands the ingenious mechanician, who invents new machinery to cheapen production and facilitate labour, — the artist, who with plastic skill designs the most exquisite forms for the furniture of our houses, — the painter, who stamps with beauty the plain creations of the loom, and enables Manchester to find a market in China and India, — all are by the present laws denied the full property in the works of their hands and brains. Is it not worth while to study why this is so, and upon what principle this is to be remedied?

The English Law, with its excellent characteristics, — trial by jury, *vivâ voce* evidence, and publicity in every stage of the proceedings, — has spread over a vast portion of the earth. In North America the English Law has crossed the Alleghanies and the Rocky Mountains with the emigrants; and on the shores of the Pacific the representative government, the municipal systems, and the Common Law of England give strength and liberty to nations. So, if we turn to India or Australia, the English lawyers may say, —

> "Quæ regio in terris nostri non plena laboris
> Est?"

In some of these new countries improvements have been made upon the Common Law, which we are slow to adopt at home. The development of the Common Law is proceeding at the most rapid rate in the United States. And our most energetic law-reformers may borrow useful bints from the latest Code of New York. There, the distinction in Procedure between Law and Equity has been abolished. And not only in the department of legal reform, but also in legal authorship, the United States of late have surpassed England. In England recently, with perhaps the single exception of John William Smith, there have been no legal authors such as Kent, Story, and Greenleaf have been in America. This may be attributed to the superior legal education which the American lawyers receive, and to the schools of law established throughout the United States.

The study of Jurisprudence is not merely concerned with the permanent progress of the human race and the amelioration of society. Many believe such ideas to be visionary. But there can be nothing more strictly practical than the consideration of such questions as the legal burdens which press upon the owners and occupiers of land, and prevent its free transfer, — the reasons for the education of the poor, and the best method to accomplish it, — the consideration of the laws which deprive inventors of the complete property in their works, — the questions of international copyright, an international law of patents, and an international commercial code, — and the reform of legal procedure. These things concern the prosperity of the entire community. And it is expedient to consider them upon scientific principles.

# BOOK II
# THE GREEK AND ROMAN JURISPRUDENCE

*Φυσει γάρ ἀνθρώπος πολιτι*
"Man is by nature a political animal. ζῶον. —*Aristotle.*

"La seconda fu la Giurisprudenza eroica di cautelarsi con certe propie parole, qual è la sapienza di Ulisse; il quale appo Omero sempre parla si accorto, che consiegua la propostasi utilità, serbata sempre la propietà delle sue parole. Onde tutta la riputazione de' giureconsulti romani antichi consisteva in quel lor *cavere*; e quel loro *de jure respondere* pur altro non era che cautelar coloro ch' avevano da sperimentar in giudizio la lor ragione, d' esporre al Pretore i fatti cosi circostanziati, che le formole dell' azioni vi cadessero sopra a livello, talchè il Pretore non potesse loro niegarle. Cosi a' tempi barbari ritornati tutta la riputazion de' dottori era in trovar cautele d' intorno a' contratti o ultime volontà, ed in saper formare domande di ragione ed articoli, ch'era appunto il *cavere, e de jure respondere* de' romani giureconsulti."

*Vico: Scienza Nuova,* lib. iv., opere vol. *v.,* 508.

"The second was the Heroic Jurisprudence composed of cautious forms with certain appropriate words. Such was the wisdom of Ulysses, who, according to Homer, always spoke so craftily as to attain his proposed end, preserving, nevertheless, the propriety of his words. Thus, all the skill of the ancient Roman jurists was expressed in the word *cavere*. And what they termed de jure respondere was nothing but advice given to those who went to law to the end that they should present the facts in such a fashion that the formulas of actions might agree with them, so that the prætor could not refuse them. Similarly on the return of the barbarous times all the skill of the doctors consisted in finding precautionary forms for the assurance of contracts and wills, and the means to elude them; all which recalls the *cavere* and the de *jure respondere* of the Roman jurists."

*Vico: The New Science*, book 4, works, vol. v., 508.

## *CHAPTER I*
## *POLITICAL PHILOSOPHY IN GREECE*

Authorities: — Van Heusde, Initia Philosophiæ Platonicæ, Leyden, 1842, 8vo.; Schleiermacher, Introduction to the Dialogues of Plato (Dobson's Translation, Cambridge, 1826, 8vo.); Tennemann's

System of the Platonic Philosophy, Leipsic, 1792, 4 vols. 4to.; Geddes' Essay on the Composition and Manner of the Writings of the Ancients, particularly Plato, Glasgow, 1748, 8vo.; Ritter's History of Ancient Philosophy; Tennemann's Manual of Philosophy, London, Bohn, 1852; Janet, Histoire de la Philosophie Morale et Politique, Paris, 2 vols. 8vo., 1858.

## 1. Political Philosophy in Greece

Great men in all ages have cultivated Jurisprudence. Most of our modern legal civilization is the result of the labours of those who from the original rudeness of savage life have developed the principles of Civil and Political Right. A true social idea, says Lamartine,[17] descended from Heaven on humanity never disappears. Once that it has germinated in certain right hearts, sound and logical minds, it bears within itself something vital, divine, immortal, which never more perishes in its entirety. Passions, vile interests, ignorance, prejudices, may crush it under their feet, may mutilate it under the sabre or hatchet; its fruits are retarded for ages; but the hand of Providence is full of ages; at the destined time, the living idea of which the seed has been spread and multiplied even by the storms, bursts forth at once in the minds of all.

In the twilight of history the magnificent despotisms of the East appear. The immobility of institutions is the chief Oriental characteristic. India and China, respectively have made but little progress in morals and legislation since Menu and Confucius flourished. And in those countries, so long celebrated for partial wealth and refinement, men endure the tyranny under which their ancestors laboured for ages. We turn from the stagnant mind of the East to the active intellect of Greece.

Throughout the annals of philosophy and legislation we find the constant aspiration to the great, the beautiful, the just, — in a word, to Progress. Greece for a time first manifested this aspiration with the greatest ardour. It is true that decay and barbarism followed there. But the decay and barbarism were only for the degenerate Greeks. The decay and barbarism were not for Rome which received the fruits of the Grecian civilization; nor were the decay and barbarism ultimately for humanity, which to this day

---

[17] Essai sur La Politique Rationelle.

preserves, as a treasure of inestimable value, some of the principles evolved by the legislators and philosophers of Greece.

In reading the political works of the ancient Greeks, we are not to judge them by modern writings. Humanity, in the conception of those philosophers, was a finished work, though we now are but beginning to understand that the world has lived only a fraction of its existence. Chivalry, Loyalty, the Purity of Woman, and her influence on society were things unknown to the old Greeks. Nulla est ars quæ singulari consummata sit ingenio — no art is perfected by one genius. The jurists, publicists, legislators, statesmen of the present age, all have before them the historical experience of twenty-two centuries since Plato wrote. From that time the human race has been labouring, not only in the academy and lyceum of the ancient in the libraries and universities of the modern schools, but also in the working life of government, legislation, and war, to solve the great question how temporal peace and happiness may best be secured. The triumphs of Alexander over Oriental despotism, — the flourishing civilization of Egypt under the Ptolemies, — the progress of the Roman Empire, and its splendid cultivation of the laws of civil society, — the feudal system, — the history of the Italian republics, — the history of the great modern nations which now maintain the progress of the civilized world — all supply us with a larger induction than Plato ever dreamed of. The brute matter of human existence is wrought into society only by length of time. A great and free state is the work of many ages, of stupendous characters, of watchful senates, of sages and heroes. To form, support, and bring such to maturity, the invention of nature must be stretched for thousands of years. We reap the fruits of all the political experiments which have cost to our ancestors time, care, and blood.

With difficulty do we picture to ourselves the Athenian civilization in which Plato lived. Some arts were then developed to a height since unattained by human genius and industry. No more do we rival the poetry of Homer or Sophocles, the oratory of Demosthenes or Æschines, the sculpture of Phidias, the painting of Appelles. But this grand cultivation of the fine arts has thrown a gloss over the traces of barbarism. Three-fourths of the population of Greece were slaves; both Plato and Aristotle justify slavery on the plea of necessity. Marriage as now understood was unknown; women were still socially slaves. In Greece the highest social types of women are Lais and Aspasia; although their poetry and fiction show that in the future marriage was anticipated. Piracy in the heroic times was an honourable profession. Later, the partially civilized Oriental nations were to the Hellenes barbarians. Even in Greece, and between Greeks, war was carried on with a ferocity now unknown in international contests between civilized nations. When one of the petty Grecian cities was taken by the enemy, it was no unusual thing that it should be burned to ashes, and all the surviving inhabitants sold as slaves. When a citizen of Greece fought, it was with the consciousness that if defeated, in all probability he would be butchered on the smoking ruins of his hearth. Such a fate as this was suffered by some of the noblest Grecian cities, which fought the bravest against the Persian, and in which were nurtured the germs of European polity and civilization. Hence we must consider it a splendid effort of the human intellect that Plato in his age wrote such works, enouncing in the most felicitous language political truths for all time; although many of his dialogues, even those which explain the most vital parts of his system, are disfigured by theories and ideas borrowed from the political experiments made by Grecian society, and which long have been eliminated from civilization by the good sense of mankind.

Among the general ideas which govern the activity of man, appear the idea of the Useful, producing mathematics, physics, industry, political economy; the idea of the Beautiful, producing Art; and the idea of the Just, producing Civil Society, the State, Jurisprudence. The Just is one of those ideas which constitute the glory of human nature. Man perceives it in the beginning; but he perceives it only as a lightning flash amidst the profound gloom of his early passions; he fees it unceasingly violated, and at every moment effaced by the inevitable disorder of conflicting interests. What Rousseau has called society in a state of nature, is nothing more than a state of war, where the right of the strongest reigns. But Justice established constitutes the State. The use of the State is to cause Justice to be respected through the means of force; and it acts in conformity with an idea which is inherent in that of Justice — that is, that injustice ought not only to be repressed but punished. Hence arises civil and political society; which is nothing else than Justice acting by means of that legal order which the State represents. The State, however, ought to take no notice of the infinite variety of human elements which were conflicting amidst the confusion and chaos of natural society; it does not embrace the whole man; it considers him only in relation to the ideas of the Just and Unjust.[18]

But the province of Justice was not so easily determined in ancient times. Even at this moment, the province of Government is the subject of the keenest inquisitions — one party of philosophers maintaining that the duty of Government is simply to maintain justice and order, another investing the Government with the direction of the whole progressive force of the people. The solution of this question is one of the most important for the happiness of mankind.

The triumph of all science is but to verify facts, and to draw from their connexion the inductions that reveal the laws to be obeyed by man under pain of being the more miserable the less he shall know or obey them. It has long been observed that the practice of a science always precedes the science itself. And with this branch of Sociology, as with all others, the art whose important principles and general rules it demonstrates was practised long before the existence of the science of Jurisprudence was ever suspected. Minos gave laws to Crete, Lycurgus to Sparta, Solon to Athens, Pythagoras to Southern Italy; but these different legislators were men rather distinguished by their strength of character, by the knowledge which they had of the state of manners, of the usages, and of the wants of the different nations for whom their laws were destined, than by the profundity of their general political views. Before their time vast monarchies had existed which have no history but the revolutions of the reigning houses. And if Minos be the first legislator whom history mentions, the cause of this honourable distinction is known. "This legislator," says the historian Ephorus cited by Strabo, "appears to have regarded liberty as the greatest good for civil societies; because that it alone can guarantee to individuals the property in the advantages which they enjoy; whilst in slavery all belongs to the man who governs, nothing to the governed." Unquestionably to these sound ideas on society and government, to the communications established between the most eminent men by their

[18] Victor Cousin.

talents, to the influence more or less direct which each of them exercised over his fellow-citizens, the Greeks owed the means of coming with glory out of the terrible crisis of the Persian invasion. The energy which they employed in defence of their liberty was the result of their ardent love of country, and of their profound consciousness of their rights as citizens of a free state.[19]

## 2. Socrates, B.C. 469-400

Four great schools of philosophy flourished in ancient Greece anterior to the time of Socrates: the Ionic, founded by Thales; the Italic, founded by Pythagoras; the Eleatic, founded by Xenophanes; and the Atomic, founded by Leucippus and Democritus. Each of these four sects was distinguished for the boldness of its hypotheses in attempting to account for the origin of the universe; and they differed from each other mainly in the principles of their solution of this one problem. The magnificence of the world without withdrew philosophers from contemplating the world within. Yet, it would be a mistake to say, as is sometimes said, that their speculations were exclusively cosmological. Thales was not a mere promulgator of physical hypotheses; but appears to have been a deep thinker, and in fact the first speculative philosopher of Greece.

The aphorism traditionally attributed to him, "Know thyself," reveals this reflective tendency. The author of the Magna Moralia again informs us that "the first to attempt the subject of Moral Philosophy was Pythagoras. His method, however, now appears absurd, for he made virtue a number, justice a cube." To Pythagoras also has been ascribed what Dugald Stewart pronounces to be "the oldest definition of Virtue of which we have any account, and the most unexceptionable, perhaps, which is yet to be found in any system of philosophy — *"Εξις τõυ δέοντος* — the Habit of Duty."

To the sect of the early natural philosophers of Greece succeeded the sophists. This class of thinkers belongs to a peculiar stage in human progress — to a period of criticism or transition. The previous sects of philosophers had failed to find any platform of truth on which the reason of man could rest satisfied. Their labours had ended and no fruits had been garnered into the

[19] Thurot, Discours Preliminaire.

treasury of knowledge. They, too, had no successors in their endeavours to solve the problem of the universe. The different views of nature, taken by the several sects, had all proved unsatisfactory, and yet seemed to have left no other possible view. This the sophists saw. The sophists were, in truth, the offspring of the thinking of these sects of naturalists. Their parentage is shown in the fact that in general they were materialists. The common doctrine of the sophists was that doubt attaches to every opinion, and that it is impossible to find certainty in any thing. They were thorough sceptics.

Here, then, begins the great era of ancient Moral Philosophy. Socrates is the leader in this period of the struggles of the mind of man with the difficulties of knowing theoretically — of construing to one's consciousness what he feels and sees within and without himself; his aim was to lay down certain laws by which men might be guided, as rational and accountable beings, to the pursuit of objects directly related to their spiritual nature, and to such a subjection of their lower faculties as should render them subservient and useful to the higher. "He was the first," says Cicero, "who invited Philosophy down from heaven, gave her a home in cities, introduced her into our domestic life, and led her to speculate on life and manners, and on all things good and evil." Baffled in his attempt to solve the mysteries of the world without, he turned his attention to the world within; for physics he substituted morals; the certitude which he failed to gain respecting the operations of nature had not shaken his conviction of the certitude of the moral truths which his conscience irresistibly impressed upon his attention. The world of sense might be fleeting and deceptive. The truths of conscience were eternal, immutable, evident. These he opposed to the scepticism of the sophists. Moral certitude was the rock upon which his shipwrecked soul was cast. From its height he could survey the world and his relation to it.

The morality of Socrates was, in fact, reared upon the basis of religion; and his lessons, communicated to us by his two most distinguished pupils, Plato and Xenophon, show that his ideas of the nature, position, and duties of man approach closely to the standard of Christian Ethics. The complete absence of selfishness distinguishes the Socratic theory. The principles of virtuous conduct which are common to all mankind were, according to this wise and good man, laws of God; and the argument by which he supported this opinion was, that no man departs from these principles with impunity.

"It is frequently possible," says he, "for men to screen themselves from the penalty of human laws; but no man can be unjust or ungrateful without suffering for his crime; hence I conclude that these laws must have proceeded from a more excellent legislator than man." He taught that true felicity is not to be derived from external possessions, but from wisdom, which consists in the knowledge and practice of virtue; that the cultivation of virtuous manners is necessarily attended with pleasure as well as profit; that the honest man alone is happy; and that it is absurd to attempt to separate things which in their nature are so united as virtue and interest.

Socrates — the first citizen of the world — incited the intellect of Greece along the path of political and ethical philosophy. He talked only — he wrote nothing; but his opinions are preserved and matured in the works of Plato. Aristotle next took up the inquiry; and with a keener and harder intellect avoided many of the errors into which Plato fell. It is necessary thus to folio w out the philosophy of the Socratic schools; no system, if completely isolated, can be understood. A system cannot be thoroughly comprehended until we know all the consequences which have actually folio wed, and which it is the business of history to trace from it in the application of principles.

With the first sages of Greece the subject of examination had been Nature, or the Kosmos, as one undistinguished whole. This vast and undefined problem had occupied the attention of the Ionic as well as the Eleatic philosophers, Pythagoras as well as Empedocles. However, under the cultivation of the Sophists, the division of labour was first applied to the sciences. It appears strange to us, knowing the degree of perfection to which the study of some of the physical sciences has advanced, that Socrates was convinced that the Gods intended the machinery by which they brought about the astronomical and other physical results to remain unknown, and that it was impious as well as useless to pry into their secrets. He therefore devoted himself to consider the rules and purposes of human life, and was the first to proclaim that "the proper study of mankind is man." He consequently desired to confine the studies of his hearers to human matters as distinguished from divine — the latter comprehending astronomy and physics. "Socrates," says Xenophon, in the "Memorabilia," "continued incessantly discussing human affairs, investigating: What is piety? — What impiety? — What is the honourable and the base? — What is the just and the unjust? — What is temperance? — What is courage or cowardice? — What is a city? — What is, the character fit for a citizen? — What is authority over man? — What is the character befitting the exercise of such authority? — and other similar questions. Men who knew these matters he accounted good and honourable; men who were ignorant of them he assimilated to slaves." The method of the Socratic examination of these important subjects was strongly to contrast the state of knowledge on the general topics of Man and Society with the state of knowledge possessed by men of their individual handicrafts and professions. Civilized men devoted to different pursuits, in the progress of the division of labour, learn accurately the matters relating to their several professions; and in the subject matter of their professions are authorities, so that no one presumes to interfere with them; but in matters of social philosophy, all are as well ignorant and confident. Since the age of Socrates and Plato, however a considerable advance has been made. Then, not only amongst the generality of civilized men were the ideas respecting morals, laws, and social economy, vague and unscientific; but also the ideas respecting physical nature were obscure, supernatural. A god was in every hill, in every fountain; the sun and moon were divinities — their motions and magnitudes as yet uncalculated with accuracy.

In the nineteenth century, as regards the physical sciences, men are content to admit their original ignorance, to seek for knowledge from the teacher, and acknowledge his proofs. And the time will arrive when the mental sciences will be brought to a similar degree of perfection, and their truths similarly admitted. Socrates was unable to draw such a comparison as is now possible for a student of the social sciences. But the comparison which he actually took, borrowed from the special trades and professions, led to one important result. He first saw and showed that as in each art or profession there is an end to be obtained, so in the general art of human living and society there is a grand and comprehensive end, the security and happiness, as far as practicable, of each and all persons in the society. Socrates resolved all virtue into knowledge, all vice into ignorance. To do right was the only way to be happy, or, at least, to avoid as much unhappiness as possible. Now this was precisely what every one wished for and aimed at, only that many persons from ignorance took the wrong road, and no man was always wise enough to take the right. But as no man was willingly his own enemy, so no man ever did wrong willingly; it was because he was not fully or correctly informed of the consequences of his own actions; so that the proper remedy to apply was enlarged teaching of consequences and improved judgment.

The method of Socrates was composed of two distinct parts — self-examination and the search after definitions. He did not employ these two processes with any perfect accuracy. Complete scientific methods belong only to very advanced stages of philosophy and society. But he certainly knew, understood, and practised both the method of internal observation and the method of definitions. He transformed into a philosophical principle the celebrated maxim, know thyself — *γνῶθι σεαυτὸν* — and declared that only in the practice of it could man be just and wise.

The search after definitions was with Socrates a consequence of self-knowledge. Perfect knowledge cannot exist without being able to give an account of our ideas, to distinguish between them, and to define them.

Socrates has defined justice as the knowledge of what has been prescribed by the Laws. But there are two sorts of Laws. The first are those which citizens make of common accord in their own country. Justice in this first sense is only obedience to the Laws of the country. It is a part of patriotism.

But the theory of Justice was elevated, when, in place of considering it as obedience to the laws of the state, Socrates displayed Justice regulated by superior laws — laws not written — laws depending not on the caprice of a people, but on the will of the Gods. The first change with men and states; the second prescribe the same things at all times, to all men, in all countries.

In his theory of Justice Socrates excelled all his cotemporaries. M. Janet has observed that in two points Socrates has surpassed all antiquity — in his ideas upon the Family, and Labour. Socrates had a far more exalted idea of domestic life than Plato. He recognised the moral equality of the two sexes — an equality which permits the ineffaceable differences of nature to exist. He gives the most admirable pictures of the Family, the Wife, and the Mother. This sentiment of domestic life led Socrates to understand another truth which antiquity never comprehended — the dignity of Labour, not merely intellectual and political labour, but the common working labour of everyday life. Socrates equally with Napoleon respected the burthen. "Whom shall we call wise?" said he. "Are they the idle, or those occupied with useful works? Whom shall we call just? the workers, or those who with folded arms dream their lives away?" Socrates relieved labour from the idea of servility attached to it by the ancients. And thus, without knowing it, he attacked slavery at its source.

In Science, Philosophy owes to Socrates its true principle — know thyself — and its true method, criticism and analysis.

The many-sided life of Socrates gave an impulse, as is well known, to a variety of schools of philosophy. It is usual to divide these into the imperfect and the perfect Socratecists; the Megarians, who represented only the dialectic element in Socrates, and the Cynics and Cyrenaics, who represented each a different phase of his ethical tradition, being considered as the imperfect Socratecists; whilst Plato is considered as the full representative and natural development of all sides of his master's thought. An account of the Megarian school belongs rather to the history of Metaphysics; the Cynical and Cyrenaic philosophies were each rather a mode of life than an abstract theory or system. It is instructive, however, to see the various points of view that it is possible to take with regard to life; and each of these schools was in fact an exaggeration of a peculiar aspect of the life of Socrates. If we abstract all the Platonic picture of the urbanity, the happy humour, and at the same time the sublime thought of Socrates, and think only of the barefooted old man, indefatigably disputing in the open streets, and setting himself against society, we recognise in him the first of the Cynics. Again, if we think of him to whom all circumstances seemed indifferent, who spoke of virtue as the science of the conduct of life, and seemed at times to identify pleasure with the good, we can understand how Aristippus, the follower of Socrates, was also founder of the Cyrenaic sect. In the Cynical philosophy there was little that was positive — there was no actual contribution to ethical science. But the whole Cynical tone which proclaimed the value of action and the importance of the individual Will was an indication of the practical and moral direction which thought had now taken; and it prepared the way for the partial discussion of the problems of the Will by Aristotle, and for their more full consideration among the Stoics. Crates, the disciple of Diogenes, was the master of Zeno. In the Cyrenaic system, again, we find a bold, logical following out of a particular view. In this respect the system is remarkable, for it is the first of its kind. The Sophists had trifled with such views, and had not followed them out. In the prominence given to the subject of Pleasure in the Ethical systems both of Plato and Aristotle, we may trace the effect of the Cyrenaic impulse.

## 3. Plato, B.C. 429-348

The personal history of some of the greatest men is but little known. The great founder of the Academy, like Shakespeare and many others, lives for us in his works. Plato, the son of Ariston and Perictione, was born in Olympiad 87. 3., B.C. 429, being about the time of the death of Pericles. It is uncertain whether Athens or Ægina was his birth-place. By his mother's side he was descended from Codrus and Solon, and connected with the most distinguished families, the greatest politicians of the age. By nature gifted with the rarest talents, he received the best physical and mental education which Athens could afford; and in his youth was distinguished alike in music, poetry, and gymnastic, exercises. By Socrates he was imbued with that spirit of true philosophy which pervades his works. Plato began to receive the instructions of Socrates when about twenty years of age, and listened to his discourses for eleven years. He had originally destined himself for public life; but the corruption of the fierce Athenian democracy drove the contemplative philosopher into the quiet groves of Academus. And thus in every line of Plato's dialogues we may discern a certain deficiency in practical contrivance — a thing only to be acquired in the working, business of life, in the actual conduct of affairs.

After the persecution and death of Socrates — "that man, the best of all in his time that we have known, and moreover the most wise and just," — Plato went to Megara, where he is said to have attended the lectures of Euclid. And, next, he spent several years in travelling, principally in Magna Græcia, Sicily, and

Egypt. At Tarentum he is said to have been initiated by Archytas into the Pythagorean mysteries. And many have attributed to this the enlarged political and social views which he afterwards unfolded in the "Republic." Chiefly at the instance of the Pythagoreans, who desired to obtain a footing in Sicily, he made two voyages to that island, where, however, his attempts were wholly unsuccessful. After suffering some vicissitudes and nearly meeting death, through the agency of Dionysius, tyrant of Syracuse, he returned to Athens, and founded his celebrated school of the Academy. There he lectured during a period of nearly forty years, only broken, it is said, by two more journeys to Sicily. Among his disciples were Xenocrates, Aristotle, Demosthenes, and Theophrastus, worthy pupils of so great a master. Such, briefly, was his uneventful life. He died Olymp. 108, about B.C. 348.

The greatest advantage in studying the works of Plato arises from the peculiar cultivation of the philosopher. In Plato we are not perusing the doctrine of one individual however great; we have the whole Greek philosophy, illustrated alike by poets, historians, sages — and by Socrates and Plato applied to the knowledge and perfection of man. Nor has Plato absorbed only the Greek philosophy. In his youth he collected the rays of civilization dispersed through the schools of Megara, Cyrene, Italy, Egypt. Thus embracing all existing knowledge, he united the religious sentiment of Asia to the metaphysics and natural philosophy of Europe; and cultivated the beginnings of political science for the instruction of the human race. The impulse so given by Plato to human thought survives to the present time. "Here is the germ of that Europe we know so well, in its long history of arts and arms; here are all its traits already discernible in the mind of Plato; and in none before him."[20]

Plato, in all his works, shows that one of the greatest causes of human corruption is bad education. He fully perceives that if knowledge be a power, ignorance is also a power — the power which keeps the savage a savage, and which commits each varied crime that disgrace civilization. His political discussions have for one of their immediate objects, the laying down of right principles of education, and enforcing them by the constitution

---

[20] Emerson.

of the laws and the power of the State. And his two great works, the "Republic" and the "Laws," may be considered as theories and plans of civic education rather than schemes of legislation and details of laws. The former inquires more particularly into the principles on which a right government may be formed; and the latter presents a systematic view of the principles of legislation; but comprising, as both works do, so much matter of a purely intellectual and ethical character, their primary object was the improvement of human nature by social institutions, expressly formed for the purpose.

Plato first divided philosophy into three parts — Dialectics, Physics, and Ethics, or the Political Science; and this division has been recognised by every succeeding age as a guide. Under Ethics he comprehended Politics, and generally the science of society. Dialectics, or Logic, was the science by which he traced the operations of the mind to certain fixed ideas inherent in the mind itself, though existing independently of it. He laid down the chief distinctions between each of these sciences, and traced their mutual dependencies. He also illustrated separately each branch of philosophy; but did not profess to give a complete system of each. In this respect his works are only suggestive of future discoveries. In his moral system he defined virtue to be the imitation of God, or the effort of man to attain to a resemblance of his original. Virtue is one, but compounded of four elements — wisdom, courage or constancy, temperance, and justice. Education is the liberal cultivation and moral discipline of the mind; and the science of politics is the application to society of the moral law; its ends are liberty and peace. Plato adopted the great Socratic principle — no one is willingly evil. He inferred from the idea of an all-perfect Deity that good is the general law, and that man is attracted to it by its nature. Evil is the result of ignorance; ignorance enslaves man with a dark cave, from which the light of knowledge alone can free him. This, then, is the first great principle, that no one is willingly evil; and the second is, that every one is capable of producing changes in his own moral character. The first has been thus exemplified by Ritter: — "As the rational soul can only involuntarily be subject to ignorance, it is only against its will that it can be evil. Every volition, by its essential nature, pursues the good; no one is willing to be subject to evil, or to become bad, inasmuch as the end of volition is not the immediate act, but the object for the sake of which the act is undertaken; and no man enters on any act or undertaking except for the sake of ultimate good. Now a man, when engaged in any act apparently good, may err, and choose the evil instead of the good; but in that case he labours under an involuntary error, and does not what he really desires, but which, in spite of his wishes, seems to him either as an immediate good, or a means to an ultimate good."

When Plato wrote, the possibility of mental science was not suspected by the vulgar, and was denied by the learned. Even at the present day, how difficult it is to convince some that there are natural principles of justice, as there are natural principles of gravitation, and that it is equally possible, although incomparably more difficult, to ascertain them with accuracy. The ancient sophists maintained that right and wrong did not exist by nature, but only by convention. "That which appears just and honourable for each city is so for that city, so long as the opinion is entertained," says Protagoras in the "Theætctes." The opinions of the sophists may have been exaggerated by their great opponent Plato: but still we may be assured that they did protest energetically against the possibility of mental science. And so, concerning Justice, Plato wrote: "Of all whose arguments are left to the men of the present time, no one has ever yet condemned injustice, or praised justice, otherwise than as respects the repute, honour, and emoluments arising therefrom; while as respects either of them in itself, and subsisting by its own power in the mind of the possessor, and concealed from both gods and men, no one has yet sufficiently investigated, either in poetry or prose writings — how, namely, that the one is the greatest of all the evils that the soul has within it, and Justice the greatest good."

But Plato's idea of the Just was so exalted, that the impossibility of its being enforced by human government has made the name of his "Republic" a symbol for a splendid political vision, whose airy outlines for ever mock the aspirations of the patriotic statesman.

On the subject of Justice, both in the individual and in the State, his views were these: — "In order that man may act rightly, there must be some end of his being, with the nature of which he ought carefully to acquaint himself. This is the real and true good, and a knowledge of it is indispensable to the moral man, and constitutes the virtue of wisdom." It is therefore necessary to be instructed in this. Virtue, so far as it rests upon science, may be learned in the same sense as science itself is teachable; that is, originally and naturally, it dwells potentially in the soul, and may be drawn out by education. And in the consideration, and practical application of this virtue the Socratic principle must never be forgotten — that no one is willingly evil.

In order, however, that this knowledge may result in action, the energy of the human soul must move. Human action requires means and co-operating causes: such is fortitude, the virtue of spirit, which is to support the reason. What Plato calls fortitude in a moral sense, does not consist merely in a contempt of death, or courage during danger, but solely in the maintenance of right opinions.

Temperance is the third virtue; and in the "Phædrus" he thus explains its essence: — Those are usually styled temperate who abstain from all excesses, and moderately indulge themselves, in order to avoid sickness, or pain, or deprivation of some other gratification, and in order to indulge their temperate indulgences as long as possible; and those are often called brave who fear not death, when they are in danger of losing other enjoyments. But the former are temperate from an intemperate desire of pleasure, the latter from the fear of losing either their honour or some other good possession. — Strange temperance that whose root is intemperance, and rare valour whose spring is cowardice! This, then, cannot be a true sacrifice to virtue which merely exchanges pleasure for pleasure, pain for pain, fear for fear, greater for less. The true coin is a right understanding of what is good.

And Justice, the fourth virtue, is employed by Plato to indicate a far higher idea than is now comprehended under the term. Justice represents the harmonious and proportional development of the inner man, by means of which each faculty of the soul, without interfering with the others, performs its due functions, and thereby produces within him complete and perfect order. It is the end and the unity by which the other three virtues co-exist and cohere; it is the harmony of wisdom, temperance, and courage. Its office is not to regulate the moral evolution of the several other virtues, but their mutual concord and adjustment.

And all the moral virtues of the citizen are closely connected with those of the individual; for even though by the aid of philosophy, a man may have preserved himself pure from all unjust and unholy deeds, he is still far from having reached the highest degree of excellence, unless it should have been his happy lot to live in a well-ordered polity; for in such a state he will both himself attain to still greater perfection, and also be serviceable to his fellow citizens.

The Platonic idea of Justice in the individual embraces the harmonious exercise of the three principal virtues of the soul, knowledge, fortitude, and temperance, — and accordingly the whole range of our temporal duties. Whilst the Platonic idea of Justice in the State is that condition of life in which each individual in the community, without interfering with the natural rights of others, discharges in the best possible manner the duty for which he is best fitted. These ideas embrace almost the whole range of human action. And from this radical mistake that the State can control or direct all human actions, have sprung the errors of Plato. His schemes of politics as detailed in the "Republic" and "Laws," approve of the system of castes: whilst they attempt to control the minutest details of domestic life. Plato advocated the system of castes, because, although perceiving that the division of labour was necessary to the existence and progress of civilization, he did not at the same time perceive that it arose spontaneously and necessarily without legislative interference. In effect, the attempts of the legislature to enforce the division of labour have only the result of arresting its complete development.

Plato considered that all human duties came within the province and control of the public authority. Justice was the harmony of the virtues; and it was the business of the state to enforce justice. Modern jurists adopt a very different opinion. In England, Adam Smith was the first to point out with distinctness that justice did not embrace all virtues, but only includes the virtues and duties which are capable of being enforced by the public authority. But assuredly, in our present imperfect state of knowledge and development, we cannot say with certainty that a time may not come when, in accordance with the theory of Plato, all the virtues may be so enforced, — or at least their transgression with propriety punished by the State. The rights of which the State takes cognizance are increasing; and the circle of human duty capable of being enforced steadily expands with the progress of mankind. In the early ages, slaves had no rights. Now, in civilized states not only is slavery abolished, but poor laws provide for the subsistence and education of the indigent; and even the lower orders of animals are protected by law from the cruelty of their masters.

In ancient times, although the natural rights to life, liberty, and property were imperfectly acknowledged in practice, philosophers extended the range of the law to the entire scope of the moral virtues, and the whole domain of the affections. Modern legislation, for the most part, attempts but to protect natural rights; and gives to the individual unrestrained liberty, checked only by laws tending to promote the greatest welfare of the community. In the works of Aristotle we perceive an approach to the modern system. But in numerous instances he is entirely swayed by the political and social opinions of his great master, Plato.

## 4. Aristotle, B.C. 384-321

Aristotle was born at Stagira, a city of the Thracian Chersonese, B.C. 384. In his seventeenth year he repaired to the school of Plato at Athens, — which rightly has been termed the then Great University of the world. There he remained twenty years; and his laborious devotion to science was appreciated by Plato, who termed him "The intellect of the School." At the death of Plato, Aristotle accompanied his fellow-pupil Xenocrates to the court of Hermias, tyrant of Atarneus in Mysia. Thence, on the overthrow of Hermias by the Persian king, he went to Mitylene. His great reputation was now shown by his appointment as tutor to the son of Philip of Macedon, — Alexander the Great, then fourteen years of age. He continued with Alexander until he set out on his Asiatic campaign, B.C. 334. And although a personal coolness had arisen between them, still Alexander placed some thousands of persons under Aristotle's directions, to make inquiries on Natural History throughout Asia and Greece. The result was the History of Animals. Returned to Athens, he taught in the Lyceum: Xenocrates or Theophrastus then occupied the Academy; and the Cynics lectured in the Cynosarges. Whilst Aristotle delivered his discourses, he was in the habit of walking up and down, — a trait of character which forcibly illustrates the restless activity of his mind; and his school has hence obtained the name of Peripatetics. He lectured at the Lyceum for twelve years. Exposed at length to the same intolerant spirit which had put Socrates to death, he fled to Chalcis, saying, "that he was unwilling to involve the Athenians in another crime against philosophy." There he died, B.C. 321, in his sixty-third year.

Aristotle errs, like Plato, in blending together the objects of moral and political science. These ancient philosophers do not so much speculate on the best laws or the best form of government as about theories on the whole of human happiness. He appears to have adopted the term Politics as the designation of all ethical investigations. And Politics comprise all those disquisitions whose object is human good, as well in the individual, the family, and the state. He therefore makes three principal divisions of politics, — Ethics, Economics, and Politics proper. The science of Ethics investigates the moral good of the individual; Economics treat of the right management of the family; Politics of the state.

The fundamental principle of the Aristotelian Ethics is, that morality m the individual, or in society, is a something which grows out of natural endowments and destination. Nature has implanted in man an impulse to action and desire without which no act ever would be accomplished; so that all the moral acts of man must attach themselves to some natural disposition as its basis. The investigations of Aristotle turn chiefly upon two principal notions, which the ethical system of Plato had largely developed — that of moral good, and that of virtue.

All men pursue some good; some things, however, are only good and desirable as means for the attainment of others; there must, therefore, be some ultimate good which is pursued solely for its own sake; the good absolutely, or the best; for otherwise, man's efforts would proceed without end, and his desire would be void and in vain. In name, at least, all men are agreed as to this object of human pursuit, and call it Happiness. Still the constituents of happiness are disputed. But it is only in the practical activity of the soul, which proceeds with reason, that the work and happiness of man consist. In order that happiness may be complete, it must exist in perfect activity, and in a perfect life. By perfect life Aristotle understood two things, — the development of life to the highest degree of perfection, and the consistency of the practical activity from its beginning to its close. And the saying of Solon is not without truth, — that we must wait till a man's death before we call him happy.

The following is a very brief Analysis of those portions of the Nicomachean Ethics which relate to Political Science.

Every art and every scientific system, and in like manner every course of action and deliberate preference, seems to aim at some good; and consequently "the good" has been well defined as "that which all things aim at."

The good appears to be the end of that which is especially the chief science. And this is political science; for it directs what sciences states ought to cultivate, what individuals should learn, and how far they should pursue them. Since, then, this science makes use of the practical sciences, and legislates respecting what ought to be done and what ought to be abstained from, its end must include those of the others; so that this end must be the good of man. For although the good of an individual and a state be the same, still that of a state appears more important and more perfect both to obtain and preserve. To discover the good of an individual is satisfactory, but to discover that of a state or nation is more noble and divine.

In the third chapter Aristotle says, as was natural in his age, that perfect exactness is not to be expected in these ethical and political subjects. Things honourable and things just, the consideration of which falls within the province of political science, admit of such vast difference and uncertainty, that they seem to exist by law only, and not in the nature of things. And this was the opinion of the sophists.

All men are agreed as to the name of the chief good; for both the vulgar and the educated call it Happiness; but concerning the nature of happiness they are at variance, some calling it health, some wealth. And conscious of their own ignorance, they admire those who say that it is something great and beyond them. Some, again, have supposed that besides these numerous goods, there is another self-existent good, which is to all these the cause of their being goods.

But happiness is neither sensual pleasure, nor honour, nor virtue, nor wealth. It is desirable, then, that it should be explained what it is. Perhaps this may be done if we take the peculiar work of man; for as to the musician, and statuary, and every artist, and all who have any work or course of action, the good and excellence of each appears to consist in their peculiar work; so would it appear to be with man, if there is any peculiar work belonging to him. What, then, must this peculiar work be? For man appears to share life in common with plants; but his peculiar work is the object of our inquiry. We must, therefore, separate the life of nutrition and growth. Then a kind of sensitive life would next follow; but this also he appears to enjoy in common with the horse, the ox, and every animal. There remains, therefore, a certain practical life of a being which possesses reason; and of this one part is, as it were, obedient to reason, the other as possessing it, and exercising intellect. But this life being also spoken of in two ways — according to energy and according to habit — we must take that according to energy. Now if we assume the peculiar work of man to be a kind of life, and this life an energy of the soul, and actions performed with reason and the peculiar work of a good man to be the same things done well and honourably, and every thing to be complete according to its proper excellence — if these things be true, it follows that man's chief good is an energy of the soul according to virtue; but if the virtues are more than one, according to the best and most perfect virtue; and besides this we must add in a perfect life: for as neither one swallow nor one day makes a spring; so neither does one day, nor a short time, make a man blessed and happy.

The second, third, and fourth books are occupied with a discussion upon virtue in general. The fifth book discusses Justice and Injustice; and is almost identically the same with the fourth book of the Eudemean Ethics.

All men mean by the term Justice that kind of habit from which men are apt to perform just actions, and from which they act justly and wish for just things; and similarly in the case of Injustice, that habit from which they act unjustly, and wish for unjust things. Justice and Injustice are used in more senses than one. The transgressor of law appears to be unjust, and the man who takes more than his share, and the unfair man; so that it is clear that the just man also will mean the man who acts according to law, and the fair man. The Just is therefore the Lawful and Fair; the Unjust the Unlawful and Unfair.

But since the transgressor of law is unjust, and the keeper of law just, it is clear that all lawful things are in some sense just;

for those things which have been defined by the legislative science are lawful. But laws make mention of all subjects with a view either to the common advantage of all, or of men in power, or of the best citizens, according to virtue, or some other such standard. So that, in one way, we call those things just which are adapted to produce and preserve happiness and its parts for the social community. This justice, therefore, is perfect virtue, not absolutely, but relatively; and for this reason, justice often appears to be the most excellent of the virtues; and neither the evening nor the morning star is so admirable; and in a proverb we say, "in justice all virtue is comprehended;" and it is more than any other perfect virtue, because it is the exercise of perfect virtue; and it is perfect, because the possessor of it is able to exercise his virtue towards another person, and not only in reference to himself; for many men are able to exercise virtue in their own concerns, but not in matters which concern other people. For this reason, the saying of Bias seems to be a good one, "Power will show the man;" for the man in power is at once associated with, and stands in relation to, others; and for this reason justice alone, of all the virtues, seems to be a good to another person, because it has relation to another; for it does what is advantageous to some one else, either to the head, or to some member of the Commonwealth. That man, therefore, is the worst who acts viciously, both as regards himself and his friends, and that man is the best who acts virtuously, not as regards himself, but as regards another; for this is a difficult task.

Universal justice being perfect virtue, considered not absolutely, but relatively, there is also a particular justice which is violated when the law is broken for the sake of gain. Particular justice is divided into two species; one distributive, being concerned in the distributions of honour, or of wealth, or of any of those other things which can possibly be distributed among the members of a political community; the other, corrective in transactions between man and man.

Distributive justice regards the relative deserts of persons, and the respective values of things: and in it geometrical proportion is observed; for in geometrical proportion it comes to pass that the whole has the same ratio to the whole which each part has to the other.

But corrective justice deals not according to geometrical but arithmetical proportion. For it matters not whether a good man has robbed a bad man, or a bad man a good one, nor whether a good or a bad man has committed adultery; the law looks to the difference of the hurt alone, and treats the persons, if one commits and the other suffers injury, as equal, and also if one has done and the other suffered hurt.

The equal is the mean between the more and the less. But gain and loss are one more and the other less in contrary ways; that is, the more of good and the less of evil is a gain and the contrary is a loss. Between which the mean is the equal, which we call the just, so that the just, which is corrective, must be between loss and gain. Hence it is that when they have a quarrel they go to the judge; but going to the judge is going to the just; for the meaning of the word judge is a living personification of the just; and they seek a judge as a mean. But the judge equalizes, and, just as if a line had been cut into two unequal parts, he takes away from the greater part that quantity by which it exceeds the real half, and adds it to the lesser part; but when the whole is divided into two equal parts, then they say that the parties have their own when they have got an equal share. But the equal is the mean between greater and less according to arithmetical proportion. For this reason also, the just is called *δίκαιον,* because it is *δίχα* (in two parts), just as if a person should call it *δίχαιον* (divided in two), and the *δικαστής* is so called, being as it were *διχαστής* (a divider).

In another place Justice is accordingly defined as a medium between excess and defect, *῾Η δικαιοσύνη μεσότης τίς ἀν εἰη ὑπερβόλης καὶ ἐλλειψέως.*

It is probable that Philology will show that a division into equal parts is the original idea of Justice in all nations and languages. Thus in Arabic *Insax,* — Justice, — literally means dividing in half: in Latin *Æquitas* means equality of division.

Commutative Justice, the Law of Retaliation, — *lex talionis,* — was the Pythagorean idea of absolute justice; but Aristotle shows its erroneousness. For a blow given by a person of rank and by an humble person is not justly punished by being simply returned. And again, the voluntariness or involuntariness of actions makes a great difference. But in the intercourse of exchange such a notion of justice as retaliation, if it be according to proportion and not according to equality, holds men together.

For by proportionate retaliation civil society is held together. For men either seek to retaliate evil — otherwise if a man must not retaliate, his condition appears to be as bad as slavery; or to retaliate good — otherwise there is no interchange of good offices; and by these society is held together.

Political Justice takes place in the case of those who live as members of society with a view to self-sufficiency, and who are free and equal either proportionately or numerically. So that all those who are not in this condition have not the political just in relation to one. another, but only a kind of justice, so called from its resemblance. Of the political just, one part is natural and the other legal. The natural is that which everywhere is equally valid, and depends not upon being or not being received. But the legal is that which originally was a matter of indifference, but which when enacted is so no longer; as the price of a ransom being fixed, and all particular acts of legislation.

After considering the divisions of offences he investigates Equity *(ἐπιεἱκια)*. Equity and justice do not seem to be absolutely the same, nor yet generally different. And we sometimes praise the equitable and the men of that character; so that we even transfer the expression for the purpose of praise to other cases, showing by the use of the term equitable instead of good, that equity is better. Sometimes again, if we attend to the definition, it appears absurd that equity should be praiseworthy, when it is something different from justice, for either justice must be not good, or equity must be not just — that is, if it be different from justice, or if they are both good, they must both be the same. The cause of the ambiguity is this, that the equitable is just, but not that justice which is according to law, but the correction of the legally just. And the reason of this is that law is in all cases universal, and on some subjects it is not possible to speak universally with correctness. When therefore the law speaks universally, and something happens different from the generality of cases, then it is proper that where the legislator has erred from speaking generally to correct the defect, as the legislator would himself direct if he were then present, or as he would have legislated if he had been aware of the case; therefore the equitable is just, and better than some kind of the just; not indeed better than the absolute just, but better than the error which arises from universal enactments. This therefore is the definition of

Equity — ἐπιεἰκια — that it is a correction of law wherever it is defective owing to its universality. And it is also clear what the character of the equitable man is. For he who does such things from deliberate preference, — who does not push the letter of the law to the furthest on the worst side (which is expressed in our proverb *summum jus, summa injuria),* but is disposed to make allowances, even although he has the law in his favour, — is equitable.

Two fundamental errors, the absolutism of the state and slavery, common to Plato and Aristotle, corrupted to the source their theory of Politics. They took for absolute truth the passing errors of an incomplete society, and did not comprehend the new signs which manifested themselves in the doctrines of Socrates, and the development of society.

There remained, therefore, two truths to introduce into the Political Philosophy of the ancients; first, to teach man that he is something dehors the state; secondly, to generalize the title of man, and to extend the friendship and sympathy which Plato and Aristotle had supposed only to exist amongst the privileged classes. This was the business of the Stoic philosophy.

The Cynical school had already burst the ties which chained man to the state. The Cynics and their success were plainly a protest of the popular classes against the aristocratic philosophy of Plato and the other Socratics. But the Cynic Philosophy was rather an enemy of the laws and society than a friend of humanity. Diogenes said he was a citizen of the world; that the only government. worthy of our admiration was the government of the universe. But these fine words only concealed a gross egotism. The Cynic was an enemy of the ties of country, family, and property. He placed virtue only in the strength to endure privations, and in the independence of all social laws. He had no principle of fraternity or sociality. Nevertheless the Cynic philosophy, in attacking social distinctions maintained by the laws, and in displaying mendicants and slaves as philosophers, served in a manner to change the ancient ideas and to prepare the way for Stoicism.

It was not until near a century after the death of Plato, that Ethics became the scene of philosophical contest between the adverse schools of Epicurus and Zeno; whose errors afford an instructive example that, in the formation of theory, partial truth is equivalent to absolute falsehood. As the astronomer who left either the centrifugal or the centripetal force of the planets out of his view, would err as completely as he who excluded both, so the Epicureans and Stoics who each confined themselves to real but partial and one-sided principles in morals, departed as widely from the truth as if they had adopted no portion of it. The two sects respectively sought a single solution for a complex problem, from not comprehending the two principles capable of solving it. The Epicureans placed the sovereign good in happiness alone; the Stoics, in the consciousness of virtue. The former identified prudence and morality — a very common error. They represented the tendency to produce happiness as the sole inducement to virtuous practice — a truth of great importance to the completeness of ethical theory. The Stoics were disposed to regard the moral sentiments, which are the motives of right conduct, as being the sole principles of moral science. The high-souled but impracticable morality of the Stoics, for the sake of vindicating Providence, declared pain to be no evil, and placed the wise man wholly out of the power of fortune. The poor and sordid philosophy of the disciples of Epicurus easily dropped by degrees the limitations by which he guarded his doctrines, and made indolent pleasure the object for which man lived, and the various affections of his chequered nature so many disguises of self-love. The true solution of this disputed problem might perhaps be found in the connexion and harmony of Virtue and Happiness as merited by Virtue. The two principles are not equivalent. Virtue is the antecedent. It is not alone the sovereign good; but it is the chief good. The eminently practical, and exquisitely balanced mind of Aristotle had not been betrayed into either of the extremes just considered. While steadily pronouncing Virtue a good in itself, he never fell into the extravagance of holding it to be man's only good. The highest good of man he regarded as consisting in the full exercise of all the faculties of mind and body in their complete perfection; and in this view he recognised the outward advantages of fortune and the enjoyment of that health which it is not always in our power to procure or preserve, as integral parts of that good which is the *τέλος τελεῖον*,for which man lives. In fact, the doctrine of the Peripatetics on this subject appears to have coincided with that of the Pythagorean school, who defined Happiness to be the Exercise of Virtue in a prosperous life — χρησις ἀρετης ἐν ἐυτυχια.

It will hereafter be seen that the two opposite moral schools of antiquity, the Stoical and the Epicurean, have had their antagonism prolonged into modern times; nor can it cease to subsist so long as there is a school of Independent Morality which, like Butler, seeks the ground of virtue or moral rightness in the faculties of man, and their relation to each other — which would regulate human action by an internal principle, as Conscience, or a Moral Faculty, or Duty, or Rectitude, or the superiority of Reason to Desire; and another school of Dependent Morality which, like Paley, looks for the criterion of rightness to external things, and asserts Pleasure, or Utility, or the Greatest Happiness of the Greatest Number, to be the true end of human action.

Sir James Mackintosh has instituted an ingenious comparative estimate of the several philosophical systems of antiquity by tracing the operation of their principles upon the lives and conduct of their most illustrious professors in the ranks of the Roman Patriciate — a case which seems to comply with all the conditions of a strict scientific experiment. The influence of the Grecian systems was tried by their effect on a body of mea of the utmost originality, energy, and variety of character, during the five centuries between Carneades and Constantine, in their successive positions of rulers of the world, and of slaves, under the best and under the worst of uncontrolled masters. "The result is the mope satisfactory, because it appears to illustrate general tendency without excluding very remarkable exceptions. Though Cassius was an Epicurean, the true representative of that school was the accomplished, prudent, friendly, good-natured time-server, Atticus, the pliant slave of every tyrant, who could kiss the hand of Antony, imbrued as it was in the blood of Cicero. The pure school of Plato sent forth Marcus Brutus, the signal humanity of whose life was both necessary and sufficient to prove that his daring breach of venerable rules flowed only from that dire necessity which left no other means of upholding the most sacred principles. The Roman orator, though in speculative questions he embraced that mitigated doubt which allowed most ease and freedom to his genius, yet in those moral writings where his heart was most deeply interested, followed the severest sect of philosophy, and became almost a Stoic. If any conclusion may be hazarded from this trial of systems, the greatest which history has recorded, we must not refuse our decided, though not undistmguishing, preference to that noble school which preserved great souls untainted at the court of dissolute and ferocious tyrants; which exalted the slave of one of Nero's courtiers to be a moral teacher of aftertimes; which, for the first, and hitherto for the only time, breathed philosophy and justice into those rules of law which govern the ordinary concerns of every man; and which, above all, has constituted, by the examples of Marcus Porcius Cato, and of Marcus Aurelius Antoninus, to raise the dignity of our species, to keep alive a more ardent love of virtue, and a more awful sense of duty, throughout all generations."

The political life of Greece being the main pillar of its speculative life, we would naturally anticipate that where that political life was departed, its speculations would become withered and heartless. And so it was. The genius of Greece fell with liberty. The Grecian philosophy received its mortal wound in the contests between scepticism and dogmatism, which occupied the schools in the age of Cicero. Energetic and original thought had expired. To that restless speculative spirit which, commencing with Thales, had informed and illustrated every phase of Grecian social existence, nothing was left but to invent a few new combinations, and re-cast certain forms of thought and language out of which the meaning had departed — to rehabilitate itself in that worn-out and cast-off skin from which the living serpent had gone forth to other lands. Philosophy, exiled from Greece, found a shelter in Rome.

# *CHAPTER II*
# *THE ROMAN LAW AND JURISPRUDENCE*

Authorities — Günther; Historia Juris Romani; Niebuhr's Roman History; Arnold's Roman History, Savigny; System des heutigen Römischen Rechts — Berlin, 1840, 8vols., 8vo — translated into French by Guenoux — Paris, Didot, 1840; Burchardt; Staats und Rechts-Geschicte der Römer — Stuttgardt, 1841; Hugo; Lehrbuch des heutigen Römischen Rechts, 1826; Thibaut; System des Pandektenrechts, 1834.

## 1. The Ancient Roman Law

The early Roman Law is a type of the blending of the popular and technical elements which exist in all laws. The whole Roman Law originally existed only by custom. Custom is converted into law when it begins to be associated with the idea of Right, when the neglect to observe the custom disappoints the general expectation, and when the state employs force to punish the violation of the custom. All Law is originally customary Law. And the legal force of custom is derived from the common consciousness of the people that they expect the things to be done which ought to be done, and are usually done by those amongst the community who strive to do Right. The early Roman Law is characterized by that religious solemnity which is found in the legislations of the most ancient as Well as the most recent states. Ceremonies are found invariably in early laws; they are all originally symbolical, but of many in time the meaning is forgotten. Symbolical forms which at first have a deep religious meaning, are finally used only to excite attention and impress the memory. The necessity which Lawyers feel for the fixing of the memory when in the progress of time they disregard the religious element in Law, leads to the introduction of the technical system. In Rome there gradually arose a technical branch of Law regulating all legal procedure; hence sprung the class of technical Lawyers; hence arose the demand for legal reform and the first Codification of the Roman Law. The first Government of Rome was composed of an elective King, a Council of nobles, and a General Assembly of the people. We have few records of the laws of the Kings, nor is it of any advantage to waste learning upon the fragments of those Laws which have been compiled by the diligence of antiquarians. I shall not enter into the question whether the legendary history of the Roman Kings contained the record of the origin of a nation or of a change of Government, by which an ancient civilized race aided in the formation of the Roman people. According to the history which we have, the prevalence of insolvency and the severity of the laws of debt created great discontent amongst the Plebeians, and they conspired against the Patricians for relief against oppression. The general discontent finally led to a proposal for a revision of the Laws. And Livy and the other Roman historians tell the mythical story that a Commission of three persons was appointed to visit Athens and other Greek cities, and to transcribe the laws of Solon. The three envoys returned in the year after their appointment. The plan of reforming the government and legislation of

Rome commenced. All the great offices of state were abrogated for a year, and the entire government, legislative, administrative, and judicial, was vested in a Council of ten to prepare a Code. Before the end of the year the Decemvirs compiled a Code from the written Greek laws and the Roman unwritten customs. They inscribed these Laws on ten tables, which were exhibited in public, and revised by the sages of the city. These laws were then sanctioned by the Senate and the vote of the people in their Assembly. We have few authentic records as to the manner in which the government of the Decemvirs in the first year became tyranny in the second year. The story of Virginia is familiar to the world. Cicero makes a broad distinction between the ten tables of the first Decemvirs and the two tables of the second Decemvirs. He says the laws of the latter were unjust; and he mentions as a novel hardship the prohibition of intermarriage between the Patricians and the Plebeians. However, the Laws of the Twelve Tables were always considered as the foundation of legal right, and they were all mentioned with equal reverence down to the latest period of Roman history. They were regarded equally by Livy and by Cicero as the fountain of all public and private right.

Some of the provisions of the Twelve Tables which were intended to protect the person and the property of private citizens are important to consider. It was enacted that any person claimed as a slave should be left at freedom until the alleged master proved his claim good. This was the Law violated by Appius in the case of Virginia. The power of a father over his children was made less absolute. By the old law the son was a slave to his father. From the time of the Twelve Tables the son might acquire independence by means of three sales, whether real or fictitious. The Twelve Tables left the law of debt in its former state of severity. But usury laws were enacted, which attempted, although erroneously, to make it possible to borrow money at a lower rate than the market price. It was made illegal to exact higher interest than ten per cent. By the Twelve Tables no private Law to impose any penalty or disability on a single citizen was possible to be enacted; there was to be an appeal to the people from the sentence of every magistrate; and no citizen was to be tried for his life except before the great Roman Assembly, the Comitia of the Centuries. These laws were repeatedly renewed and were finally consolidated more than two centuries later by the famous Porcian laws, by which it was enacted that no Roman citizen should be put to death or scourged without trial before the Centuries. These laws may be compared to the English Acts of Habeas Corpus. Under the English law no man can be imprisoned by the sovereign or his officers without having his person produced in open court and allowed a fair trial. However, as in England, in times of rebellion, the Habeas Corpus Act is suspended, so in Rome the laws of appeal were occasionally suspended. This was done in the earlier times by the appointment of a Dictator, and afterwards by a resolution of the Senate, that the Consul should take heed that the Republic suffered no injury. Under this resolution the Consuls were invested with the supreme dictatorial power.

On the whole, the Legislation of the first Ten Tables was fair; and it really tended to introduce equal rights both in Law and Government for the entire nation. But some laws had a directly contrary effect. These have been attributed to the two last tables of the Code. The old law prohibiting intermarriage between the two orders of Patricians and Plebeians was now formally re-enacted, and thus the aim of the promoters of the Decemviral Code was defeated so far as they sought to procure an equalization of the two orders. Such an equalization was impossible so long as the National Code of Law proclaimed the two orders of Patricians and Plebeians to be of different races, unfit to mingle with one another. The license of public libel was restrained by the law of the Twelve Tables, which subjected libellers to the deprivation of civil rights. But though the Twelve Tables enacted many useful reforms, they left one matter untouched. No attempt was made to distribute the public land more justly. Hence the introduction of agrarian laws remained as a constant source of the most violent civil commotions.

From a motive of national pride the Roman historians wished to believe that before the Twelve Tables were enacted the Roman deputies visited Athens, and consulted the Grecian laws. However, all the Grecian memorials and history are silent on the subject, and there is no authentic record that the embassy ever took place. In any comparison of the Twelve Tables no more resemblance is found to the Grecian laws than may be found to all laws of civilized nations in the same phase of legal existence.

Whatever was the origin of the Twelve Tables, so long as Roman law prevailed, they obtained amongst the Roman lawyers a blind and partial reverence; they were committed to the memory of students, they were illustrated by the labours of the learned, they had escaped the conflagration of the city by the Gauls, they subsisted to the time of Justinian, and their subsequent loss has not been restored. Subsequently the acts and new laws before the time of the consolidation under Justinian exceeded three thousand in number, and many of the acts contained over one hundred chapters.

The Decemvirs had been elected and the Twelve Tables were sanctioned by the Assembly of the Centuries, in which riches preponderated against numbers. Ninety-eight votes were assigned to the first class of Romans — the proprietors of one hundred thousand pounds of copper, equal to five thousand pounds sterling of English money, and only ninety-five more votes were left for the six inferior classes. However by degrees the Assembly of the Centuries was superseded by the Assembly of the Tribes, in which the vote of each Roman citizen, poor or rich, was of equal value. Originally the votes were given in public; but "a method of secret ballot abolished the influence of fear and shame, of honour and interest, and the abuse of freedom accelerated the progress of anarchy and despotism."

## 2. The Agrarian Laws

The law of real property in Rome was in a state of more advanced development than under the feudal system. At Rome property was derived from political rights rather than political rights from property. In this the ancient system of privileged castes still prevailed. But contrary to the feudal method, the proprietor of land was the absolute owner of it in his lifetime; and could bestow it absolutely on his death. The rights and duties of a Roman citizen were derived not from his possession of property, but from his being a member of the society to whose law he owed his property. A vast proportion of the Roman territory was land acquired by the sword. In ancient times when a state was conquered, the private rights of its inhabitants to their landed property were commonly disregarded. And this land so conquered in war constituted the ager publicus of the Roman people. But in the progress of society there is an inevitable tendency to the individual appropriation of common or public land. This is natural, necessary, and ultimately beneficial. Land so held in common, loses a great portion of its value to the copartners, and occasions perpetual disputation. Cultivation cannot proceed; nor will expensive buildings be erected where the proprietor is a mere usufructuary, and the property is not absolute in him. The powerful patrician families obtained large grants of the public land, and endeavoured to make their property in them absolute in themselves, or hereditary in their families. The plebeians as constantly strove to keep the land public, in the hopes of sometimes obtaining a share of the spoil. The occupation of such public land could be transmitted from father to son as an inheritance, and could be sold. But the occupant remained in law a precarious tenant whom the State had a right to dispossess when occasion required. The Licinian Law, B.C. 366, provided that no one should possess more than five hundred jugera of this public land. Although numerous divisions of the land had taken place in small portions among the victorious soldiers of Rome, still there was a constant tendency to the accumulation of landed property in the hands of the nobles. The ravages of war in Italy continually annihilated the small farms. And slavery rendered the cultivation of immense tracts of land easy and profitable. Thus when Tiberius Sempronius Gracchus, on his march to Spain, passed through Etruria, he saw far and wide no free labourers, but numbers of slaves in chains; whilst the population of Rome was becoming more and more pauperised.

The remedy proposed by the elder Gracchus for these things was in the social state which characterized that period of history impracticable. This public land had been in the possession of families for one hundred, and in some cases for two hundred years. Where the lands had not been in the possession of the same family, others had bona fide purchased them. When some of the lands had been ravaged by war, and their possessors slain, the neighbouring proprietors had occupied them, and changed them by expenditure of their capital and labour into olive-fields and plantations. Others, on the faith of long-continued possession, had built on the lands. Thus divers equities had arisen difficult to be encountered by those who sought a re-division of the public land.

Tiberius Gracchus, B.C. 132, carried a law, constituting

three commissioners to inquire into the administration of the public lands and the violations of the Licinian Law. His plan was, that no one should occupy more than 500 jugera of the public land for himself, and 250 for each of his sons — "ne quis plus mille agri jugera haberet." He further wished to enact that the lands thus recovered by the State should not be allowed to be gold; and this clause he desired to introduce in order to prevent the wealthy Romans from acquiring them. It is plain that this enactment would have been wholly nugatory. Where two free agents wish to effect a transfer of property, it is almost impossible for a law to prevent them. Again, buildings erected on lands according to this law to be taken from their possessors, were to be valued, and.the price to be given in money to the owners of the buildings. But persons who had bona fide purchased from the occupants their interest in the public lands, grounded on their long possession, would have lost their money. This agrarian scheme of confiscation, combined with the political reforms meditated by Gracchus, called forth the bitter exasperation which ended in his murder.

Notwithstanding the great authority of Niebuhr, the agrarian bill of Tiberius Gracchus must be considered an interference with the rights of private property. In name the domain land was public, and the State had a right to resume it. But labour had certainly conferred rights of property upon the persons who had been for so many years permitted to occupy the land; and purchasers for value unquestionably had preferable rights to the needy populace of Rome. Even if Gracchus had proposed to estimate fairly all the improvements, and to pay the full value to the occupants of the land, it seems uncertain whether it would not have been preferable to divide the money raised for such a purpose amongst the plebeians, than first to dispossess the occupants of the public land, then to compensate them for their loss, and, after all the confusion and distress unavoidable from such a scheme, finally to divide the land amongst the plebeian populace of Rome, poor, unused to agriculture, and without the means to stock their farms.

The value of houses and all other buildings on agricultural estates is most imperfectly transferable. In recent experience in Ireland mansions built at an expense of £20,000 and £30,000, and which, to the families of their owners, had a far higher value, have not produced, at a sale by auction in the Incumbered Estates Court, under the most favourable circumstances, one third of their original cost. Therefore it is to be considered that the plan of Gracchus, if completed, would have destroyed so much of the value of the agricultural property which it proposed thus compulsorily to transfer. It is to be regretted, that instead of devoting his splendid talents to the scheme of forcibly substituting a system of small farming for the system of large estates cultivated by slaves, he did not at once apply his energy to the abolition of slavery.

The great reforms effected by the Twelve Tables were the establishment of the legal equality of all Roman citizens, and the enactment that there should be an appeal to the people from the sentence of every magistrate, and that all capital trials should be conducted before the Comitia of the Centuries. However, the aristocracy still preserved the exclusive eligibility to the consulship. And the caste system was still maintained in the prohibition of intermarriages between the patricians and plebeians. Thus the fusion of Patricians and Plebeians into one united people remained incomplete.

From the recognition of the equality of all citizens by the twelve tables, the plebeians rapidly progressed in the development of their civil rights. The Consul Valerius, B.C. 446, passed a law giving legislative force to the plebiscita, the votes of the Commons in the Comitia Tributa, — "ut quod tributim plebes jussisset, populum teneret." The Tribune Canuleius, B.C. 445, repealed the marriage-law in the last of the twelve tables. The office of the quæstors or secretaries of the Public Treasury was thrown open to the plebeians, B.C. 418. The Licinian Law, through the influence of the great Camillus, opened the consulship to the plebeians, B.C. 366. And the plebeians were admitted to the Dictatorship, B.C. 353 — to the Censorship, B.C. 334. The Ogulnian Law, B.C. 300, threw open the priesthood to the Commons; and thereby finally abolished the distinctness of the patrician caste.

## 3. Cicero, B.C. 107-44

Authorities: — Plutarch, Life of Cicero; Morabin, History of Cicero, Paris, 1745, 2 vols. 4to.; Middleton, Life of Cicero; Hulseman: De Indole Philosophicâ M. T. Ciceronis, Luneb. 1799, 4to; Dunlop's

History of Roman Literature, London, 1824; Ritter's History of Ancient Philosophy, book iii. cap. ii.

The Romans were essentially a nation of warriors. Of themselves they acquired no speculative philosophy, and for six centuries were ignorant of the very name. They were Strangers to the various systems of legislation, to those rhetorical treatises on jurisprudence, whether composed upon aristocratic or democratic principles, which the Greeks possessed in abundance. But in their laws, and especially in their ancient political system, they displayed a practical sense, almost an instinct in legislation. Thus the tribunate introduced that element of constitutional opposition which has been developed with such success in England in the system of government by parties. However, with wealth and conquest appeared Philosophy. In the year of the city 586 when Perseus of Macedon was finally conquered the philosopher Metrodorus followed in the train of the victorious army to Rome. Other Greeks soon accompanied him, and were favoured by the most enlightened Romans — Lælius, Scipio, and Scævola. Still the unlettered senate regarded the new philosophy with distrust, and, U.C. 592, publicly banished it from Rome. But philosophy soon returned in a more honourable guise. Athens sent an embassy to Rome U.C. 598, and selected for the purpose her then most distinguished sages, The envoys were — Diogenes, then the head of the Stoics; Critolaus, the head of the Peripatetics; and Carneades, the Cyrenæic, the head of the New Academics. During their embassy they gave public lectures, attended by crowds of the youthful patricians. Diogenes in particular was supported by the jurisconsults, who from that time cultivated the trenchant logic of the Stoic philosophy, and introduced many of its principles into the Civil Law. But before Cicero no Latin writer on the principles of Law and Politics had appeared in Rome, so that the entire of this noble domain of literature was open for one worthy of it.

This great man was born in an age which the universal testimony of mankind has called one of the most illustrious in the world. Rome culminated in the height of her power, and from the freedom of her institutions there was the noblest career for talents which any state had ever yet presented in the history of mankind. Cicero was not compelled to struggle with the same difficulties as Demosthenes. Humble birth or ruined fortunes did not obstruct him in the pursuit of fame; and the provident care of a father gave him that best of gifts, a good education. It is, however, a question whether in the grand pursuits of ambition some difficulty at the outstep of life be not an advantage to genius, as it is an incentive to industry. Before Cicero were the seductions of that city where the most extravagant wealth urged the keenest intellects to ransack the world for new inventions of luxury. But he applied his wealth to wealth's noblest task, the cultivation of the intellect. When Rome had given him all that could be taught by her poets and orators, he went to Athens and the cities of the Lesser Asia; and they too unfolded to him all the treasures of their wisdom, all that art could teach or inspiration bestow. He spent long years in the study of eloquence, in the endeavour to acquire a correct fluency of style. For, Cicero, whose works are so voluminous, whose style is so beautiful, himself tells us that at the commencement of his career he was unable to speak or write correctly the Latin language.

All that illustrates the career of the great men of antiquity is amongst the most useful lessons left to us by the olden times: —

> "Lives of great men all remind us,
> We can make our lives sublime,
> And departing leave behind us
> Footsteps on the sand of time;
> Footprints that, perhaps, another,
> Sailing o'er life's solemn main,
> A forlorn and shipwrecked brother,
> Seeing shall take heart again."
>
> — LONGFELLOW.

There exists for us little real of the old world except those collossal intellects which still rise above the waters of oblivion. Classical Borne, the one sole object of all Cicero's hopes, and fears and wishes, is no more! The pinnacles of the Capitol, gilded with barbaric gold and seen afar as a crown, have fallen. The poet grandly prophesied that the sacrifice wherein the priest with the silent virgin ascended the Capitol should not be discontinued for all eternity, — the very rites have faded from human memory in a, little space of time. The grass grows in the deserted forum, and the peasant's plough turns up the fragment of a column, — memorial of those eternal structures where Roman citizens sate in judgment upon kings. Capitol and temple, forum and shrine empire and religion, are gone, but the words of Cicero have survived the fragile objects that inspired them.

But we cannot here dwell upon the details of Cicero's history; nor upon the orations that entranced the ancient world, and have been the delight and instruction of every succeeding age; nor upon the miserable end of his arduous life. The great Roman orator, though more successful in public affairs than Demosthenes, like him found a grave beneath the ruins of his country's liberty: —

"Eloquio sed uterque perit orator; utrumque
Largus et exundans letho dedit ingenii fons."

Reflecting on the wretched deaths of the greatest men in the ancient world, modern statesmen may congratulate themselves on living in an age and country where a change of ministry does not involve confiscation, exile, and death to the defeated party. Late in life, when the combinations of his enemies had succeeded in driving him from the public stage of politics, he applied himself again to philosophy, and laboured to transplant into Italy the most perfect theories of the Grecian schools. Like Socrates and Plato, Cicero raised himself beyond the details of local politics, and extended his philanthropy to mankind. Amongst human virtues, he writes, nothing is more beautiful than the union between men, this association, this community of interest, this love of the human race, — caritas humani generis — which, commencing with the family, spreads itself progressively over parents, friends, neighbours, fellow-citizens, and thus finally over the human race.

Cicero combined in himself the characters of the learned lawyer, the enlightened statesman, and the profound philosopher. He lived and took a leading part in one of the most eventful and splendid periods in history. His friends and enemies were the captains and statesmen of the age. There is, therefore, in his political philosophy a practical turn which renders it more useful than the poetical aspirations of Plato, or the hard abstractions of Aristotle. With Cicero, eloquence was an aid to worldly honour, political philosophy a guide to actual legislation.

The celebrated treatise De Republicâ was rescued from oblivion by the learned Cardinal Maio, when librarian of the Vatican. He discovered the work in a palimpsest volume containing a part of Augustin's Commentaries on the Psalms, and published the greater portion of it at Rome in 1822. In the De Republicâ, Cicero shows first that the study of philosophic truth should be made as practicable as possible, and applied to the interests of philanthropy and patriotism. It is not sufficient to possess virtue as an art except we use it. An art, indeed, though we may not use it, may still be possessed in knowledge; but virtue absolutely consists in its use, and its noblest use is the government of the Commonwealth. For nothing is said by philosophers, so far as it is said rightly and honestly, which has not been discovered and confirmed by those who have given laws to States. For whence is piety? — from what sources religion? — whence the Law of Nations, or that which is termed the Civil Law? — whence justice, faith, equity? — whence modesty, continence, the horror of baseness, the emulation of praise and honour? — doubtless from those who instilled some of these principles by education, confirmed others by manners, and sanctioned others by laws. Xenocrates when asked what his disciples learned from him replied, "to do spontaneously what they might be compelled to do by the laws." Therefore that citizen, who by the authority and sanction of laws obliges all to do that to which the philosophers by their eloquence could scarcely persuade a few, is to be esteemed before such doctors. For what speech of theirs is so exquisite as to be preferred before a well-constituted state, public justice, and good manners? In these books Cicero undertakes a discussion on the State and first argues against the hesitation of philosophers to enter into public affairs. If there be any who are moved by such authority, let them attend to those whose authority and glory are greatest amongst the most learned men; whom I consider, even though themselves have not conducted the Government, still, since they have investigated and written much concerning public affairs, have discharged a species of political duty. And the seven whom the Greeks named wise absolutely employed themselves in the midst of public affairs. Nor is there any thing in which human virtue approaches nearer to the power of the Gods than in the founding of new States, or preserving those already founded: — Neque enim est ulla res, in qua propius ad deorum numen virtus accedat humana, quam civitates aut condere novas, aut conservare jam conditas.

Scipio Africanus, the son of Paulus Æmilius, Quintus Tubero, and Lælius, are then introduced as spending the Latin holidays in the gardens of the first, and their conversation upon political science is given as related by Rutilius at Rhodes to Cicero in his youth. After some preliminary conversation, Scipio, on the request of the others, gives his views on the management of public affairs. The study of astronomy is contrasted with politics. What. can he deem splendid in the affairs of men who has penetrated the realms of the gods, — or what can he deem durable who knows what is eternity, — or what can he deem glorious who sees how paltry is, first, the entire earth, next that part of it which men inhabit? And can we, placed in a small part of it, unknown to most nations, still hope that our name can circulate to the widest extent? How fortunate is he to be considered who may claim all things as his own. not by the law of the Quirites, but by the right of philosophers; not by the civil bond, but by the common law of nature, which forbids any thing to be the property of any man unless of him who knows how to treat and use it; — how fortunate is he to be deemed who considers military commands and consulships as necessary, not desirable things, to be undertaken in order to discharge a duty, not to be sought for glory and emolument; who, in fine, as Cato was wont to say of Africanus, deemed himself never more busy than when he did nothing, never less alone than when alone. After some further discussion Scipio proceeds to define the Commonwealth, — *res publica.* The Commonwealth is the state of the people. But the people is not every association of men gathered together in every way, but the association of a multitude allied by the compact of justice and the communion of utility. And the first cause of union is not so much weakness as the natural association of man: Est igitur, inquit Africanus, res publica res populi: populus autem non omnis hominum cœtus quoque modo congregatus, sed cœtus multitudinis juris consensu et utilitatis communione societas. Est autem prima causa coeundi non tam imbecillitas, quam naturalis quædam hominum quasi congregatio. Every commonwealth in order to last must be governed by a certain authority. This authority must either be deposited in the hands of one monarch, be entrusted to certain delegates, or be undertaken by the multitude. All these single forms of government are liable to the greatest dangers. Therefore a fourth species of government is most to be approved, moderated and combined out of the three former. Itaque quartum quoddam genus rei publicæ maximè probandum esse sentio, quod est ex his quæ prima dixi moderatum et permixtum tribus. And the state is such as is the nature or will of the governing power; wherefore liberty has no domicil in any other state unless in that in which the power of the people is supreme. After discussing the merits of the monarchical, democratical, and aristocratical systems, Scipio declares again that he approves of none separately, but prefers the system united of the three. Yet if one of the simple forma is to be preferred, that is the monarchical. But a revolution in an absolute monarchy is most certain. When the long begins to be unjust, that species of government perishes. If the nobles have overcome the king, as frequently happens, the state obtains the second constitution of the three, a council of the aristocracy consulting for the public benefit. If the people of themselves expel or clay a tyrant, so far as they are wise they are moderate, and strive to protect the commonwealth established by themselves. But if they raise their strength against a just king, or deprive him of his realm, or taste the blood of the nobles, and subject the whole commonwealth to their licence, no sea or fire is more difficult to appease than the unbridled insolence of the multitude. From the extreme licence which alone they call liberty, Plato declares a tyrant must arise; for as from the excessive power of the nobles springs the destruction of the nobles, so this excessive liberty visits with slavery a people too free. All things in excess generally turn to their contraries; and this most of all happens in political affairs: for from this indomitable and capricious people is chosen some chief against their expelled leaders, — audacious, impure, insolently prosecuting those who have deserved best of the state, gratifying the people with both the property of others and his own. Finally, such men stand forth the tyrants of those by whom they were raised; which despots if the good citizens crush, the constitution is re-established; but if the wicked, faction becomes another species of tyranny. Thus tyrants snatch the sovereign power as a ball from the hands of kings; but from them the nobles or the people; from whom either factions or tyrants. Nor is the same constitution of government long maintained. A mixed government is, therefore, the best. There should be in the commonwealth something pre-eminent and regal: something should be assigned to the authority of the nobles; some things reserved for the judgment of the multitude. This constitution possesses that great equality which free men cannot long be deprived of; secondly, stability, because the other forms easily change into their contraries: so that a tyrant starts up from a king, a faction from an aristocracy, a mob from a people. But in the united and mixed constitution of the commonwealth this cannot happen without the greatest vices in public men.

In the second book Cicero reviews the history and development of the Roman constitution. Cato used to say that the constitution of Rome on this account excelled all others, because in them individuals had established the state by their own laws and ordinances, as Minos that of the Cretans, Lycurgus that of the Spartans Theseus, Draco, and Solon, and others, that of the Athenians. But the Roman constitution was not established by the genius of one man, but of many; nor in the life of one man, but in many ages and centuries. For he said there never yet existed an intellect that nothing could escape.

After the history of the Roman Commonwealth, the second book concludes with an eulogium on the gradation of ranks proper in a state. The statesman must never cease from instructing and contemplating himself, so as to summon others to his imitation, in order that by the splendour of his intellect and life he may offer himself as a mirror to his fellow-citizens. For, as in lutes or harps, and as in song itself, a certain harmony must be obtained out of the distinctive tones, which, when changed or discordant, practised ears cannot bear; and that harmony is made concordant and consonant out of the modulation of dissimilar notes; so, from the highest, and lowest, and middle, and intervening ranks, as sounds, the state becomes harmonious from the concord of its dissimilar elements. And what is called by musicians harmony in song, this is concord in the state, the closest and best bond of security in every commonwealth. And this cannot exist without justice. But all that has been said concerning the government of the state is nothing, unless this is established, that without the strictest justice no government can be long conducted.

In the third book — one of the most magnificent relics of ancient philosophy — Cicero, in imitation of Plato discusses whether justice be natural and immutable, or whether it rest only in opinion. Philus, in his argument against the inherent nature of justice, supports the character which the Sophists undertake in the Dialogues of Plato. Nature has treated man less like a mother than a step-dame. He has been cast into mortal life with a body naked, fragile, and infirm; and a mind agitated by troubles, humbled by fears, weakened by labours, prone to the passions. In which, however, there lies, as it were hidden, a divine fire of genius and intellect. The pleasing tie of speech united men first divided. By this same intellect, a few characters having been invented, the infinite sounds of the voice are all designated and expressed, by which also converse is held with the absent, the symbols of our ideas and the memorials of the past recorded. Political science and the discipline of nations, whether discovered by men practised in the variety of public affairs, or treated in their literary leisure, is to be honoured. In great intellects it attains an incredible and divine virtue; and if to these faculties of soul which are here received from nature or developed by social institutions there be added learning and an extensive knowledge of affairs, persons so gifted must be preferred to all others. For what can be more admirable than the management and practice of the grand affairs of state united to the study and knowledge of the arts? What can be more perfect than a Scipio, a Lælius, a Philus, who, omitting nothing that pertained to the glory of the greatest men, joined to the examples of our countrymen and ancestors the foreign philosophy of Socrates. Wherefore he has attained all things towards glory who has willed and accomplished the cultivation of himself, as well by the institutions of our ancestors as by learning. But if either path of wisdom is to be chosen, still, though the tranquil mode of life passed in the most excellent studies and arts may seem the more happy, this political science is the more laudable and illustrious, in which life the greatest men become glorious, like M. Curius, whom neither gold nor iron could subdue, — "Quem nemo ferro potuit superare nec auro." Between philosophers and politicians there is this principal difference, that the former have developed the principles of nature by their writings and technical systems, the latter by their institutions and laws. But Rome has produced, if not sages, at least men worthy of the highest praise, since they have cultivated the precepts and discoveries of sages. Philus, following out the argument of Carneades the Sophist, asks, if it be the duty of a just and good man to obey the laws, what are the laws?

Are they all laws indifferently? But virtue does not permit inconsistency, nor does nature allow variety; and the laws are sanctioned by punishment, not by our fear of justice. Wherefore there is no natural right, and men are not just by nature. Alexander asked of a pirate by what audacity he infested the sea with one brigantine? He answered, "By the same with which you infest the world." This same Alexander, how could he, without taking the property of another, rule, enjoy so many pleasures, and reign supreme? Justice commands us to spare all, to consult for mankind, to give each one his own. But worldly wisdom teaches us to gain wealth, power, riches from all. The answer to this sophism is obvious. Many things long existed in nature before they were perceived by human intelligence. Wherever a circle was, all the radii which sprang from its centre were equal, although it required the cultivation of mathematical studies in the brain of a clever man to perceive this fact.

Lælius replies to the sophisms of Philus in the celebrated passage on natural justice. There is a true law, a right reason, conformable to nature, diffused through all, constant, eternal, which by its commands summons to duty, by its prohibition deters from wrong; which, however, neither in vain commands or forbids the good, nor by its commands or prohibitions deters the wicked. This law it is not right to contradict, nor to derogate from any part of it, nor entirely to repeal it; nor can we be released from this law by the senate or by the people; nor is another expounder or interpreter of it to be sought; nor shall it be one law at Rome, another at Athena — one now, another hereafter. But the one eternal, immutable law must embrace all nations in all time, and be the common master and Lord of all. God himself is its author, promulgator, enforcer. He who shall not obey this law shall fly from himself, and, despising the nature of men, shall on this account suffer the greatest punishments, even if he escape the other usual misfortunes, — Est quidem vera lex, recta ratio, naturæ congruens, diffusa in omnes, constans, sempiterna, quæ vocet ad officium jubendo, vetando a fraude deterreat, quæ tamen neque probos frustra jubet, nec improbos jubendo aut vetando movet. Huic legi nec obrogari fas est, neque derogari ex hac aliquid licet, neque tota abrogari potest; nec vero aut per senatum aut per populum solvi hac lege possumus; neque est quærendus explanator aut interpres ejus alius; nec erit alia lex

Romæ, alia Athenis, alia nunc, alia posthac; sed et omnes gentes et omni tempore una lex et sempiterna et immutabilis continebit; unusque erit communis quasi magister et imperator omnium; deus ille legis hujus inventor, disceptator, lator; cui non parebit, ipse se fagiet ac naturam hominis aspernatus hoc ipso luet maximas pœnas, etiam si cetera supplicia quæ putantur effugerit. The virtue which obeys this law nobly aspires to glory, which is virtue's sure and appropriate reward — a prize she can accept without insolence and forego without repining. When one is inspired by virtue such as this, what bribes can you offer him? — what thrones, what empires? He considers these but mortal goods, and esteems his own divine.

Lastly, Cicero shows that patriotic statesmen will not only be rewarded on earth by the approval of conscience and the applause of the virtuous, but that they shall hereafter enjoy eternal happiness.

The great works of Cicero, De Legibus and De Republicâ, were neglected by his contemporaries, and under the Empire were, we may imagine, almost proscribed. The ideas of eternal and immutable justice, of moral duty, of pure reason and liberty, were impossible to be understood by a people degraded in vice and ignorance. The scholiasts commented upon the grammar of Cicero's writings, yet were unable to perceive their spirit. But the Christian Fathers of the Church first understood these admirable compositions. Whilst Diomedes Nomius and Aulus Gellius only analyzed the metaphors and ellipses used by Cicero, St. Augustine quotes the passages of the De Republica, and in magnificent language comments upon their philosophy.

Many things in the politics of Cicero are to be censured; he justifies the sway of the Roman people over the conquered provinces on the same principles which enable him with Plato and Aristotle to justify slavery; he did not understand the natural rights of man, the idea of which was reserved for a later and a Christian age. Much of his political system is but a paraphrase of the Grecian philosophy adapted to the larger induction of Roman history. But this is wrought out by him in the most splendid language, with all his most wonderful powers of composition. These sublime political truths so enounced were recognised and published by the Christian Fathers. And thus Cicero had an important result upon general civilization. Those who popularize certain axioms in politics do as much for mankind as those who discover and scientifically adjust them.

Cicero's treatise, De Legibus, was composed by him when in his fifty-sixth year, about two years after the publication of his treatise De Republicâ, to which it forms a supplement. It was written in imitation of his favourite model, Plato. The Greek philosopher wrote two dialogues on Government and Laws; the Roman felt an irresistible compulsion to do the same. The treatise on Laws was divided into six books, like the treatise on Government. Of these only three have come down to us. In the first he discusses the origin of laws and the sources of obligations, which he derives from the universal nature of things; or, as he explains it, the consummate reason and will of the supreme God. In the second and third books he gives a body of laws conformable to his own plan of a well ordered state.

The theory, in fact, which he announces in the first book is briefly this, that man being linked to a supreme God by reason and virtue, and the whole species being associated by a communion of feelings and interests, laws are alike founded on divine authority and natural benevolence. Reason prescribes the law of nature and nations. In the second book of the De Legibus, Cicero proceeds to set forth a body of laws. And since all law is divine or human, but regard should be paid first to the divine law, he first lays down the laws relating to religion and the worship of the gods. The third book contains the laws of the magistrates. The work, after the Platonic fashion, is cast in the form of a dialogue, in which Cicero, his brother Quintus, and Atticus are the speakers; and the introduction is directly imitated from the Phædrus of Plato. The scene is laid at his villa near Arpinum, his birthplace, on the banks of The Liris, beneath a shady grove, where grew an ancient oak. This oak reminds Atticus of the oak in the poem which Cicero wrote in eulogy of Marius; Quintus says as long as the Latin language is spoken this oak of Marius will not lose its reputation. But the poem which Cicero hoped to be immortal has long since perished with the oak.

The conversation then turns upon History; and Cicero, upon the plea of want of time, declines to write a history of the Roman Empire; but consents to give his sentiments on the subject of Universal Justice. From this investigation the Epicureans must retire who care not for the Republic. The New Academy must be silent, for her objections would destroy the well ordered structure of his lofty system. Zeno, Aristotle, and the disciples of Plato are the teachers who best prepare a citizen for social life. They had many great men in Rome who were wont to expound to the people the nature of law and explain its doctrines. But though they professed great things, they were practised in trifling. What can be grander or nobler than Jurisprudence? or what can be more insignificant than the practice of lawyers? — necessary as it is for the people. In no kind of discussion can we more advantageously investigate the faculties which man owes to nature, and the capacity of the human mind for the noblest enterprises. The true objects of thought and action should be discussed for which we were born into the world, and the beautiful association and fellowship which bind men together by reciprocal charities; when we have fathomed these grand and universal principles of morals, we shall discover the true fountain of laws and rights. Not in the edict of the prætor, not in the laws of the Twelve Tables, but in the depths of philosophy, must the knowledge of jurisprudence be sought. With respect to the true principles of justice, it is laid down: — Law is the highest reason implanted in nature, which prescribes those things which ought to be done, and forbids the contrary; — Lex est ratio summa, insita in naturâ, quæ jubet ea, quæ facienda sunt, prohibetque contraria. Some have, therefore, conceived that moral prudence is a law, the force of which is to command us to do good, and forbid us to sin. They have thought also that law is called by the Greek name *νόμος*, which is derived from *νεμώ* to distribute, from giving to every man his due. But Cicero considers that the moral essence of Law is better expressed by its Latin name, lex, which conveys the idea of selection or discrimination. For as the Greeks placed the essence of Equity, so the Romans placed the essence of selection, in Law. But nevertheless both these characteristics are proper to Law; which, if it be correct, the origin of justice is to be sought in this Law, meaning thereby the eternal Law of Morality. This, indeed, is the true energy of nature, the very soul and essence of wisdom, the role of right and wrong. And the principles of justice must be established on that supreme law which bad its origin before all the ages, before any law was written or government constituted.

Man is the only creature amongst so many races of animated

beings, who has a share in that reason and thought, in which the rest are deficient. And what is there, not in man alone, but in all heaven and earth more divine than reason, which when it has grown to maturity and become perfect, is rightly termed wisdom.

There exists, therefore, since nothing is better than reason, and since this is the common property of God and man, an original partnership in reason between God and man. Now, virtue is the same in the Deity and in man. This virtue is nothing else than a nature perfect in itself, and developed to the highest degree of perfection. There exists, therefore, a similitude between God and man; nor can any knowledge be more appropriate and sterling than what relates to this divine similitude. Nature, attentive to our wants, offers us her treasures with the most graceful profusion. And we may easily perceive that the benefits which flow from her are true and veritable gifts, which Providence has provided' on purpose for human enjoyment; and not the fortuitous productions of her exuberant fertility. Innumerable arts have likewise been discovered by the teaching of nature; for reason doth imitate her, and skilfully discover all things necessary to the happiness of life.

Man himself this same Nature has not only adorned with activity of mind, but has also bestowed on him the senses as guardians and messengers; and she has laid bare the necessary understanding of many obscure principles, as the foundations of some knowledge, and given us a mould of frame suitable and fit for the human mind. It is not necessary to dwell upon these faculties and capabilities of the body, — the modulation of the voice, — the power of speech, which is the greatest harmonizer of human society, — orationis vim quæ conciliatrix est humanæ maximè societatis.

Of all things which are the subjects of discussion amongst learned men, nothing is certainly more important than that it should be plainly understood, that we are born for Justice, and that Right is not founded on Opinion, but in Nature, — nos ad justitiam esse natos neque opinione sed naturâ constitutum esse jus. Although Cicero had borrowed so much from the Greek philosophy, his mind revolted at many of its disfiguring errors. The system of castes adopted by Plato and Aristotle is rejected by Cicero. He expressly holds the principle, that in the conduct of life every one ought to look to his own nature; every one ought to choose a mode of life and vocation agreeable to his natural disposition; one will rightly devote himself to philosophy, another to war, a third to oratory, and others to such occupations as they may severally deem to be becoming a free citizen. Blindly to follow a paternal profession, or to do a thing because it is the general fashion, is highly foolish. Ritter has observed that in perusing the political writings of Cicero, it should be borne in mind that many doubts would naturally suggest themselves to the mind of a politician who had not entirely withdrawn from public life, of the expediency of promulgating his own opinions of the constitution of his country, and its administration, and deter him from expressing openly and unreservedly the peculiar instructive and valuable conclusions which his long experience had enabled him to form.

## 4. Roman Jurisprudence

The development of the Roman law in itself had the most important effect upon the cultivation and progress of Jurisprudence. For Rome was the first state that gave to law a complete organization. Under Oriental despotisms, Law never could have permanence; nor could be raised to the dignity of system. The irresponsible Eastern Judges decided through prejudice, bribery, or chance. Under the turbulent democracies of Greece, with their tribunals composed of hundreds of unaccountable citizens swayed by the politics of the hour, Law could have no stability or systematic and coherent form. In both cases the precedent of to-day would be set aside by the caprice of to-morrow. But from the contests of the equally balanced parties, the patricians and plebeians; from the labours of the patrons in the service of their clients; from the long succession of the Jurisconsults; from wealth, security, and centralization arose, first, the importance and cultivation of the Roman Law.

Its magnificent development arose from other causes. The liberties of Rome were destroyed by Augustus; and all the avenues to political distinction were closed to independent merit under the empire. Then those who in former times would have been the captains and statesmen of the Commonwealth were driven out of the sphere in which their ancestors had shone. But they had recourse to other pursuits: eloigned from politics, they endeavoured by the study of Jurisprudence to keep alive some traditions of the Republic, to pay the debt which Lord Bacon holds we all owe to our profession, and to entitle themselves to the gratitude of their countrymen. Similarly on the Continent at present in France, Germany, and Italy, where political liberty is almost extinct, Law is studied as a science, and cultivated with enthusiasm. In Great Britain and Ireland all but its immediate practitioners neglect the study of the law; and with them it is only a profession.

The Civil Law is one of the greatest triumphs of the human intellect. The rich treasures of its ancient wisdom must be left unused by us no longer. There are numerous and important reasons for its cultivation. To classical students who purpose to pursue the legal profession, no part of their labours will be so useful as the study of the laws and constitution of Ancient Rome. To those who have the taste and leisure for the most extended classical studies, a knowledge of the elements of the Civil Law is essential for the proper application of Cicero and many other Roman authors. Again, the study of the Civil Law ought to be cultivated, because in it is the origin of most of the systems now prevalent in European countries; and in order that the laws which regulated and are the types of the ancient civilization may be compared with the laws governing the present complicated combinations of society. In the admirable forms of some portions of the Civil Law are suggestions which might be useful to modern legal reformers. By studies such as these the student will readily obtain a quick perception of legal fitness and analogy; in no other way will he so speedily form a legal mind.

At the same time unqualified praise must not be given to the Civil Law. The value of the Civil Law is not to be found in questions that relate to the connexion between the government and the people, or in provision for personal security, and a fair trial in criminal cases. In all that concerns civil and political liberty, it is not to be compared with the free spirit of the English Common Law. But, to use the words of Sir William Jones, in questions of Natural Law, no cause can be assigned why we should not shorten our own labours, by resorting occasionally to the wisdom of ancient jurists, many of whom were the most ingenious and sagacious of men. What is good sense in one age must be good sense in another, all circumstances remaining the same; and pure unsophisticated reason is the same in Italy and

England, in the mind of a Papinian and a Blackstone. Upon all subjects relating to private rights, personal contracts, and the duties flowing from them, there is no system of law in which principles are investigated with more good sense, or declared or enforced with more impartial justice.

The scientific development of the Roman law is best evidenced by the definitions given by the learned jurists who accomplished its great codification under Justinian. In the Institutes are found the following definitions — "Justitia est constans et perpetua voluntas jus suum cuique tribuere. Jurisprudentia est divinarum atque humanarum rerum notitia, justi atque injusti scientia." This is a correct definition of the virtue of justice as the constant and perpetual disposition to give every man his right. But it is not a correct definition of justice as capable of being enforced by the government of a country, inasmuch as only a limited class of rights and their correlative duties is capable of being protected and enforced by the public authority. The details of domestic life, the exercise of the virtues of benevolence and gratitude, the duties we owe to society in good conduct and the beneficent administration of property — these things are all beyond the sphere of justice as possible to be administered in our courts of law. The following is Justinian's definition of natural law — "Jus naturale est quod natura omnia aimalia docuit. Nam jus istud non humani generis proprium est, sed omnium animalium quæ in cœlo, quæ in terrâ, quæ in mari nascuntur." According to this definition the term natural law embraces all the principles of nature common to all animals. But natural law, as now understood, only implies the theory of that part of our duties which is capable of being enforced. The phrase, *jus gentium,* as used by the Roman jurists, corresponds more nearly to the modern term natural law. "Jus autem gentium omni humano generi commune est." And so the phrase appears to designate the natural principles of right common to all. The Law of Nations was almost unknown to the Romans, nor have we any important records of their *jus feciale.*

The edicts of the Prætors and other Judicial magistrates in time supplied the deficiencies of the Common Law of Rome. The edicts appeared to have sprung from the inherent power which every supreme court has to enact rules for its own guidance; but the edicts of the Roman Prætors gradually went far beyond this limited jurisdiction, and built up a system of Equity which finally completely superseded the ancient Roman Common Law. In the time of the Emperor Hadrian the perpetual edict was composed, and superseded the Twelve Tables as the invariable standard of Civil Jurisprudence.

As the number of the acts and constitutions of the Emperor, the edicts of the Prætor, and the commentaries of the learned increased, the rules of Law became more difficult to ascertain, until these different laws were compiled in the Gregorian, the Hermogenean, and the Theodosian codes.

Gibbon remarks that among savage nations the want of letters is imperfectly supplied by the use of visible signs which awaken attention and perpetuate the remembrance of any public or private transaction. The Jurisprudence of the first Romans exhibited the scenes of a pantomime; the words were adopted to the gestures, and the slightest error or neglect in the forms of proceeding was sufficient to annul the substance of the fairest claim. The period of a thousand years from the Twelve Tables to the reign of Justinian may be divided into three periods almost equal in duration, and distinguished from each other by the mode of instruction and the character of the lawyers. The periods were first mentioned by Gibbon, and they have been adopted by Hugo. During the first period the Roman Law was confined within the limits of the consultations between the patrons and their clients. The second period extended from the time of Cicero to the reign of Alexander Severus; then a system was formed, schools were instituted, and books were composed. During this period lawyers and professors compiled the enormous number of treatises on law which were afterwards digested in the Pandects. The third period of Roman Jurisprudence is between the reigns of Alexander Severus and Justinian. During this period legal authorship ceased. Lawyers were content to repeat the lessons taught by their predecessors, and the law was finally consolidated under Justinian. Long after the development of the Roman law had finally ceased the complete consolidation of the Roman law took place. The Codification of law is impossible until the development of the society and the law has been arrested.

The four compilations executed by the commissioners under the direction of Justinian are the *Code, Pandects* or *Digest,* the *Institutes,* and the *Novels.* These four constitute the Corpus Juris

Civilis. The Code was the collection of the Im
tions. When the legislative power of the senate and of the several comitia was abolished, the laws drawn up by the Imperial ministers and promulgated by the Imperial authority alone were termed Constitutiones. The Code occupied only one year, in the compilation, and was published A.D. 529. The Digest was a compilation from the *responsa prudentum.* Sixteen commissioners in three years selected 9,000 extracts from 2,000 different treatises on law. This was published A.D. 533. The. Institutes were designed as an elementary treatise for the use of students and candidates for the civil services of the Roman Empire. They are based upon the Institutes of Gains, and were digested by Theophilus, Dorotheus, and Tribonian. The latter celebrated minister superintended the whole system of codification accomplished by Justinian. The Institutes were published A.D. 533. The Novels — novellæ constitutiones — were the new constitutions published between 534 and the death of Justinian, 564. "The vain titles of the victories of Justinian have crumbled into dust; but the name of the legislator is inscribed on a fair and everlasting monument."

The consolidation of the Roman law under Justinian was certainly one of the greatest achievements ever accomplished in the history of the world. We have no authentic record whether the original idea of this scheme was owing to Justinian himself or to his celebrated minister Tribonian. In the first year of Justinian's reign Tribonian and nine other commissioners received instructions to revise the Imperial constitutions from the time of Hadrian in the Gregorian, Hermogenean, and Theodosian codes; to retrench whatever was obsolete or superfluous; and to select those laws best adapted to the practice of the tribunals and the use of the subjects. These constitutions of the emperors exactly corresponded to the English acts of parliament. The Code of Justinian was a digest of the statute law of the Roman Empire, and as such was transmitted to the magistrates of the European, Asiatic, and African Provinces.

The Code was by no means exhaustive of the body of the Roman law. No matter under what arbitrary principle the laws of a country may be enacted or administered there will be always besides the statute law a common law, whose external forms are seen in the decisions of the judges, the opinions of the learned, and the customs of the people. These were digested in the Pandects.

## 5. The Institutes of Justinian

I have thought right to give an analysis of the Institutes of Justinian. In its principles it is law in England, France, Germany, and Italy. An old writer has said — "Time hath his revolutions; there must be a period and an end to all temporal things — finis rerum — an end of names and dignities, and whatever is terrene; for where is Bohun? where is Mowbray? where is Mortimer? — nay, which is more and most of all, where is Plantagenet? They are entombed in the urns and sepulchres of mortality." So the names of those who compiled the Institutes are forgotten. But the legal works of the old Romans to this day influence the life of every citizen in Europe and America.

The Institutes commence with a short statement of the reasons for their publication.

The imperial dignity should not only be supported by arms, but guarded by laws, that the people may be properly governed in time of peace as well as war; for a Roman emperor ought not only to be victorious in the hostile field, but should take every legal course to expel the iniquities of men regardless of law; and become equally renowned for a religious observance of justice, as for warlike triumphs. When the hitherto confused mass of imperial constitutions had been arranged and brought into lucid harmony, attention was directed to the numerous volumes of ancient law. So soon as, by the blessing of God, this was accomplished, Tribonian Theophilus, and Dorotheus, men of known learning and tried fidelity, were enjoined to compose the Institutes that the rudiments of law might be more effectually learned, that the minds of students for the future should not be burdened with obsolete and unprofitable doctrines but instructed in those laws only which are allowed and practised. When, therefore, by the assistance of Tribonian and other illustrious persons, the fifty books called Digests or Pandects had been compiled, it was directed that the Institutes should be divided into four books, which serve as elements of the science of law. The four books of Institutes thus compiled by Tribonian, Theophilus, and Dorotheus, from all the institutions of the ancient law, but chiefly from the commentaries, institutions, and other writings of Caius, were read and diligently examined, and received the approbation of the Emperor at Constantinople on the eleventh day before the calends of December, in the third consulate of the Emperor Justinian. (21st Nov., A.D. 533.)

The first title is — De Justitia et Jure. — Justice is the constant and perpetual disposition to render every man his due. Jurisprudence is the knowledge of things divine and human; the science of what is just and unjust.

The precepts of the law are, to live honestly, to hurt no one, to give to every man his due. The law is divided into public and private. Public law regards the state of the commonwealth: but private law, of which we shall here treat, concerns the interests of individuals; and is tripartite, being collected from natural precepts, from the law of nations, and from municipal regulations.

The second title is — De Jure Naturali, Gentium, et Civili. — The law of nature is a law not only to man, but likewise to all other animals, whether produced on the earth, in the air, or in the waters.

Civil law is distinguished from the law of nations, because every community governed by laws, uses partly its own, and partly the laws which are common to all mankind. That law, which a people enacts for its own government, is called the civil law of that people. But that law which natural reason appoints for all mankind, is called the law of nations, — jus gentium, — because all nations make use of it. The people of Rome are governed partly by their own laws, and partly by the laws which are common to all men.

Civil laws take their denomination from that city in which they are establislied; it would not therefore be erroneous to call the laws of Solon or Draco, the civil laws of Athens: and thus the law which the Roman people make use of, is styled the civil law of the Romans. Whenever we mention the words civil law, without addition, we emphatically denote our own law: thus the Greeks, when they say the poet, mean Homer, and the Romans Virgil. The law of nations is common to all mankind, and all nations have enacted some laws, as occasion and necessity required; for wars arose, and the consequences were captivity and servitude; both which are contrary to the law of nature; for by that law all men are born free. But almost all contracts were at first introduced by the law of nations, — jus gentium, — as, for instance, buying, selling, letting, hiring, partnership, a deposit, a loan, and others without number.

The Roman law is divided, like the Grecian, into written and unwritten. The written consists of the plebiscita, the decrees of the senate, ordinances of princes, the edicts of magistrates, and the answers of the sages of the law — responsa prudentum.

A law is what the Roman people enact at the request of a senatorial magistrate; as a consul. A plebiscitum is what the commonalty enact, when requested by a plebeian magistrate, as a tribune. The word commonalty differs from people, as a species from its genus; for all the citizens, including patricians and senators, are comprehended under the term people. The term commonalty, includes all the citizens except patricians and senators. The plebiscita, by the Hortensian law, began to have the same force as the laws themselves.

A senatorial decree is what the senate commands and appoints; for, when the people of Rome became so increased, that it was difficult to assemble them for the enacting of laws, it seemed right, that the senate should be consulted instead of the people. The ordinance of the prince has also the force of a law; for the people by the lex regia, make a concession to him of their whole power. Therefore whatever the emperor ordains by rescript, degree, or edict, is law. Such acts are called constitutions. Of these, some are personal, and are not to be drawn into precedent; for, if the prince has indulged any man on account of his merit, or inflicted any extraordinary punishment on a criminal, or granted some unprecedented assistance, these acts extend not beyond the individual. But other constitutions being general, undoubtedly bind all. The edicts of the prætors are also of great authority. These edicts are called the jus honorarium, because the magistrates who bear honours in the state have given them their sanction. The curule ædiles also, upon certain occasions, published their edicts, which became a part of the jus honorarium. The answers of the lawyers are the opinions of persons authorized to give answers on matters of law. For anciently, public interpreters of the law were licensed by the emperors, and were called juris-consulti; and their opinions obtained so great an authority, that it was not in the power of a judge to recede from them.

The unwritten law is that which usage has approved; for daily customs, established by the consent of those who use them, put on the character of law. Nor is it an inelegant division of the law into written and unwritten; which seems to have taken rise from the peculiar customs of the Athenians and Lacedemonians. For the Lacedemonians trusted chiefly to memory for the preservation of their laws; but the laws of the Athenians were committed to writing. The laws of nature observed by all nations, inasmuch as they are the appointment of divine providence, remain fixed and immutable. But the laws which every city has enacted for itself, suffer frequent changes, either by tacit consent of the people, or by some subsequent law. All laws relate to persons, things, or actions.

After the division of persons into freemen and slaves another is given. And the eighth title is — De his, qui sui vel alieni juris sunt. — Some persons are independent, and some are subject to the power of others. Of those who are subject to others, some are in the power of parents, others of their masters. All slaves are in the power of their masters, a power derived from the law of nations; for it is observable among all nations, that masters have always had the power of life and death over their slaves, and that whatever the slave acquires is acquired for the master. All subjects are now forbidden to inflict any extraordinary punishment upon their slaves, without legal cause. For, by a constitution of Antoninus, whoever causelessly kills his own slave, is to be punished equally as if he had killed the slave of another. The too great severity of masters is also restrained by another constitution of Antoninus, who being consulted by certain governors of provinces concerning slaves, who take sanctuary either in temples, or at the statues of the emperors, ordained, that if the severity of masters should appear excessive, they might be compelled to make sale of their slaves upon equitable terms, so that the masters might receive the value, and properly; inasmuch as it is for the public good, that no one should be permitted to misuse even his own property.

The ninth title is — De Patria Potestate. — Children, begotten in lawful wedlock, are under our power. Matrimony is a connexion between a man and woman, implying a mutual and exclusive co-habitation during life. The power over children is peculiar to the citizens of Rome; for no other people have the same power over their children. The citizens of Rome contract valid matrimony, when they follow the precepts of the law; males when they arrive at puberty, and females, when they attain to a marriageable age. The males whether patres familiarum, fathers of a family, or filii familiarum sons of a family; but, if they are sons of a family they must first obtain the consent of the parents, under whose power they are. For reason, both natural and civil convince that the consent of parents should precede marriage.

Not only all legitimate children are subject to paternal power, but those also who are adopted. Adoption is made two ways, either by imperial rescript, or authority of the magistrate. The imperial rescript empowers all to adopt persons of either sex, who are sui juris, (i.e. independent), and this species of adoption is called arrogatio. But it is by the authority of the magistrate that persons actually under the power of their parents are adopted, whether they are in the first degree, as. sons and daughters; or in an inferior degree, as grandchildren, or great grand-children.

The twelfth title is — Quibus modis jus Patriæ Potestatis solvitur. — Let us now inquire how persons can be freed. Those who are under the power of a parent become independent at his death; yet this rule admits of a distinction. When a father dies, his sons and daughters are, without doubt, independent; but, by the death of a grand-father, his grand-children do not become independent, unless there is an impossibility of their ever falling under the power of their father. Therefore, if their father is alive at the death of their grandfather, in whose power the father was, they then become subject to the power of their father. But, if their father is either dead or emancipated before the death of their grand-father, they then cannot fall under the power of their father, but become independent. If a man, upon conviction of some crime, is deported into an island, he loses the rights of a Roman citizen; and it follows, that the children of a person thus banished, cease to be under his power, as if he was naturally dead. And by parity of reasoning, if a son is deported, he ceases to be under the power of his father.

Of those who are not under the parental power, patria potestas, some are under tutelage, some under curation, and some under neither. Let us inquire what persons are under tutelage and curation; for thus we shall ascertain who are not subject to either. And first of persons under tutelage. Tutelage, as Servius has defined it, is an authority and power, given and permitted by the civil law, over such independent persons, as are unable, by reason of their youth, to protect themselves. Tutors are those who have this authority and power; and they take their name from the nature of their office. For they are called tutors, quasi tuitores, defenders.

The Agnati, by a law of the Twelve Tables, are appointed tutors to those to whom no testamentary tutor was given; and these tutors are called legitimi, tutors by law. Agnati are those who are collaterally related to us by males, as a brother by the same father, or the son of a brother, or by him a grandson; also a father's brother, or the son of such brother, or by him a grandson. But those who are related to us by a female, are not agnati, but cognati, bearing only a natural relation to us.

The authority or confirmation of a tutor is in some cases necessary, and in others not. When a man stipulates to make a gift to a pupil, the authority of the tutor is not requisite; but, if a pupil enters into a contract, it is so; for the rule is, that pupils may better their condition, but not impair it, without the authority of their tutors. And therefore in all cases of mutual obligation, as in buying, selling, letting, hiring, mandates, deposits, etc., he who contracts with a pupil is bound by the contract; but not the pupil, unless the tutor hath authorized it.

The first book of the Institutes treated of persons; the second book is entitled — De Rerum Divisione, et Acquirendo Earum Dominio. — Things may be divided into such as are, and such as are not within our patrimony for some things are in common by the law of nature; some are public; some universal; and some there are to which no man can have a right. But most things are the property of individuals, by whom they are variously acquired, as will appear hereafter. Things common to mankind by the law of nature are the air, running water, the sea, and, consequently, the shores of the sea; no man, therefore, is prohibited from approaching any part of the sea-shore, whilst he abstains from damaging farms, monuments, edifices, etc. which are not in common as the sea is. Rivers and ports are public; hence the right of fishing in a port or in rivers are in common. Theatres, ground appropriated for a race, or public exercise, and things of this nature, which belong to a whole city, are public, and not private property. Things sacred, religious, and holy, belong to no individual: for that which is of divine right is not private property. Things which have been duly consecrated by the pontiffs, are sacred; as churches, chapels, and movables, properly dedicated to the service of God. Wild beasts, birds, fish, and all animals, bred either in the sea, the air, or upon the earth, so soon as they are taken, become by natural law the property of the captor; for natural reason gives to the first occupant that which had no previous owner; and it is not material whether a man take wild beasts or birds upon his own, or upon the ground of another: although, whoever has entered into the ground of another, for the sake of hunting or fowling, might have been prohibited by the proprietor if he had foreseen the intent. Whatever of this kind you take is regarded as your property while it remains under your coercion; but when it has escaped your custody, and recovered its natural liberty, it ceases to be yours, and becomes the property of the first who seizes it. It is understood to have recovered its natural liberty if it has escaped your sight; or, although not out of sight, yet if it cannot be pursued and retaken without great difficulty.

The second title of the second book is — De Rebus Corporalibus et Incorporalibus. — Things are corporeal, others incorporeal. Things corporeal are tangible; as lands, slaves, vestments, gold, silver, and others innumerable. Things incorporeal are those which are not tangible, but consist in rights and privileges; as inheritances usufructs, uses, and all obligations however contracted; nor is it an objection that things corporeal are contained in an inheritance; for fruits gathered from the earth are corporeal; and that also is generally corporeal which is due to us upon an obligation; as a field, a slave, or money; for, the right to an inheritance, the right of using and enjoying any particular thing, and the right of an obligation are undoubtedly incorporeal. To these may be added the rights (or qualities) of rural and city estates, termed servitudes. The rights or servitudes of rural estates are: a path, iter; a road, actus; an highway, via; and an aqueduct, or free passage for water. A path is the right of passing and repassing on foot over another man's ground, but not of driving cattle or a carriage over it. A road implies the liberty of driving either cattle or carriages; hence he who hath a path hath not a road, but he who hath a road hath inclusively a path; for he may use such road when he doth not drive cattle. A highway imports the rights of passing, driving cattle, etc., and includes in it both a path and a road; and an aqueduct imports the right of leading water through the grounds of another. The servitudes of city estates are such as appertain to buildings; they are so called because we call all edifices city estates, though built upon farms or in villages. It is required by city servitudes that neighbours should bear the burdens of neighbours, and by such services one neighbour may be permitted to place a beam upon the wall of another; may be compelled to receive the droppings and currents from the gutters of another man's house, upon his own house, area, or sewer; or may be exempted from receiving them; or may be restrained from raising his house, so as to darken the habitation of his neighbour. Among rural servitudes we ought to reckon the right of drawing water, watering and feeding cattle, burning lime, digging sand, in the ground of another.

Usufruct *is* the right of using and enjoying without consuming or destroying, things which are the property of another. It is a right over a corporeal substance; if the substance perish, the usufruct must cease. The usufruct and the naked use of a thing are constituted and determined by the same means. Less right appertains to the use of a thing than the usufruct; for he who has but the use of lands is understood to have nothing more than the liberty of using so much of the herbs, fruit, flowers, hay, straw, and wood, as may be sufficient for his daily supply; and he is permitted to be commorant upon the land, on condition that he neither becomes troublesome to the owner, nor impedes the labours of the husbandmen. Neither can he let, sell, or give his right to another, which an usufructuary may.

By the civil law, whoever had fairly obtained a thing from one whom he supposed the true owner, (although in reality he was not), and, if a moveable, had possessed it bona fide for one year, either in Italy or the provinces; or, if immoveable for two years within the limits of Italy, could prescribe to such thing by use; and this was held to be law, lest the dominion or property of things should be uncertain. But although it was thought by ancient legislators that these periods were sufficiently long to enable every owner to search after his property, yet a better opinion occurred to Justinian, that the true owners be not defrauded or too hastily excluded by the circumscription of time and place, from recovering their just due; Justinian therefore provided that things moveable may be prescribed to after the expiration of three years, and that a possession, during a long tract of time will also found a prescription to things immoveable — that is to say, ten years, if the parties are present, (i. e. in the province), and twenty years if either of them be absent. Property may thus be acquired not only in Italy, but throughout the Roman dominions, if the possession was honestly obtained at first. No prescription lies for things that have been stolen or seized by violence, although they have been possessed bona fide during the length of time required by our constitution; for prescription to things stolen is prohibited by a law of the Twelve Tables, and by the law Atilia; and the laws Julia and Plautia forbid a prescription to things seized by violence.

Donation or gift is another mode of acquiring property; it is of two kinds; on account of death, and not on account of death. A donation mortis causa is made under apprehension of death; as, when any thing is given upon condition that, if the donor dies, the donee shall possess it absolutely; or return it if the donor should survive, or should repent of having made the gift; or if the donee should die before the donor. Donations made without apprehension of death, called donations inter vivos, admit of no comparison with legacies: for when once perfected they cannot be rashly revoked: they are esteemed perfect when the donor has manifested his will either in writing or otherwise.

A testament is so called from testatio; because it testifies the determination of the mind. But, lest ancient usage should be forgotten, it is necessary to observe, that formerly there were two kinds of testaments; one practised in times of peace, and named calatis comitiis, because made in a full assembly of the people; and the other when the people were going forth to battle, and this was the procinctum testamentum. A third species was afterwards added, called per æs et libram, being effected by emancipation; which was an alienation made by an imaginary sale in the presence of five witnesses, and the libripens or balance-holder, all citizens of Rome, above the age of fourteen; and also in the presence of him who was called the emptor familiæ, or purchaser. The two former kinds of testaments have been disused for many ages; and that which was made per æs et libram, although it continued longer in practice, has now ceased in part to be observed. These three kinds of testament, originated from the civil law; but afterwards another kind was introduced by the honorary or prætorian edict; whereby the signatures of seven witnesses was decreed sufficient to establish a will without any emancipation or imaginary sale; but this signature of witnesses was not required by the civil law. When the civil and prætorian laws began to be blended partly by usage, and partly by the emendation of imperial constitutions, it became a rule that all testaments should be made at one and the same time according to the civil law; that they should be sealed by seven witnesses according to the prætorian law, and that they should also be subscribed by the witnesses, in obedience to the constitutions. Thus the law of testament seems to be tripartite; for the civil law requires witnesses to make a testament valid, who must all be present at the same time without interval; the sacred constitutions ordain that every testament must be subscribed by the testator and the witnesses; and the prætorian edict requires sealing, and settles the number of witnesses. To all these solemnities, additional security of testaments, and for the prevention of frauds, was added by Justinian, that the name of the heir shall be expressed by the handwriting, either of the testator or of the witnesses; and that every thing shall be done in conformity to the tenor of the Roman constitutions.

The before-mentioned strict observance of formalities in the construction of testaments, is dispensed with by the imperial constitutions in favour of all military persons, on account of their unskilfulness in these matters. For, although they should neither call the legal number of witnesses, nor observe any other solemnity, yet they may make a good testament if they are in actual service.

A man by testament may appoint many degrees of heirs; as thus: if Titius will not, let Seius be my heir. And he may proceed in such a substitution as far as he shall think proper; and lastly, in default of all others, he may constitute a slave his necessary heir.

A testament, legally made, remains valid until it be either broken or rendered ineffectual. A testament is broken when the force of it is destroyed, while the testator still remains in the same state. For if, after making his testament, he should arrogate an independent person by license from the emperor, or in the presence of the prætor, should adopt a child under the power of his natural parent, by virtue of the constitution, then that testament would be broken by this agnation, or quasibirth of a proper heir. Testaments legally made are also invalidated if the testator suffer diminution (that is change his condition). In case of diminution, testaments are said to become irrita (ineffectual); although those which are broken, or which, from the beginning, were not legal, are equally so.

Since parents often disinherit their children without cause, or omit to mention them in their testaments, it has therefore been introduced, that children who have been unjustly disinherited or omitted may complain that such testaments are inofficious, under colour that their parents were not of sane mind when they made them; not that the testator was really insane, for the testament may have been well made, but that it is not consistent with the duty of a parent. For if a testator were really insane at the time, his testament is null.

Heirs are divided into three sorts — necessary, proper and necessary, and strangers. A slave instituted by his master is a necessary heir; and he is so called because, at the death of the testator, he becomes instantly free, and is compellable to take the heirship; he, therefore, who suspects his circumstances commonly institutes his slave to be his heir in the first, second, or some other place; so that, if he does not leave a sum equal to his debts, the goods which are seized, sold, or divided among his creditors, may rather seem to be those of his heir than his own. Proper and necessary heirs are sons, daughters, grand-sons or grand-daughters by a son, or other direct descendants, in the power of the deceased at the time of his death. All other heirs, not subject to the power of the testator are called strangers; thus, children, not under the power of their father, but who are constituted his heirs, are strangers in a legal sense; and so are children instituted heirs by their mother, for a woman is not allowed to have her children under her own power. A slave, also, whom his master had instituted by testament, and afterwards manumitted, is so accounted.

A legacy is a gift directed by the deceased, and to be fulfilled by the heir. Anciently there were four kinds of legacies in use, namely, per vindicationem, per damnationem, sinendi modo, and per præceptionem. To each of these was assigned a certain form of words, by which their different species were signified; but these fixed forms have been wholly taken away by the imperial ordinance. A testator may not only bequeath his own property or that of his heir, but also the property, of others; and if the thing bequeathed belong to another, the heir can be obliged either to purchase and deliver it, or to render the value of it, if it cannot be purchased.

An obligation is the chain of the law, by which we are necessarily bound to make some payment, according to the laws of our country. Obligations are primarily divided into two kinds, civil and prætorian. Civil obligations are such as are constituted by the laws, or by any species of the civil law. Prætorian obligations are such as the Prætor hath appointed by his authority, and are also called honorary. The second or subsequent division of obligations is four-fold — by contract, by quasi-contract, by malfeasance, and by quasi-malfea-sance. Those which arise from contract are also fourfold; for obligations are contracted by the thing itself, by parol, by writing, or by consent of parties.

An obligation may be founded on the thing itself, as by the delivery of a loan or mutuum. He, also, to whom the use of any particular thing is granted or commodated, is bound by the delivery of the thing, and is subject to the action commodataria. But such person widely differs from him who hath received a mutuum; for a commodatum, or thing lent, is not delivered with the intent that it should become the property of the receiver and therefore he is bound to restore the identical thing received. A person intrusted with a deposit, depositum is bound by the delivery of the thing, and is subject to an action of deposit, because he is under an obligation of making restitution of that very thing which he received. But a depositary is only thus answerable on account of fraud; for where a fault only can be proved against him, such as negligence, he is under no obligation; and he is, therefore, secure, if the thing deposited be stolen from him, even although it were carelessly kept. For he who commits his goods to the care of a negligent friend should impute the loss, not to his friend, but to his own want of caution. A creditor, also, who hath received a pledge, pignus, is bound by the delivery of it; for he is obliged to restore the very thing which he hath received, by the action called pigneratitia. But, inasmuch as a pledge is given for the mutual service of both debtor and creditor, (of the debtor, that he may borrow more readily, and of the creditor, that repayment may be better secured), it will suffice, if the creditor shall appear to have used exact diligence in keeping the thing pledged; for if so, and the pledge be lost by mere accident, the creditor is secure, and is not prohibited from suing his debt.

A verbal obligation is made by question and answer, when we stipulate that any thing shall be given or done; hence arise two actions, viz., the condictio certi, when the stipulation is certain; and the condictio ex stipulatu, when it is uncertain. This.obligation is called a stipulation, because whatever was firm was termed stipulum by the ancients; probably from stipes, the trunk of a tree.

Sometimes others bind themselves for the promissor. Such sureties are called fide-jussors, and are generally required by creditors for their greater security. Fide-jussors may be received in all obligations, whether contracted by the delivery of the thing itself, by words, by writing, or the mere consent of parties; nor is it material whether the obligation be civil or natural; for a man may intervene and oblige himself as a fide-jussor or surety, even on behalf of a slave; and this may be done whether the person who accepts the fide-jussor be a stranger or the master of the slave, when the thing due is a natural debt or obligation. A fide-jussor is not only bound. himself, but by his death transmits the obligation to his heir. A fide-jussor may be accepted either before or after an obligation is entered into. Where there are fide-jussors, however numerous, each is bound for the whole debt; and the creditor may choose from whom he will demand it. But, by a rescript of the Emperor Adrian, a creditor may be obliged to demand separately from every fide-jussor who is solvent at the time of the suit, his share of the debt pro rata; and if any of the fide-jussors at the time of the suit are not solvent, the burden falls upon the rest. But, if a creditor obtain his whole demand from one of the fide-jussors, the whole loss shall be his, if the principal be insolvent, for such fide-jussor must blame himself, since, under the rescript of the Emperor Adrian, he might have prayed that no action should be given against him for more than his share of the debt, as surety.

Obligations or contracts are made by consent, in buying, selling, letting, hiring, partnerships, and mandates. An obligation thus entered into is said to be contracted by consent; because neither writing, nor the presence of parties is absolutely requisite. The contract of buying and selling is perfected as soon as the price is agreed upon, although it be not paid, nor even an earnest given; for earnest does not constitute a contract, but serves only as proof of it.

Locatio and conductio, i.e. letting and hiring, are nearly allied to emptio and venditio, i. e. buying and selling; and are governed by the same rules; for as the latter contract is completed when the price is agreed upon, so the former is contracted when the hire is once fixed by the parties. The locator, or person who lets, is entitled, if aggrieved, to an actio locati, and the conductor or hirer may have his actio conducti against the locator.

Buying and selling, and letting and hiring, are so nearly connected that in some cases it has been difficult to distinguish the one from the other; as when lands have been demised for ever, upon condition that if a certain yearly rent be paid to the proprietor it shall not be in his power to take these lands from the tenant or his heirs, or from any other person to whom such tenant or his heirs shall have sold, or granted, or given them as a marriage portion or otherwise. But as this contract, concerning which the ancient lawyers had great doubts, was by some regarded as an emption and vendition, and by others as a location and conduction, the Zenonian law was enacted, which settled the proper nature of an emphyteusis, making it to be neither the one nor the other, but a contract supported by its own peculiar covenants; and ordaining that whatever is agreed upon by the parties shall take place as a contract.

It is common for persons to enter either into a general partnership, or what the Greeks call a community of goods; or into a particular partnership, respecting some single species of commerce, as that of buying and selling slaves, oil, wine, or corn. If no express agreement be made by the partners concerning their shares of profit and loss, the loss and the profit must be equally divided. But if an express agreement be made it must be observed. A partnership lasts so long as the partners persevere in their consent so to continue; and if one of them renounce, the partnership is dissolved. A partnership is also dissolved by the death of one of the partners. Also when a man in partnership, being pressed by debts, makes a cession of his goods, and they are sold to satisfy either public or private demands, the partnership is dissolved.

The twenty-eighth title of the book is — De Obligationibus quæ quasi ex Contractu Nascuntur. — When one person transacts the business of another, who is absent, they reciprocally obtain a right to certain actions, called actiones negotiorum gestorum; i.e. on account of business done: and it is manifest that these can arise from no proper or regular contract; for they take place only when one man assumes the care of the affairs of another without a mandate; and they for whom business is transacted are thus bound without their knowledge; and this is permitted for the public good, because the business of persons absent in a foreign country, who have not intrusted their affairs to any particular person, would otherwise be totally neglected: for no man would take this care upon himself if he could not afterwards bring an action to recover what he had expended.

The fourth book is — De Obligationibus, quæ ex Delicto Nascuntur. — These are of one kind only; for they all arise ex re, that is, from the crime or malfeasance itself, as from theft, robbery, damage, injury, furtum, rapina, damnum, injuria. Theft is the taking, using, or possessing any thing by fraud for the sake of gain. Robbery is the taking by force.

The action for injurious damage is given by the law Aquilia; which enacts in the first chapter that if any man injuriously kills the slave, or the four-footed beast of another which may be reckoned among his cattle, he shall be condemned to pay the owner the greatest price which the slave or beast might have been sold for at any time within a year preceding. A man who kills an other without proper authority is understood to kill him injuriously: but he is not subject to the law who kills a robber lying in wait, if there was no other way of avoiding the danger threatened. Nor is he liable under this law, who has killed another by accident, if no fault can be imputed to him. But the law holds a man equally liable for negligence or fraud. But if a man, by throwing a javelin for his diversion or exercise, happen to kill a slave who is passing, we must in this case make a distinction: for if the slave be killed by a soldier, while exercising in a place appointed for that purpose, the soldier is guilty of no fault; but if any other person should accidentally kill a slave by throwing a javelin, he is guilty; and even if a soldier should kill a slave accidentally by throwing a javelin in any other place than that appointed for soldiers to exercise in, he also is guilty of a fault, (i.e. culpable negligence.) If a man lopping a tree, chance to kill a slave who is passing, he is an offender if he worked near a public road, or in a way leading to a village without giving proper warning; but if he made due proclamation, and the other did not take care of himself, the lopper is exempt from fault: and he is equally so, although he did not make proclamation, if he worked apart from the high road, or in the middle of a field: for a, stranger has no right of passage through such places. Also if a surgeon having performed an operation on a slave, should neglect or forsake the cure, by reason whereof the slave dies, he is guilty of culpable negligence. The want of professional skill is also regarded as culpable: as if a physician occasion the death of a slave by an unskilful incision, or a rash administration of medicine. If a mule-driver from want of skill, is unable to manage his mules, and a slave is run over by them, the mule-driver is in fault; and if he want strength to rein them in when another man is able to do it, he is then equally culpable: and the same may be said of a rider who, through want either of strength or skill, is not able to manage his horse.

An injury may be done not only by beating and wounding, but also by slanderous language, by seizing the goods of a man, as if he were a debtor, when the person who seized them well knew that nothing was due to him; by writing a defamatory libel, poem, or history; or by maliciously causing another so to do; and by various other means too numerous to be specified. The punishment of an injury, by the Twelve Tables, was a return of the like injury if a limb was maimed; but if a blow only was given, or a single bone broken, then the punishment was pecuniary, the ancients living in great poverty. The Prætors afterwards permitted the parties injured to fix their damages at a certain sum, which might serve as a guide to the judge, but not preclude him from lessening the estimate at his discretion. It must be observed concerning every injury, that the party injured may sue either criminally or civilly. If civilly, the damage must be estimated, and the penalty awarded as we have before noticed: but if he sue criminally, it is the duty of the judge to inflict an extraordinary punishment upon the offender.

An action is nothing more than the right of suing in a court of law for our just demands, jus persequendi in judicio quod sibi debetur. All actions, whatever be the subject-matter of them, whether determinable before judges or referees, may be divided into real and personal; for the plaintiff must sue the defendant, either because the defendant is obliged to him by contract, or has been guilty of some wrong; and, in this case, the action must be personal, in which the plaintiff alleges that his adversary is bound to give or to do something for his benefit; or some other matter, as the occasion requires; or otherwise, the plaintiff must sue the defendant on account of some corporeal thing when there is no obligation; in which case the action must be real; as, for example, if a man possess land which Titius affirms to be his property, the other denying it, Titius must bring a real action for the recovery.

Actions are also farther divided into those which are given to recover the specific thing in dispute; those which are given for the penalty only; and mixed actions.

Interdicts were certain forms of words, by which the prætor either commanded or prohibited something to be done; and were chiefly used when any contention arose concerning possession, or quasi possession. The first division of them is into prohibitory, restoratory, and exhibitory interdicts. Prohibitory are those by which the prætor forbids something to be done, as when he forbids force to be used against a lawful possessor; or against a person who is burying another, where he hath a right; or when he forbids an edifice to be raised in a sacred place or hinders a work from being erected in a public river, or on the banks, which may render it less navigable. The restoratory direct something to be restored, as the possession of goods to the universal successor, who has been kept out of possession by one who hath no right; or when the prætor commands possession to be restored to him who hath been forcibly ejected. And the exhibitory interdicts are those by which the prætor commands some exhibit to be made, as of a slave, for example, concerning whose liberty a cause is depending; or of a freed-man, from whom a patron would exact the service due to him; or of children to their parent, under whose power they are.

## 6. The Stoic Philosophy

Such is the analysis of the Institutes. The work may be regarded as an abstract of the legal part of the Stoic philosophy developed in the Roman law. Stoicism was equally manifested in the Roman politics. At Rome Stoicism remained popular in its most striking features — in its energy, and in its contempt of pleasure and of death. All the great political characters of Republican Rome were Stoics. And from the first to the last Stoic philosopher — from Antisthenes to Epictetus — manly independence is the characteristic of the school. The principle of internal liberty sufficient in itself for happiness, conducted Stoicism to the separation of the man from the citizen, and to his enfranchisement from the state. The stranger, the barbarian, the slave might be a man: the citizen might not. The wise man who alone is king, alone is citizen. The other Stoic principle conducted to the same consequences. The principle of the unity of the human race rested on another still more general — the universal order and harmony of the universe. There is, says the Emperor Marcus Aurelius, but one God, one world, one law, one truth. The study of politics at Rome ceased with Cicero. The Stoic philosophy of the Empire was only a philosophy of independence and resistance. Later it animated two of the greatest emperors. But driven from politics, the logic of the Stoics was used as the most trenchant weapon of the Roman Law. Cicero first applied philosophy to law. He was the first who combined the two characters of a practising barrister and of a jurist who studied the Science of Right. The great jurisconsults of Rome, Gaius, Paul, Papinian, Ulpian, were all educated in the school of Stoicism. And they introduced into law the maxims which had been hitherto buried in the books of philosophers. The strict law of ancient Rome, and the privileges of the Roman citizens based upon immemorial injustice, were incompatible with the maxims of justice, that every man was to live honestly, to injure no one, and to render to every one his own. But whilst equality of rights was extended to all, and the name of a Roman citizen became allied with the doctrines of equity and equality and lost the idea of privilege, absolute power triumphed. The pleasure of the prince has the force of law, says Ulpian. And this maxim, prominently advocated in the Institutes, was taught for centuries to all the young men who entered the Civil Service of the Empire. Ancient Greece and Republican Rome rested on the two principles of political liberty and civil slavery. The jurisconsults of the Roman Empire reversed both these doctrines. For political liberty they substituted absolute power: to civil slavery they opposed the natural equality of all men.

## 7. The Civil Law in England

Notwithstanding that in the feudal monarchies the authority of the civil law was greatly lessened, and in some places annihilated, the systems of the civil jurists to this day survive in many of the most important portions of our Jurisprudence. During the greater part of three centuries Britain was a Roman province; from the year 82, when Agricola reduced the Britons to subjection, down to the year 403, when the Roman legions were finally withdrawn to assist Honorius against the Goths under Alaric. During this time the judicial tribunals of Roman Britain was fashioned upon the Roman models. And the corporations invented by the Roman jurists were unquestionably the origin of the municipal institutions by which England in every age has been distinguished. Papinian, the celebrated Roman jurist under Septimus Severus, presided in the forum of Eboracum, York. Ulpian and Paulus also are considered by Selden to have exercised the functions of prætors in the tribunals of Roman Britain. But the invasion of the Anglo-Saxons swept away the monuments of Roman genius and civilization.

After the Norman conquest the study of the Civil Law was first prominently introduced into England in the reign of Stephen. Archbishop Theobald, the immediate predecessor and instructor of the celebrated Chancellor and Archbishop Thomas-a-Becket, brought Vacarius, an Italian priest, to England, A.D. 1143. Vacarius first brought the Pandects into England, and shortly afterwards, A.D. 1149, established a school of Civil Law at Oxford. There he taught with the greatest success; and the school so founded has continued to the present day. Soon after the establishment of this school different learned persons compiled treatises on the Laws of England. And to this school, perhaps, may be attributed the origin of that scientific system of Jurisprudence which arose, as Sir William Blackstone has remarked, in the interval between the reigns of Henry II. and Edward I. In the reign of Henry II. was published the treatise compiled under the direction of Glanville, who was, in 1189, *capitalis justiciarius totius Angliæ.* In the reign of Henry III., Bracton, Doctor of Civil Law, who also was one of the King's Justices Itinerant in 1244, collected, though not professedly by authority, the laws and customs then prevailing in England.

Bracton introduced many of the terms of the Roman into the English Law. Thus the celebrated "latitat" derived its name from the perpetual edict, "Qui fraudationis causâ latitaverit." In the reign of Edward I., from whose time, according to Lord Chief Justice Hale, the whole scheme of English Law may date its existence, many treatises appeared.

Fleta, — seu Commentarius Juris Anglicani — was written about the year 1285, the thirteenth of the reign of Edward I. Breton, written in the same reign, is merely an abridgment of Bracton's work interspersed with new matter. Ranulph de Higham and Gilbert de Thornton, both Chief Justices, also wrote in the same reign. The summary of the latter is an abridgment of Bracton. Most of these writers from Glanville downwards have not only adopted much of the style and matter of Justinian, but also appear to have been much struck with his Proemium, which they invariably copy.

Justinian says: "Imperatoriam majestatem non solum armis decoratam, sed etiam legibus oportet esse armatam, ut utrumque tempus, et bellorum et pacis recte possit gubernari; et Princeps Romanus non solum in hostilibus præliis victor existat, sed etiam per legitimos tramites calumniantium iniquitates expellat; et fiat tam juris religiossisimus, quam victis hostibus, triumphator magnificus."

So Glanville says: "Regiam Potestatem non solum armis contra rebelles et gentes sibi regnoque insurgentes, oportet esse decoratam, sed et legibus ad subditos et populos pacificè regendos decet esse ornatam; ut utraque tempera, pacis et belli, gloriosus rex noster ita feliciter transigat, ut effrænatorum et indomitorum, dextra fortitudinis, elidendo superbiam, et humilium et mansuetorum, æquitatis virgâ, moderando justitiam, tam in hostibus debellandis semper victoriosus existat, quam in subditis tractandis æqualis jugiter appareat."

Bracton, too, says: "In rege qui recte regit, necessaria sunt duo hæc, arma videlicet et leges quibus utrumque tempus bellorum et pacis, rectè possit gubernari; utrumque enim istorum alterius indiget auxilio, quo tam res militaris possit esse in tuto, quam ipsæ leges usa armorum et præsidio possint esse seirvatæ, si autem arma defecerint contra hostes rebelles et indomitos, sic erit regnum indefensum; si autem leges, sic externimabitur justitia, nec erit qui justam faciat judicium."

So Fleta says: "Regiam Potestatem non solum armis contra rebelles et gentes sibi regnoque insurgentes oportet esse decoratam sed legibus ad subditos populosque pacificos regendos decenter ornatam esse."

Glanville, though in stating the principles which govern the important subject of contracts, he has evidently borrowed from the Institutes of Justinian, avoids all notice of the sources whence they were obtained. Bracton, in his treatise De Legibus et Consuetudinibus Angliæ, introduces from the Institutes of Justinian the leading principles of justice — "Justitia est constans et perpetua voluntas jus suum cuique tribuere," and numerous other Roman maxims. He also adopts the title and method of the Institutes. He uses the term Prætor to designate a Common Law Judge, and distinguishes between the jus civile and jus prætorium. He also, in numerous instances, expressly quotes the Institutes, the Digest, and the Code. In fact, Sir William Jones has said, "When I rely on the authority of Bracton I am perfectly aware that he copied Justinian almost verbatim."

In the same reign was published a treatise called the Mirror of Justices. Mr. Blaxland has noticed as a curious coincidence, that most of the Germanic nations have their Mirror of Justice. In Germany, about the year 1220, appeared the Speculum Saxonium, or Sach Senspiegel. In France, about 1280, Guillaume Durant published his Speculum Justitiæ. Of the same period, or a little later, in England, is the Miroir des Justices. And this latter book. is supposed to have been formed by Andrew Horne on the basis of an older law tract called the Speculum Justitiariorum, said to have been written in the time of the Saxons.

We must now consider the reasons which led to the separation of the English Common Law in terms from the Roman system. Glanville, Bracton, and the other fathers of English legal history had quoted largely from the Roman books of authority; and even laid down that where an express rule was wanting in our law, recourse might be had to the rule of the Civil Law. So in the reports of cases decided during the reigns of Edward I. and Edward II. the rules of the Imperial Law are quoted and relied upon as good authority. Edward I. openly encouraged the study of the Civil Law, and invited to England Franciscus, son of the celebrated Accursius, to lecture at Oxford. But a jealousy speedily arose between the Common Lawyers and those who cultivated the Civil and Canon Laws. The Norman ecclesiastics were always regarded with dislike by the native nobles and clergy. The Civil Law unquestionably did not contain those principles of a just organization of judicial tribunals — namely, vivâ voce evidence and trial by jury, the peculiar characteristics of the English Common Law system; whilst the political portion of the Roman Law, as exemplified in the Lex Regia, left no independence to the feudal nobles or liberty to the subject. I quote this passage again: Quod principi placet, legis habet vigorem; ut-pote cum lege regia, quæ de imperio ejus lata est, populus in eum omne suum imperium et potestatem conferat — What pleases the prince has the force of law; inasmuch as by the Royal Law, which was passed concerning his authority, the people conferred upon him all their power and authority. Passages such as these if incorporated with the laws of England would soon have destroyed that feudal liberty which the nobles cherished. And once the Roman Law was understood in its political portion and as regarded the public law of the empire to be founded upon the most arbitrary principles, it ceased to be cultivated professedly as the Roman law. Though with respect to property and the rights of private persons the opinions and decisions of the Roman lawyers do not seem in any degree to have been perverted by the nature of their government.

From the time of Stephen the English nation was divided into two parties. The clergy, who, from the Norman Conquest, had engrossed the learning of the age, were particularly distinguished by their knowledge of law — Nullus clericus nisi causidicus, says William of Malmesbury. Even before the Conquest the judges had been selected from the clergy, and all the inferior offices of the law were filled by the lower orders of the clergy — a fact which has occasioned their successors to be denominated *clerks,* i.e., clerics. The bishops and clergy applied themselves wholly to the study of the Civil and Canon Laws. The nobility and laity adhered with equal pertinacity to the old Common Law. After the reign of Edward II. the Civil Law ceased to be quoted in the Common Law courts, and the lawyers did not hesitate to boast of their ignorance of it. Thus in the Abbot of Torum's case Sergeant Skipwith declares a title in the Civil Law to be devoid of meaning — in ceux parolx, contra inhibitionem novi operis, ny ad pas entendment. And in a more remarkable case at the

Parliament of Merton, 20 Henry III., when the prelates endeavoured to procure an Act to declare all bastards legitimate in case the parents intermarried at any time afterwards, because the Canon Law had adopted this doctrine from the Civil Law, all the earls and barons, says the Parliament Roll, with one voice answered — Nolumus leges Angliæ mutari. The same jealousy prevailed above a century afterwards, when the nobility declared, "that the realm of England hath never been unto this hour, neither by the consent of our lord the king and the lords of parliament shall it ever be ruled or governed by the Civil Law." This with other reasons led to the withdrawal of the clergy from the temporal courts. Early in the reign of Henry III. episcopal constitutions were published, forbidding all ecclesiastics to appear as advocates in foro sæculari. The Civil Law now permanently retired to the universities and the ecclesiastical courts.

The great event which gave a place to the common lawyers to unite and develop their system was the fixing, at Westminster, of the Court of Common Pleas, the grand tribunal for disputes of property. Formerly this court was held, like all the other superior courts, before the King's Chief Justiciary in the aula regis, or such of his palaces wherein he resided, and removed with his household from one end of the kingdom to the other. To remedy the consequent inconvenience to suitors, the eleventh chapter of Magna Charta enacted, that Common Pleas should no longer follow the king's court, but be held in some certain place. This place was fixed in the Palace of Westminster, now for centuries the principal seat for the administration of justice in England. The professors of the Common Law, then first brought together at Westminster, and excluded from studying their own science at Oxford and Cambridge, formed themselves into a society, purchased houses called the hostels, hotels, or inns of Court and Chancery, and raised a legal university. Here exercises were performed, lectures read, and degrees were at length conferred in the Common Law, as at other universities in the Canon and Civil. The degrees were those of barristers, first called apprentices, from apprendre, to learn, which degree of barrister or apprentice answered to the bachelor's degree conferred at the universities, as the state and degree of a sergeant — serviens ad legem — did to that of doctor.

Notwithstanding this formal denunciation of the Civil Law,

many portions of the Civil Law have been incorporated into the laws of England and Ireland; and the law of Scotland is more immediately founded upon the Roman procedure. The study of these portions is directly practical for the education of an English lawyer. From the Civil Law has been derived much of the doctrine and practice of Equity; and the Civil jurists have constantly been cited by the most eminent English Chancellors. At Law and in Equity the great names of Lord Chief Justice Hale, Lord Chief Justice Holt, Lord Hardwicke, Lord Mansfield, Lord Stowell, Sir William Grant, and Lord Brougham, show that the knowledge of the Civil Law is an aid to the cultivation of the most powerful intellect, to the formation of the soundest legal mind.

Uses were directly borrowed from the fidei commissa of the Civil Law, although it is true that in their introduction the ecclesiastical chancellors extended the Roman principles. During the latter years of the Roman Republic various prohibitory laws existed as regarded successions and legacies. Among them, in particular, was the Voconian law, U.C. 584, which precluded the appointment of a female, even an only child, as heir. Vinnius shows that exiles and unmarried persons also were incapable even of taking a legacy under the testament of a Roman citizen. A practice, therefore, arose of constituting by will a qualified citizen as heir, or universal devisee and executor, with a precatory request that he would give the inheritance, or part of it, to the intended legatee or devisee, who could not take it by direct appointment. Quibus enim non poterunt hereditatem vel legata relinquere, si relinquebant, fidei committebant eorum qui capere ex testamento poterant. This was called a fidei commissum, of which the form has been preserved in the Institutes. The person thus constituted heir was called hæres fiduciarius; and the person to whom the testator directed the inheritance to be given was called hæres fidei commissarius. Before the time of Augustus, such trusts were left to the honour of the person so selected. But Augustus, moved by the solicitations of individuals, and by some gross breaches of confidence that had occurred, first ordered the Consuls to compel the performance of such trusts as fidei commissa. Next, he created a Prætor at Rome, to whom was given the jurisdiction over them. The Emperor Augustus thus gave a legal sanction to the violation of existing laws, without repealing them. However, this plan ultimately had the most singular effect upon the English legal system, giving origin to the distinction between legal and equitable estates. Thus, a person at one side of Westminster hall is the owner, at the other a trespasser. The Emperor Justinian completed the system introduced by Augustus, and extended the rights of the hæres fidei commissarius by a law which enacted, that if a testator should direct the person whom he constituted his heir to give either the whole or a part of the inheritance to another, and if this circumstance could not be proved either by the written will of the testator, or the testimony of five witnesses, in case the person constituted heir should refuse to comply with the intention of the testator, he was compellable either to make a solemn oath that the testator had not created a fidei commissum, or else to execute the trust reposed in him. Thus, the right of the person having the beneficial interest — cestui que use, which was originally only jus precarium, one for which the remedy was only by entreaty or request, became jus fiduciarium, entitled to a remedy from a court of justice. The history of the introduction of uses into England is well known. They were originally employed to evade the statutes of Mortmain. Corporations, and especially the ecclesiastical corporations, were by the policy of the law prohibited from the purchase of land, unless a licence in Mortmain were previously obtained. The Mortmain statutes were constantly evaded by different expedients, one of which was to obtain grants, not to the religious houses directly, but to some person to hold to the use of the religious houses. Now, the principle of the feudal tenure was to look no further than the actual and ostensible tenant, and to consider him alone as proprietor. In the Courts of Common Law the use was a nonenity, and so it escaped the statutes of Mortmain. But the Chancellors, who were then almost invariably ecclesiastics, acting on the principles of the Roman law, maintained that these gifts were binding on the conscience, and ought to be like the fidei commissa. As regarded the religious corporations, this contrivance of uses was of little avail; for immediately there passed a statute, 15 Ric. II. c. 5., which enacted that, for the future, uses should be subject to the statutes of Mortmain, and forfeitable like the lands themselves, unless the licence of the Grown were duly obtained. But the uses continued. It soon, however, appeared that the assumed jurisdiction of Chancery was not sufficient; for whenever a positive declaration of a use could not be proved, the Court of Chancery could not compel the feoffees to uses to execute them, there being no legal proof that they held the land for the use of any other person. To remedy this evil, the precedent of the Emperor Justinian's reform of the system of procedure in respect to the fidei commissa was exactly followed. John Waltham, Bishop of Salisbury, and Chancellor to King Richard II., took advantage of the privilege given him by the Statute of Westminster, 2. (13 Edw. I. c. 13.), of inventing new writs, and invented a new writ of subpoena, returnable, into the Court of Chancery only, to compel the appearance of a defendant, and to oblige him to answer upon oath the allegations of the plaintiff, contrary to one of the first principles of the Common Law — that no man can be compelled to charge himself — nemo tenetur prodere seipsum. Such has been the introduction of uses into the English Law. Blackstone has considered that this was the origin of the equitable jurisdiction of the Court of Chancery; and says, that this writ of subpoena, returnable into Chancery only, in order to make the feoffee to uses accountable to his cestui que use, was afterwards extended to other matters wholly determinable at Common Law. But Sir James Mackintosh has shown his inaccuracy; he says, in his life of Sir Thomas More, "It would seem that this device [of the subpœna] was not first employed as has been hitherto supposed, to enforce the observance of the duties of trustees who held lands, but for cases of an extremely different nature, where the failure of justice in the ordinary courts might ensue, not from any defect in the Common Law, but from the power of turbulent barons, who, m their acts of outrage and lawless violence, bade defiance to all ordinary jurisdiction." Sir James Mackintosh then proceeds to show that in the earliest cases in Chancery there are statements of the age and poverty of the complainants, and of the power, and even of the learning of the supposed wrongdoer, topics addressed to compassion, or at most to equity in a very loose and popular sense of the word. It may be difficult to imagine how the clerical chancellors could have moulded into a regular form this very anomalous branch of Jurisprudence. But many of the ecclesiastical order, originally the lawyers, were eminently skilled in the Civil and Canon laws, which had attained an order and precision unknown to the digests of barbarous usages then attempted in Great Britain.

The English system of Common Law Pleading is directly derived from the technical system used in the more ancient Roman Law, whilst the system of Equity Pleading was derived from the method used under the Jus Prætorium. The ancient Roman Law was all stricti juris. The mode of procedure under the ancient Roman Law was by actio — the two principal classes of which were the actio in personam, and the actio in rem; to which was added the actio mixta. So in English Law Pleading, actions are real, personal, or mixed. In the actio in rem the actor — plaintiff sued the reus — defendant, for the recovery of some particular thing — for example, a landed estate, not in respect of any contract, but because the actor claimed the better title. It was an action to try the right to the property. In the actio in personam the actor sued the reus in respect of some obligation arising either from a contract, ex contractu, or from a wrong, ex delicto. The analogy of our Law Pleading to this system will at once be traced by every student. This system was full of the most technical subtlety; and as in our Law Pleading, the slightest slip was fatal to the action. A modification was introduced in which the actor proceeded by formula. According to this method the actor obtained from the Prætor a precept which, together with the subsequent pleadings, were delivered to the Judge who afterwards tried the cause. Similarly in England original writs were sued out from the office of Chancery. In proceedings by formula it was originally necessary to state the cause of action by some name recog-nised by the law, as empti, venditi, locationis. However, as many cases were without the strict letter of the law, the intentio of the formula was allowed to be so framed as to state the facts in a form settled by a Jurisconsult. Hence arose the distinction between actiones præscriptis verbis and actiones in factum. In the English system the word actor has not been retained. It has been translated into the word plaintiff, derived from the proceeding by plaint in the Saxon County Courts. The word defendant has been taken from the commencement of a plea in an action at law. "And the said C.D. comes and defends the wrong and injury." — the word defend — as defendere in Latin — meaning in old English to deny. When the reus, — defendant, merely denied the plaintiff's case, no form of pleading was necessary. But when he relied on distinct matters of defence these were stated in the exceptio, plea. Exceptiones were either dilatoriæ, dilatory — such as went to defer the action, or to dispute the plaintiff's capacity to sue — similar to our Pleas in Abatement; or they were peremptoriæ, peremptory, denying the right of action, similar to. our Pleas in Bar. The exceptio might, prima facie, bar the plaintiff's right; but he might be able to state some new fact avoiding the prima facie bar. This was done by the replicatio — replication. To this the defendant might similarly answer by a duplicatio, — rejoinder. And this again might be answered by the plaintiff's triplicatio — surrejoinder. In this way the parties proceeded as in the English system of Law Pleading until they came to a direct contradiction whether of law or fact. When this was accomplished the litis contestatio was said to ensue; the parties were at issue, ad exitum, at the end of the pleadings. Ultimately the whole of this technical system was abolished by the Emperor Constantius, A.D. 352; and all causes were heard before the Prætor according to the system in his court. I have given the above sketch of the Civil Law in England as an illustration. But the Roman Law has had a similar effect upon the development of every legal system in every nation of Europe.

# BOOK III
# THE CULTIVATION OF CIVIL LAW AND OF JURISPRUDENCE, UPON
# REVIVAL OF LEARNING
# A.D. 1100 — 1600

"Wenn ein wissenschaftliches Gebit, so wie das unsrige, durch die unterbrochene Anstrengung vieler Zeitalter angebaut worden ist, so wird uns, die wir der Gegenwart angehören, der Genuβ einer reichen Erbschaft dargeboten. Es ist nicht blos die Masse der gewonnenen Mahrheit, die uns zufällt; auch jede versuchte Richtung der geistigen Kräfte, alle Bestrebungen der Vorzeit, mögen sie fruchtbar oder verfehlt sehn, kommen uns zu gut als Muster oder Warnung, und so steht es in gewissem Sinn bei uns, mit der vereinigten Kraft vergangener Jahrhunderte zu arbeiten. Wollten wir nun diesen natürlichen Bortheil unsrer Lage aus Trägheit oder Eigendünkel versäumen, wollten wir es auch nur, in oberflächlichem Verfahren, dem Zufall überlassen, wie Viel aus jener reichen Erbschaft bildend auf uns einwirken soll, dann würden wir die unschäßbarsten Güter entbehren, die von dem Wesen wahrer Wissenschaft unzertrennlich sind: die Gemeinschaftlichkeit wissenschaftlicher Überzeugungen, und daneben den steten, lebendigen Fortschritt, ohne welchen jene Gemeinschaft in einen todten Buchstaben übergehen könnte."

*Savigni: System des heitigen Römischen Rechts*, Vorrede, 1.

"A domain of science, like Law, cultivated by the unbroken continuity of many ages, is for the present time a rich inheritance. There is not merely the mass of truths accomplished; but the efforts of scientific minds, all the attempts of our predecessors, whether they have been fruitful or failures, are either guides or warnings; and thus we are enabled to labour with the united strength of the ages that are past. Were we through indifference or presumption to neglect this natural advantage of our position, and to abandon to chance the influence which it ought to exercise over us, then should we throw away an inestimable advantage, the indissoluble substance of true science, the community of scientific convictions, and the living progress without which that community would degenerate into a dead letter."

*Savigny: History of She Modern Roman Law*, Preface, I.

# CHAPTER I

## 1. The Italian Schools of Civil Law, 1100-1500

The last conspicuous form of ancient philosophy was that which it assumed at Alexandria. The city chosen by the pupil of Aristotle to bear his name, and to rise to scientific, commercial, and political importance over others, even as its founder overcame empires, became the scene of great thinkers and mighty schools. Plotinus resuscitated Plato; Proclus gave the world another Aristotle. The spirit and tendency of their speculations, however, render it unnecessary to make more than a passing allusion to them. The closing of the Athenian Schools by Justinian, and the death of Boëthius may be considered the last events in ancient philosophy. Nothing can be more unfounded than to suppose because Boëthius is usually styled the last of ancient philosophers, and Descartes the first of modern, that, therefore, from the sixth to the seventeenth centuries, there had been no philosophical activity. We have too much disregarded the philosophy of the so-called dark ages. It is usually the least explored, but by no means the least instructive period of European history, as it has been traced in the disquisitions of Montesquieu, Ranke, Hurter, Voight, Hallam, and other philosophical inquirers. The feudal and legal systems of Europe arose. Independently of mere abstract investigations on mind, and of the principles of doctrinal theology, all the most important laws and institutions of European society were dug out of the mine of that ponderous and inexhaustible mass of human speculation. There, even more than among the ancients, may be found the well-springs of our modern speculative doctrines and controversies. In fact, no age in the world's history was more productive of great men. It was the age of William the Norman, of the well-taught Lanfranc, of Abelard, and Bernard of Clairvaux, of the learned Mussulmans of Spain, of Roger Bacon, of Albertus Magnus, of St. Thomas Aquinas, of Duns Scotus, of Alexander Hales, of Occam, and of Bradwardinus, of Thomas the Rhymer and Marco Polo, of Sir William Wallace and Edward the First. It was the age of rising cities, of consolidated feudalism, of literature beginning to breathe, of liberty struggling to be born. It is a universal law of nature that a new organization shall always be preceded by the entire dissolution of what has gone before. The mineral will crystallize anew only after it has been completely dissolved. The vegetable and the animal must be decomposed before their elements can recombine into other forms of life. So, too, a new society can arise only when the old one has been wholly dissolved, its atoms freed from each other, and its old arrangements broken up, that every particle may be at liberty to become part of the new living frame, according to some other law than that which governed the formation of the old social unit. The Roman world had to be ground down and dissolved by barbarian and Christian influences before the formation of modern society became possible. When the decomposing process was completed society may be said to have ceased, whilst each family and individual, passing also through a modified chaos, acquired new ideas, and tended to new organizations. To use the language of electrology, each atom then acquired a new polarization. Then the Church set about the task of reorganizing a body of knowledge, of pouring her vivifying and purifying light through all the powers and capacities of thought which were slumbering in the minds of men, so as to arouse them to exercise themselves in the various pursuits of arts and sciences. Philosophy meditated on the deep truths of religion, and endeavoured to arrange them in logical order and sequence. An acute and penetrating logic, like the naming sword of Paradise, turned every way to guard the sanctuary of religious truth.

Upon the fall of the Roman empire, the study of the civil law was abandoned, an age of darkness for a time covered Europe with a cloud. Upon the revival of learning in Europe, the term Jurisprudence was not used to designate that department of mental science which treats of the rules of universal justice. In its primary sense, the word Jurisprudence was used to denote the knowledge of the Roman Law. The science of Law in Europe dates from the twelfth century. It was then associated with theology and scholasticism. Irnerius was the contemporary of Abelard. During four centuries from the year 1100 the Civil Law was zealously cultivated in Italy; and simultaneously the Feudal and Canon Laws acquired a systematic form. The Feudal system obtained complete dominion over the tenures of land. The Canon Law regulated the ecclesiastical relations of the States of Europe; and having been originally but the rule of the Christian Church, it acquired the stability and authority of Positive Law under

Gregory VII., in the thirteenth century.

The first professors of the Civil Law appeared in the Italian cities. Irnerius, — Werner, by universal testimony, was the founder of all learned investigation into the Laws of Justinian. He gave lectures at Bologna soon after the commencement of the twelfth century. The freedom of the Italian Republics rendered the profession of the Law honourable; and the Doctors of the Law were frequently called to the office of Podesta, or Criminal Judge. Irnerius commenced the custom of making glossaries, which long continued to be the only attempts at legal literature. A gloss properly meant a word from a foreign language, or any difficult word which required interpretation. It was afterwards used for the interpretation itself. The first glosses were interlinear; they were afterwards placed in the margin, and were finally extended to a sort of running commentary on the entire book. An example of this latter kind of glossary is the commentary of Coke upon Littleton's Tenures. Thus Italy, the cradle of the Roman Law, was also the theatre of its renovation. The prosperity of the Lombard cities, and their love of independence, gave to civil and political life new events and new activity. The old laws of the barbarians could not satisfy the novel principles which struggled for development, and the study of the learned was directed to the Roman Law. During the space of a century from the time that Irnerius commenced the system of glossaries, each glossator wrote much to show his independence and genius; the glosses had multiplied into a huge and inconsistent bulk, and a digest was required. This work was accomplished by Accursius the Florentine. Accursius was born in 1182, and died in 1260. The best edition of his works is that of Denis Godefroi, Lyons, 1589, 6 vols. fol. The digest of Accursius — Corpus Juris Glossatum — is described by Eichhorn as remarkable as well for its barbarous style and gross mistakes in history, as for the solidity of its judgments and practical distinctions. Savigny, however, speaks but slightingly of this laborious compilation. To these succeeded Bartolus (born 1302, died 1359). He appears at the head of the scholastic jurists. The fame of the schoolmen excited the emulation of the lawyers to use the dialectic method. Thus, during three centuries spent in the study of the Roman Law the science of Law had not yet passed out of a trivial exegesis, which employed in its service neither history nor literature. And this school of jurists, feebly cultivating only the Civil Law lingered to the close of the fifteenth century.

Next after the attempts of the Italian civilians in the Middle Ages, some of the first essays upon Jurisprudence were directed to the consideration of International Law. The Law of Nations was unknown as a science to the ancients. The Jus Feciale amongst the Romans could have been of but little importance, since not the faintest trace of its doctrines has survived to modern times. Their Jus Gentium was what we term Natural Law. Thus Ulpian says: — Jus gentium est quo gentes humanæ utuntur; quod a naturali recedere facile intelligere licet; quia illud omnibus animalibus, hoc solis hominibus inter se commune est. Nor had Tribonian, or the other jurists who compiled the Institutes and Digest from the writings of the classical jurisconsults of Rome, any other idea of the Law of Nations than that comprised in Ulpian's definition. As the revival of Western civilization arose in the commercial republics upon the coast of the Mediterranean, accordingly the first rules of International Law appear in the customs of Venice, Genoa, Marseilles, Barcelona, and the other trading republics of the Middle Ages during their mutual wars. Machiavelli, a citizen of Florence, early in the sixteenth century, wrote systematic political treatises. Vasquez and Suarez, the learned Spanish Jesuits, wrote on Jurisprudence. And these are among the first eminent authors in modern history treating of the science of Law. For from the sixth to the fifteenth century, both inclusive, not a single writer of any note either upon General Jurisprudence or the Law of Nations appears.

There is a great distinction to be observed between the methods of Melancthon, Oldendorp, and other early writers on Natural Law, and the systems of Grotius and his followers. The authors who precede Grotius understand Natural Law as a special science, but in intimate union with the dogmas and precepts of the Christian religion. Natural Law is derived from human nature; but as this nature has been perverted by original sin, and as reason has been obscured, this science requires the aid of Theology, and Reason must be strengthened by Revelation. There is thus a double state of man, before and after the Fall. Hence, there is a two-fold natural law — that of the first state of integrity in which Natural Law is blended with Religion and Morality, and in which the institutions rendered necessary by the

Fall do not yet exist, such as property, social inequalities, contracts, — and that of the latter state in which there remains only a portion of primitive law to protect which the positive laws exist. But, after Grotius, Natural Law was understood as a science independent of Positive Religion.

In 1539, Oldendorp, afterwards professor at Marburg, published a work, which may be considered as the first system of Natural Law. The title is, Isagoge, seu elementaria introductio Juris Naturæ, Gentium, et Civilis. Oldendorp perceived the distinction between the Jus Gentium and the Jus Nature; but he had no accurate idea on the subject.

## 2. The French School of Law

Ulric Zazius, a professor at Friburg, and Garcia d'Erzilla, who flourished 1515, according to Andrès, have the merit of extricating the Roman Law from the glossators and scholastics. Alciati, of Milan, however, has more generally the reputation of the introduction of a better system. He taught, from 1518 to 1550 in the universities of Avignon, Milan, Bourges, Paris and Bologna. Alciati has had the merit of being the first modern jurist to write with purity and elegance. And the French school of jurists, so founded, has produced Cujas, L'Hopital, Godefroi, Domat, D'Aguesseau, and Pothier.

French Jurisprudence commenced in practice, and its first monuments were Laws. In the last year of the eleventh century the usages and customs of France were collected under the name of The Assizes of Jerusalem, Many brief compilations of the French Law were made during the ensuing three centuries. Under Charles VII., Louis XI., and Charles VIII., Laws were consolidated, the numbers of local customs reduced; and this labour continued during the sixteenth century. Thus practice everywhere prevailed. Jurists only wrote as to the daily application of the law. Italy brought into France the cultivation of the theoretical science of law. Alciatus, after having been a professor whilst very young at Avignon, came to Bourges on the invitation of Francis I., and founded a new school of law.

Fifteen years after the arrival of Alciatus at Bourges, Cujas opened at Toulouse a course of lectures on the Institutes, and rapidly assembled together a number of illustrious disciples. After some years of a free professorship he demanded from his native city a Chair of Law. But Toulouse had not felt the revolution which Alciatus had accomplished at Bourges in Jurisprudence. The school of Bartolus reigned there without a rival, whilst Cujas, inspired by his own genius, as well as by the example and the works of Alciatus, studied the texts and explained the Institutes of Justinian with the assistance of literature and philosophy. Afterwards he lectured on law at Bourges, at Paris, and at Turin; then he returned to Bourges, where he died. The historical labours of Cujas were important. Before his time jurists regarded the body of the Roman Civil Law as a code of laws and homogeneous legislation which it was necessary to study as time had made it; it never entered into their minds to decompose so complicated a machine into its constituent parts. But Cujas attempted this. Tribonian had confounded the principles of science, the history of antiquities, the philosophy of the juris-consult; and corrupted the purity of the Roman traditions with the pretentious barbarism of Byzantium. But Cujas understood that each jurist, the dispersed fragments of whose works Justinian presents to us, represents a system, and that it was impossible to seek for unity in a compilation which subsisted only byaunion of contradictory elements. Cujas then endeavoured to recompose the Roman Law, by attaching to each jurist his own part. Hence he annotated Ulpian and Paulus, and restored Papinian. Cujas is the true founder of the historical school of law. Towards the last period of his professorship Cujas pronounced in his school a discourse on the method of teaching law. By this it is easy to see how much he was deficient in method and rational criticism, and in that power which generalizes ideas; he finds scarcely any thing to say, except that the professor should be always nominated by the authorities. He displays an elegant latinity, gives numerous quotations from Euripides and Aristotle, but has scarcely a universal conception or a philosophical thought on the science of law.

Doneau taught a contrary doctrine to that of Cujas. With him law was a sort of geometrical system and method of deciding all civil and political affairs. Thus he wrote only treatises, whilst Cujas only wrote commentaries. Doneau, whilst studying the Roman Law, isolated himself from the Roman jurists and their fragmentary works, and composed true, dogmatical treatises upon each considerable portion of the Civil Law. Cujas, in a brilliant style followed antiquity and the ancient jurists. Doneau, a profound thinker and an indefatigable logician, lays down principles and deduces consequences. He is the model of the dogmatical method applied to texts. Thus these two jurists had a cordial antipathy for one another. But time has associated them in the history of law. Now, in France, Doneau is almost entirely unknown. In Germany he is reprinted, admired, and studied.

In the sixteenth century the French Law received the same impulse in its study and development which the Roman Law had already received. Dumoulin, advocate at the parliament of Paris, was no less indefatigable in study than ardent in dispute. He mingled law with business, and brought Jurisprudence into the discussions of the age. Exiled from France, he went from court to court and from university to university; he taught law successively at Basle, Geneva, Strasbourg, and many other places. The weakness of his health prevented him from pleading in public; but he was constantly consulted in chamber, and was one of the most learned men that appeared in the early history of the French Bar. Whilst the school of Civil Law at Bourges cultivated the historical study of the Roman Law, the French Law, scattered in the customs of the different provinces, received at last some stability from Dumoulin. By his Commentary on the Customs of Paris he established the principal rules of French Law and prepared the way for the labours of Pothier. This period has been termed the golden age of French Jurisprudence. Montesquieu says the Roman Law was then the object of the study of all who were destined for civil employments. Persons, then, did not make a boast of being ignorant of what they ought to know, and of knowing what they ought to be ignorant of Lerminier considers the French Bar in the sixteenth century to have been at its height of development. In the following century the language was purified, but learning was deteriorated. The eighteenth century had oratorical talents, but little study or labour. It was in the sixteenth century that the French Bar displayed its most vivid energy beside the school from which it proceeded.

The science of law required to be translated into legislation by a powerful, learned, and good man. L'Hopital was a practical and reforming minister of France. He did his best to accomplish the amendment of the law of judicial procedure, and to unite and calm the great French political parties. Amongst the fierce passions of the times some persons at last perceived that liberty of conscience ought to be respected. This truth is plain for us. It was novel in the sixteenth century. One of the first who conceived its principles and applied them was the Chancellor L'Hopital. In 1570 he composed his treatise on the end of war and peace, in which he expressed with eloquence the ideas of union and reconciliation of which he is the representative at this epoch. The end of war, he says, is peace. But how is peace to he obtained? Is it by compromise, or by full and complete victory? He shows that this complete victory cannot be hoped for; that insurgents, who fight for their personal defence, will yield only to extermination; that they are still very powerful and numerous; that the prolongation of war can only fill France with destruction and massacre; that prolonged civil war produced contempt for the authority of the king; that already many of the lords openly violated the oath of fidelity which they had taken; if, then, victory were impossible, or at least very difficult; if it could be obtained only by a war of extermination, which would introduce barbarism in manners, disorder in laws, and rebellion everywhere, what remained if not to obtain peace by a compromise. But it was said on the other side the king is ordered to do justly, and to punish by the sword those who with the sword have unjustly raised themselves to trouble his state. Rebels, as they are, it is necessary to cut off these corrupted members. To this violent policy L'Hopital opposes the argument of humanity. As medicine tends to cure, so does justice tend to the glory of God, not to cruelty. It is true it is necessary to cut off a corrupted member, but only when there is no hope of cure. Without siding with the rebellion, L'Hopital excuses the rebels. It is necessity, he says, the most just and inviolable of all laws, which has put arms into their hands; and since they are men, and not angels, do we find it strange that as men, in whose heart is divinely engraven the first law of nature, to defend life and liberty against oppression, they wished to defend themselves against those who desire to ruin and oppress them. On the other side it was argued, against the idea of compromise, that this was to ask royalty to capitulate with its subjects. For, said they, in such case the king will grant them conditions, which, without arms, they would not have obtained. L'Hopital replies, these conditions are not contrary to the dignity of the king, his power, or authority. If the king in doing this relinquished any of his right, I could only reply that, to speak freely, it is no longer a right if it prevents the public good; but how could that be a humiliation of the king before the rebels, when he only gives them liberty of conscience, or rather leaves them their conscience at liberty — liberty of conscience is the greatest and purest of all liberty.

Montaigne sometimes treats of law, and develops many correct judicial principles. Thus he denounces the French method of administering justice: "What can be more outrageous than to see a nation where by lawful custom the office of a judge is to be bought and sold; where judgments are paid for with ready money; and where justice may be legally denied to him that has not wherewithal to pay?" What can be more strange than to see a people obliged to obey and pay a reverence to laws they never heard of, and to be bound in all their affairs, both public and private, as marriages, donations, wills, sales and purchases, to rules they cannot possibly know, being neither writ nor published in their own language, and of which they have of necessity to purchase both the interpretation and the use. However, he adopted the sceptical arguments against the intrinsic natural distinctions between right and wrong, and argues against the theory of natural law. But they are pleasant, he says, when, to give some certainty to the laws, they say that there are some given perpetual and immoveable, which they call natural, that are imprinted in human kind by tile condition of their own proper being; and of these some reckon three, some four, some more, some less. Now, the only likely sign by which they can argue or infer some natural law is the universality of approbation. Yet we should, without doubt, follow with a common consent that which nature has truly ordained us. Not only every nation, but every private man, would resist the force and violence that any one should do him who would tempt him to any thing contrary to this law.

Stephen de la Boetie, the friend of Montaigne, died in 1563, but his treatise, "Le Contre un ou discours de la servitude voluntaire," was not published until 1578. He was probably the only Republican in France before the period of the First Revolution.

Francis Hottman published the Franco Gallia in 1577. This is chiefly a collection of passages from the early French Historians to prove the share of the people in the Government, and especially their right of electing the Kings of the first two races.

An anonymous treatise, "Vindiciæ contra Tyrannos, auctore

Stephano Junio Bruto Celta, 1579," is commonly ascribed to Hubert Languet, the friend of Sir Philip Sidney. The author explains in his preface the nature of his work, — to refer the government of princes and the right of nations, to their legitimate and certain principles, that the power of both may be confined within certain limits, on either side of which a correct administration cannot go: — Principum imperium et jus populorum ad sua legitima certaque principia referre: intra certas fines utrorumque potestatem conclusum iri quos ultra citraque recta reipublicæ administratio plane non possit consistere. He thus lays down the most difficult problem in social science: but professes to teach it with delusive geometrical accuracy. He will employ, he says, the geometrical method which from a point passes to a line, from a line to a surface, from a surface to a body. Such is the scientific method which Languet pretends to employ. But the execution is by no means equal to the design. In the Vindiciæ the following questions are successively treated: — 1. Should subjects obey their prince when he commands any thing against the law of God? 2. Is it permitted to resist a prince who commands any thing against the law of God? 3. Is it permitted to resist a prince who oppresses the state? 4. Have neighbouring princes the right of assisting subjects of other princes oppressed for sake of religion or by manifest tyranny? Languet has the merit of having originated the idea of the social contract: and he sought to establish it by examples taken from sacred history. In the development of the third question he extends the right of resistance to the defence of all natural rights. We enter into the domain of modern politics. The new political rights are discussed, whence arise the revolutions of England, America, and France. The principle of this political doctrine is not novel: it is that the people created the kings. This principle was admitted by the greater part of the jurisconsults, who explained the origin of the empire by a grant of the Roman people. But this cession, it was said, implied the idea of the abandonment of the sovereignty. The people were said to have lost their rights, whether by a tacit abandonment or by a want of exercise. Hubert Languet answers this objection. There is no prescription against the people. Kings die: the people die not; they are like a river that flows for ever. If their leaders have allowed tyranny to be strengthened, their weakness cannot prejudice the people. Time adds to the wrongs of kings; but takes nothing from the rights of the people: — Nec demunt anni quidquam juri populi sed addunt injuriæ regis. The people may have surrendered their power; but they cannot give themselves a master except for the sake of a great advantage. The institution of civil power has for its end to defend individuals against one another by means of justice, and to defend the entire body against external attacks by force. The sole end of government is the advantage of the people. Government is not an honour, but a charge; not an immunity, but a duty; not a leisure, but a mission: — Non honos, sed onus; non immunitas sed munus; non vacatio sed vocatio. Kings being instituted to do justice are then only the guardians and preservers of the law. It is asked whether law depends on the king, or the king on the law. Without doubt, if the kings were always just, there would be little necessity to make laws; but as this is impossible, laws have been instituted by wise and prudent magistrates to the end that they should be the rule according to which princes ought to judge; and, to prevent the prince from violating the law, they have associated with him the great men, the magistrates, and the public council that we meet in all forms of government.

Courtiers have given princes the right of life and death over their subjects. But the prince is only the minister and executor of the law. He ought to strike only those whom the law strikes; otherwise he is not a king but a tyrant; he is not a judge, but a brigand. Subjects are not the serfs of the king. Together they are the sovereigns of the king: united they are his brothers — ut universi domini ita singuli loco fratrum censendi sunt.

As regards property, we constantly hear at the Court of Princes that all belongs to the King. Thus what he takes he does not rob; what he docs not take he gives. But is it true that men who each love so much their property would have given themselves a master in order to abandon what they had gained with so much trouble? Neither is the king the proprietor of the public domain. The treasury of the prince is one thing, the public treasury another. Without doubt, princes are the proprietors of their private fortune, like other citizens; but in no point of view can they be considered as the proprietors of the royal domain. The royal dignity is not a possession, it is a function. The king is only the curator and administrator of the public wealth. The people, therefore, has ceded the sovereignty only on the conditions that the king should use it for their good. In this sort of contract it is the people that stipulates; it is the king who promises. In return the people promises implicitly to obey, if the conditions have been well executed, and the king on his side promises to fulfil them. Thus the people is engaged under conditions. The king is absolutely engaged; but when a condition is inserted in a contract, it is evident that the contract is not complete, when the condition is not executed. We cannot then call a people perjured which refuses obedience to him who has violated the conditions of his contract. The right of resisting tyrants, that is to say violators of the primitive compact being once established, it remains to know to whom, how, and by what means it is permitted to resist them. It is necessary to distinguish two species of tyrants. This distinction, familiar in the sixteenth century, was already found in Bartolus De Tyranno. There is the tyrant without title, and the tyrant in practice. The first is he who procures power without title, this is a usurper; the second possesses power with a legitimate title, but abuses it. The conduct of the people ought to be different with regard to these two species of tyrants. Against the first, natural law, the law of nations, and the civil law permit us to take up arms, for natural law authorizes us to defend our life and our liberty when threatened. No contract, no obligation binds us to a tyrant of this species; even a private person can raise himself against this species of tyranny; but if after having obtained power in an illegitimate manner the usurper obtains the approbation of the people, this consent ought to hold the place of a title.

As regards legitimate kings who abuse their power, we must not for every abuse or negligence call them tyrants and declare war against them; even when we have to do with a declared tyrant who openly violates the laws, we must at first endure him, and employ all means before arms, for a remedy may happen worse than the disease; but if he persists in his tyranny, he must be treated as a rebel, and deposed as such. Now, the people is superior to the prince; it has then the right to depose him. Such a revolt could not be accused of sedition, for there are just and unjust seditions. The just, says Bartolus, are those which overthrow an unjust Government, the unjust are those which overthrow a just Government; and in truth the overthrow of a bad Government cannot be called a sedition. But Languet always insists that the right of resistance belongs only to the magistrates. As for private persons, he refuses to them all right to take the initiative. The republic has not been confided to the protection of individuals, for these are not the persons to defend the state who cannot protect themselves. If they draw the sword they are seditious, for it is only the whole of the citizens who constitute the sovereignty, and individual persons do not. The people ought then only resist through the intervention of their magistrates. If these do not act, the people must remain quiet, and not forget that the best physicians often leave it to nature to cure maladies.

Languet concludes his system by a brief summary. Princes are chosen by God, but constituted by the people. The prince is superior to each individual, but inferior to all, and those who represent all — that is to say, magistrates or the nobles. In the institution of sovereignty, a contract takes place between the prince and the people — a contract tacit or express, natural or civil, of which the officers of the king are the guardians. He who violates this contract is a tyrant in practice. The magistrates have a right to bring him back to his duty by force, if they cannot otherwise; but private men have not the right of drawing the sword against a legitimate sovereign, even though he be a tyrant; in fact, as regards the tyrant without a title, as there is no contract entered into with him, all, even private persons, may rise against him.

# *CHAPTER II*

## 1. Machiavelli, 1469 — 1527

Authorities: — Sismondi's History of the Italian Republics: London, 1832. Macaulay's Essays: London, 1843. Characteristics of Men of Genius; Chapman: London: Hallam's Literature of Europe. Histoire de L'Economie Politique en Italie, par le Compte J. Pecchio, traduite par Gallois: Paris, 1830. Schlegel's Lectures on the History of Literature. Guizot: Histoire de la Civilization.

Works: — Opere di Niccolo Machiavelli, Cittadino e Segretario Florentino, vol. x. 1826. Œuvres Complêtes de Machiavel, traduites par J. V. Perier, Paris, 1825. Machiavel, son Génie et ses Erreurs, tom. xi. Par A. F. Arland, 1833. The Works of the famous Nicholas Machiavel, Citizen and Secretary of Florence. London, Starkey, 1675. London, Bohn, 1851.

As in Italy the study of the Civil Law was first revived, so Political Jurisprudence here first received an elaborate scientific cultivation. And the first great writer on politics, after the revival of learning, is the celebrated Niccolo Machiavelli.

Few political treatises had appeared before Machiavelli. The De Monarchia of Dante, another illustrious Florentine, is not, however, a treatise on monarchical government compared with other forms. It is a demonstration of the doctrine cherished by the imperial jurists, that the universe should have only one chief; that in the designs of God this one chief is the Roman people, or its heir, the Emperor; and that in the temporal order of things he has no superior. Two points are remarkable in this work. Dante employs the metaphysics of the Peripatetic Philosophy and its most subtle principles in the demonstration of a political thesis. Next, the work is a sort. of philosophy of history, resting on the authority of poetry and science, and which plainly suggested many things to Machiavelli and to Vico. Dante defines monarchy as the government of one chief over all men and over all things. The definition implies that monarchy embraces the universality of the human race and the universality of human interests. He demonstrates the necessity and the right of such a power. To determine the nature of government, the end of political society ought to be known. Politics is a practical not a speculative science. So far as science is practical, it is busied with actions. The nature of an action is related to the end of the action. For example, the action of him who builds a house is determined by the end which he proposes to himself in constructing the house. The end of man is not simply existence, or life, it is the manifestation of intellectual power. It remains to know how this power passes into action. Dante cites Averroès, and seems to admit with him that there is a universal consciousness spread through the human race; and which is realized not in the individual, but in the totality of mankind. This idea has been developed by Savigny in his History of the Roman Law, where he states the origin of Law to be in the common consciousness of the people. Dante proceeds to say that this intelligence acts in two ways — by practical intellect, and by speculative intellect. The end of the first is action and production. The end of the second is pure and simple knowledge, the most perfect of all things. And these metaphysical premises are introduced to arrive at the end that what is true of a part is in this case true of the whole, and that as an individual can arrive at wisdom only in a state of peaceful rest, so the human race can arrive at its end only in a state of Peace. Dante had reason to proclaim the necessity of Peace: for the middle ages were nothing but continual war. A universal monarchy is the condition most favourable to Peace and Justice. Such is Dante's theory; but the proofs and illustrations are most incomplete. The most general doctrine of the jurisconsults of the middle ages was the theory of the divine right of kings. They were almost without exception the partizans of absolute power. But one in particular advocated ideas singularly advanced for the age. Marsilius of Padua wrote the Defensor Pacts in 1314. The greater part of his work is only a commentary on Aristotle. But he terminates by conclusions opposed to the doctrines of the glossators and jurisconsults. He establishes definitely the principle of the sovereignty of the people — Legislatorem humanum, solam civium universitatem esse, aut valentiorem illius partem. The true legislative authority, where the people is sovereign, is the whole body of citizens, or a part of them elected by all. For the utility of a measure is more certain when the entire body of citizens devote to it all their intelligence and energy. And also no one willingly injures himself — nemo sibi nocet scienter. Thus the entire community alone is fit to judge if a measure be conformable to the instincts of one, or of some, or of all. Besides a law is better observed by citizens, when they believe it to be imposed by themselves. The state is a society of few men. This would not be the case if one person, or a few enacted laws of this private authority over all citizens, for then they would be the masters of the rest — aliorum despotes essent. Thus, according to Marsilius of Padua, the people is not only the source of the imperial power, as most of the jurists of the middle ages admit, in the sense of having conferred upon the Emperor the sovereignty, but the people is, of right, the sovereign and true legislator. He goes farther. He gives the people the legislative and also the executive power, and the right of determining by election who shall exercise the executive power of the state, and of deposing from office for just cause. The three essential points of the entire democratic doctrine are thus found in the writings of Marsilius of Padua, as well as in those of St. Thomas Aquinas — that legislative power belongs to the people — that the legislative power institutes the executive power — that the people may judge, change, or depose the executive power whenever it is wanting in its duties. Such were the theories of Marsilius; and in reading them we might almost suppose that we were perusing a page of Bentham or Mill.

Of all writers on Political Philosophy, none have received so general a condemnation as Machiavelli. The treacheries of the tyrants of the age in which he lived have been attributed to his political writings; and he has been commonly described as the discoverer of ambition and revenge — the original inventor of perjury among princes. Yet, even if his political works on the whole displayed nothing but the scientific atrocity in which Milton's fiends would have exulted, it would still be necessary for the historian of Jurisprudence to peruse and consider them as the results of the political experience and political wisdom of the age in which they were composed. The vices of the Italians of the middle ages, like those of the Greeks in their decline, sprung from the necessities of their position. They possessed the highest civilization of the age in which they lived. Almost alone of nations, they cultivated literature and the arts. But the merchant aristocracy of Florence, Pisa, Genoa, and Lucca were unable to furnish from their republics soldiers to cope with the rude barbarians of France, Switzerland, and Arragon. Open force they were compelled to meet with secret teachery. Barbarian violence they sometimes defeated with poison and assassination. By such policy on the part of their rulers, the civilization of the Italian republics was for a time preserved. Let that civilization atone to the world for the treacherous policy by which its rulers, for a time, maintained themselves in power. The names of Dante, Petrarch, and Boccaccio, Cimabue, Raffaelle and Michael Angelo, outweigh the cruelties of the Borgias. And let not the age which has witnessed the splendid triumph of Louis Napoleon be too severe on the author who scientifically treated of that princely dissimulation without which perchance princes could not have then existed. The political enemies of Louis Napoleon will always assert his power to have originated in treachery and murder. But they must admit that power has been used to forward the greatness of France. The French, as a nation, appear unsuited for parliamentary government. They require a despotic master of the school of Machiavelli. Political truth can only be discovered by the study and analysis of the past. Succeeding centuries will regard even the open wars of the nineteenth century with the same detestation which we entertain towards the secret crimes of the Borgias. To the jurist, the study of the history of the Italian Republics is peculiarly interesting. With them first, after the dissolution of the Roman empire, began the science of governing men for their advantage. Former governments had been but the tyrannies of armies over subjected slaves. In the petty Italian republics victors and vanquished were fused into one people, united by a single bond — the public good. To one element in particular was the precocious development of the Italian burghs into powerful republics due. Italy had never been wholly in the power of the barbarians. The South was dependent on the Greek Emperor. Even that part of the North which the barbarians occupied had all been cleared and cultivated; so that forests no longer remained for the barbarian nobles to enjoy the chase or lead their old country life. Even those hordes that remained were broken in power. The Ostrogoths were defeated by Belisarius. The Lombard Kingdom was destroyed by the Franks. The barbarians, then, were never exclusive masters of the territory and society of Italy; and but a feeble feudalism was established beyond the Alps. The preponderance, therefore, instead of passing to the inhabitants of country districts, adhered to the towns. When this became decided, a considerable number of the fief-holders settled within the cities. The barbarian nobles became burghers. They brought their energy, in dependence, and fiery spirit of freedom with them; whilst at the same time they relieved their fellow burghers from the terrors of feudal tyranny. Hence arose their great and precocious superiority. The Italian cities for the most part date the commencement of their liberties from the invasion of Otho the Great in 951. For three centuries, during which history is almost silent concerning them, they laboured, and flourished in their labour. At the close of the thirteenth century a degree of prosperity had been attained which Italy may now look back to with regret. Then were perfected the great works of industry which still fertilize the land. The Naviglio Grande of Milan, which yet spreads the clear waters of the Ticino over Lombardy, was begun in 1179, and terminated in 1262. If we turn to the cities, we see them adorned by the palaces of the aristocracy, enriched with the finest works of sculpture — the streets paved with broad flag stones. Whilst, at the same time, the nobles of Germany and England, in building their castles, thought not of beauty, but only of defence, and the streets of Paris were almost impassable from mud. The crusades had brought to the Republics of Italy a large increase of wealth. The great maritime states of Venice, Genoa, and Pisa, united their fleets to fight the Turks and pirates, — or, delivered from those foes, they fought amongst themselves for supremacy. "Genoa la superba" had already built the palaces now, after six centuries, the wonder and admiration of travellers. She maintained military and mercantile colonies at St. Jéan d'Acre in the Holy Land; at Pera, opposite Constantinople, and in the Crimea, in the Black Sea. Pisa was already celebrated for the "profusion of marble, the patrician towers, and the great magnificence." She had conquered Sardinia and the Balearic Isles; and was the first to introduce into Tuscany the arts which ennoble wealth. Her Dome, her Baptistery, her leaning tower, and her Campo Santo, had been successively built from the year 1063 to the end of the twelfth century. The churches of Santa Croce and Santa Maria were begun. They are not finished yet. Giovanni Villani has given us an ample and precise account of the state of Florence in the early part of the fourteenth century. The great manufacture of wool alone employed two hundred factories, and thirty thousand workmen. The cloth annually sold produced a sum equal in exchangeable value to two millions and a half of our money. Eighty banks conducted the commercial transactions of Florence. The city and its environs contained one hundred and seventy thousand inhabitants. At the commencement of the fourteenth century the revenue of the Republic amounted to three hundred thousand florins of gold, more than, three centuries afterwards, England and Ireland united produced to Queen Elizabeth. But during the period of this greatest prosperity of Florence, culminating in the age of Lorenzo the Magnificent, England was distracted by the Civil Wars of the Roses. The battles of Northampton, Wake-field, St. Albans, Towton, Barnet, and Tewkesbury, are the historical events. France was desolated by the English wars and the Jacquerie. Both countries exhibit a miserable spectacle of poverty and barbarity. In both the name of scarcely a single great man appears. These miseries then existed in France and England, now the seats of the most flourishing nations, — the most advanced and refined civilizations. But Florence, built of marble, and robed in the silks of the East, was then successively ennobled by the divine melancholy of Dante, the mirth of Pulci, the political wisdom of Machiavelli, the magnificence of Lorenzo de Medici.

Not only had the Italian Republics prospered before modern political science arose, but they put in practice many of the ideas which this science cultivates, explains, and brings to perfection for the wealth and prosperity of nations. Amalfi introduced a maritime code, which became the law of all navigators; to this city also is attributed the discovery of the compass. Milan from the year 1260 had practised a census of the land. Venice towards the end of the twelfth century discovered a new financial resource in the public loans, and also authorized the circulation of paper-money. Venice also promulgated the wisest sanitary laws, and adapted statistics to administrative science. The Florentines, who were the first to have banks in most parts of Europe, were also the first to arrange the expenses of the state according to the annual revenue and expenditure. The gonfalonier, Pierre Soderini, in rendering an account of his administration, submitted, in 1510, to the examination of the Great Council, the table of the revenue and expenses of the eight preceding years. Genoa gave the first example of exclusive privileges accorded to a company in payment of the loan which the state obtained from the company. The monts-de-pietè were another invention useful in their generation. Finally, all the Republics honoured commerce by dignities and distinctions; and nobles did not consider themselves disgraced by engaging in trade.

The prodigious prosperity of these states, and all these useful discoveries, were not the work of blind empiricism, they were the work of liberty. Experience alone, without liberty or science, does not furnish sufficient means of instruction, and brings men to prosperity but slowly. Liberty is not an empty word, an imaginary being created by the poets, but a powerful and real benefactress of the nations. She works prodigies, multiplying a hundred-fold the forces of the imagination and the soul, stimulating the keen rivalry which she excites, offering to person and property that certainty without which there can be neither industry nor commerce, finally making all ideas and all interests converge towards the common good.

A great blot appears upon all this Italian prosperity. The refined Italian merchants had not the leisure which then was necessary to men who desired to be trained as soldiers. The strength of armies lay in their cavalry. These were covered from head to foot with iron, and armed with ponderous lances. No infantry of the day was supposed capable of withstanding their charge. But it required the labour of years to train the man-at-arms to sustain his armour and wield his spear. It would have been well for the prosperity of the Italian States if they had had political wisdom to adopt the expedient of standing armies; — if some portion of their own citizens had been armed by them for the common defence. Then some patriotism animates the soldier, and he is unwilling to imbrue his sword in his country's blood. But they do not appear to have thought of this modern discovery in political science. Mercenary foreign soldiers alone were employed; ever ready to sell their lances to the best bidder, and to turn them tomorrow against the State which employed them to-day. From the difficulties of their position arose the character of the statesmen of the Tuscan and Lombard Republics. They were traitors and assassins. They knew not and despised military courage — the sole virtue of the licentious and drunken soldiers who came from beyond the Alps. But at the same time they cultivated eloquence, poetry, and the fine arts with complete success. Machiavelli, in his public conduct, was upright and honourable; but because amongst his own discoveries in political science he scientifically treated of the opinions current in the fashionable morality of the day, he has been gibbeted by posterity.

In times such as these he flourished. Niccolo Machiavelli was born at Florence on the 5th of May, 1469, of a poor, old, and noble family. We know nothing about his youth, and all that can be gathered from his own writings consists of a few brief allusions to his dependence and poverty. His talents must have rapidly attracted the notice and commendation of the statesmen of the time; and we find him in 1498, being then only twenty-nine years of age, appointed by the "Ten of Liberty and Peace" the secretary of the Florentine Republic. This was the government, the remnant of the ancient oligarchy, which ruled Florence between the expulsion of the Medici in 1494, and their return in 1512. For fourteen years he was thus employed as secretary, or exercised his diplomatic policy in the numerous embassies which Florence despatched to the Courts of Europe. But when the popular government was overthrown, and the Medici returned to

Florence supported by the arms of Spain, Machiavelli was arrested on a charge of conspiracy against the new government, imprisoned, and tortured with "the cord." Immediately after this he composed his great political works; but none of his writings were published during his life, and they first appeared in Rome in 1532, with an approbation of the Pope. "The Prince," — the work by which Machiavelli is best known to those who unsparingly condemn him, — was dedicated to Lorenzo de Medici. This book was written in 1513, after the fall of the Republican Government at Florence; when Machiavelli, living in retired poverty, and despairing of the liberty of his country, was disposed to support any government which might secure her independence. He naturally felt the reluctance of every man of talent who has once been employed in political affairs to waste the best years of his life in idleness. And he wrote "The Prince" to recommend himself to the notice of the Medici. He thought it better to serve some master usefully for the State than to remain in poverty and obscurity.

"The Prince" commences with a dissertation upon the several sorts of government, which Machiavelli divides first into commonwealths and monarchies, and these again into hereditary and mixed. The latter term he applies to a monarchy in which are territories lately annexed to the dominion of the conqueror. He also applies the term to cases where the new acquisition arises from the talent of a prince in subverting the liberties of a people and acquiring absolute power for himself. In the third chapter occur some of the politic maxims of kingcraft, which have been so censured. Thus, speaking of the manner in which to treat a conquered province, he says: It is to be observed, men are either to be flattered and indulged, or utterly destroyed; because for small offences they do usually revenge themselves, but for great ones they cannot; so that injury is to be done in such a manner as not to fear any revenge.

Again, he says in chapter iii.: That it is very obvious, and no more than natural, for princes to desire to extend their dominion, and when they attempt nothing but what they are able to achieve, they are applauded, at least not upbraided thereby; but when they are unable to compass it, and yet will be doing, then they are condemned, and indeed not unworthily. If France then with its own forces alone had been able to have enterprised upon Naples, it ought to have been done; but if her own private strength was too weak, it ought not to have been divided; and if the division of Lombardy, to which she consented with the Venetians, was excusable, it was done because to get footing in Italy. But this partition of Naples with the king of Spain is extremely to be condemned, because not pressed or quickened by such necessity as the former. Louis, therefore, committed five faults in this expedition. He ruined the inferior lords; he augmented the dominion of a neighbour prince; he called in a foreigner as puissant as himself; he neglected to continue there in person; and planted no colonies; all which errors might have been no inconvenience whilst he lived, had he not been guilty of a sixth, and that was depressing the power of the Venetians. If indeed he had not sided with the Church, nor brought the Spaniards into Italy, it had been but reasonable for him to have taken down the pride of the Venetians; but pursuing his first resolutions, he ought not to have suffered them to be ruined, because whilst the Venetian strength was entire, they would have kept off other people from attempting upon Lombardy, to which the Venetians would never have consented, unless upon condition it might have been delivered to them, and the others would not in probability have forced it from France, to have given it to them; and to have contended with them both, nobody would have had the courage... So then King Louis lost Lombardy, because he did not observe one of those rules which others have followed with success in the conquest of provinces, and in their desire to keep them; nor is it an extraordinary thing, but what happens every day, and not without reason. To this purpose I remember I was once in discourse with the Cardinal d'Amboise, at Nantes, at the time when Valentine possessed himself of Romagna. In the heat of our conference he telling me that the Italians were ignorant of the art of war; I replied that the French had as little skill in matters of state; for if they had had the least policy in the world, they would never have suffered the Church to come to that height and elevation. And it has been found since by experience that the grandeur of the Church and the Spaniard in Italy is derived from France, and that they in requital have been the ruin and expulsion of the French. From hence a general rule may be deduced, and such a one as seldom or never is subject to exception, viz., that whoever is the occasion of another's advancement is the cause of his own diminution; because that advancement is founded either upon the conduct or power of the donor, either of which becomes suspicious at length to the person preferred.

The chapters on the military force of a state are interesting; the first assumes, as an unquestionable truth, that good laws and good arms are the principal foundation of every state. Machiavelli describes the different kinds of troops then in use; in bold and powerful language paints the destruction which is inevitable to any state that relies upon foreign mercenary forces; and in chapter xiii. draws the conclusion, that without having proper and peculiar forces of his own, no prince is secure, but depends wholly upon fortune, as having no native and intrinsic strength to sustain him in adversity.

Chapter xvii. is headed "Of Cruelty and Clemency, and whether it is best for a Prince to be beloved or feared." He says, —

Every prince is to be esteemed rather merciful than cruel, but with great caution, that his mercy be not abused. Cæsar Borgia was counted cruel, yet that cruelty reduced Romagna, united it, settled it in peace, and rendered it faithful; so that if well considered, he will appear much more merciful than the Florentines, who, rather than be thought cruel, suffered Pistoia to be destroyed. A prince, therefore, is not to regard the scandal of being cruel, if thereby he keeps his subjects within their allegiance and united, seeing by some few examples of justice you may be more merciful than they, who, by a universal exercise of pity, permit several disorders to follow, which occasion rapine and murder; and the reason is because that exorbitant mercy has an ill effect upon the whole universality, whereas particular executions extend only to particular persons... And from hence arises a new question, "Whether it be better to be beloved or feared, or feared than beloved?" It is answered, both would be convenient, but because that is hard to attain, it is better and more secure (if one must be wanting), to be feared than loved; for in general men are ungrateful, inconstant, hypocritical, fearful of danger, and covetous of gain: whilst they receive any benefit by you, and the danger is at a distance, they are absolutely yours; their blood, their estates, their lives, and their children (as I said before), are all at your service; but when mischief is at hand, and you have present need of their help, they make no scruple to revolt. And that prince, who leaves himself naked of other preparations, and relies wholly upon their professions, is sure to be ruined; for amity contracted by price, and not by the greatness and generosity of the mind, may seem a good pennyworth, yet when you have occasion to make use of it, you will find no such thing. Moreover, men do with less remorse offend against those who desire to be beloved, than against those who are ambitious of being feared, and the reason is because love is fastened only by a ligament of obligation, which the ill-nature of mankind breaks upon every occasion that is presented to his profit; but fear depends upon an apprehension of punishment, which is never to be dispelled.

But in the eighteenth chapter the principles of this crooked policy are carried to the utmost extent. He says, —

How honourable it is for a prince to keep his word, and act rather with integrity than collusion, I suppose everybody understands; nevertheless experience has shown in our own times, that those princes who have not pinned themselves up to that punctuality and preciseness have done great things, and by their cunning and subtlety not only circumvented and directed the brains of those with whom they had to deal, but have overcome and been too hard for those who have been so superstitiously exact. For further explanation you must understand that there are two ways of contending, by law and by force; the first is proper to men, the second to beasts; but because many times the first is insufficient, recourse must be had to the second. It belongs therefore to a prince to understand both, when to make use of the rational, and when of the brutal way... A prince, therefore, that is wise and prudent, cannot nor ought not to keep his word, when the keeping of it is to his prejudice, and the causes for which he promised removed. Were men all good tills doctrine was not to be taught; but because they are wicked, and not likely to be punctual with you, you are not obliged to any such strictness with them; nor was there ever any prince that wanted lawful pretence to justify his breach of promise. I might instance in many modern examples, and show how many considerations, and peaces, and promises have been broken by the infidelity of princes, and how he that best personated the fox had the better success. Nevertheless, it is of great consequence to disguise your inclination, and play the hypocrite well; and men are so simple in their temper, and so submissive to their present necessities, that he that is neat and cleanly in his collusions, shall never want people to practise them upon. I cannot forbear one example which is still fresh in our memory. Alexander VI. never did nor thought of any thing but cheating, and never wanted matter to work upon; and though no man promised a thing with greater asseveration, nor confirmed it with more oaths and imprecations, and observed them less, yet, understanding the world well, he never miscarried. A prince, therefore, is not obliged to have all the forementioned good qualities in reality; but it is necessary to have them in appearance; nay, I will be bold to affirm, that having them actually, and employing them upon all occasions, they are extremely prejudicial — whereas, having them only in appearance, they turn to better account. It is honourable to seem mild and merciful, and courteous and religious, and sincere, and indeed to be so, provided your mind be so rectified and prepared that you can act quite contrary upon occasion. And this must be premised, that a prince, especially if come but lately to the throne, cannot observe all those things exactly which make men be esteemed virtuous, being oftentimes necessitated for the preservation of his state, to do things inhuman, uncharitable, and irreligious; and therefore it is convenient his mind be at his command, and flexible to all the puffs and varieties of his fortune; not forbearing to be good, whilst it is in his choice, but knowing how to be evil when there is a necessity. A prince, then, is to have particular care that nothing falls from his mouth but what is full of the five qualities aforesaid, and that to see and to hear him he appears all goodness, integrity, humanity, and religion; which last he ought to pretend to more than ordinarily, because more men do judge by the eye than by the touch, for everybody sees, but few understand; everybody sees how you appear, but few know what in reality you are, and those few dare not oppose the opinion of the multitude who have the majesty of their prince to defend them; and in the actions of all men, especially princes, where no man has power to judge, every one looks to the end. Let a prince, therefore, do what he can to preserve his life and continue his supremacy; the means which he uses shall be thought honourable, and be commended by everybody; because the people are always taken with the appearance and the event of things, and the greatest part of the world consists of the people; those few who are wise taking place when the multitude has nothing else to rely upon. There is a prince this time in being (but his name I shall conceal), who has nothing in his mouth but fidelity and peace, and yet had he exercised either one or the other, they had robbed him before this of his power and reputation.

This passage has condemned Machiavelli as a blackhearted traitor. Yet most of the other principles in the book are good. He advises economy to the prince, that he may not be the oppressor of his subjects. He should cultivate rigid and severe justice as the surest road to mercy. He should preserve respect for religion, avoid flatterers, secure the free advice of the wisest of his subjects. In truth, all the political philosophy of Machiavelli will bear the light and experience of the nineteenth century, save the passages which show the means whereby absolute power is to be acquired and preserved. And if a statesman were now to write how absolute power is to be acquired and maintained, he would write the same as Machiavelli did three centuries and a-half ago. In fact, all the acts of tyranny which we read of in Machiavelli had been previously unfolded by Aristotle. What is, in its nature, repugnant to truth and justice, can only be maintained by perjury and injustice. The commentary of Machiavelli on absolute power merely places in a scientific formula a digest of the principles of tyranny. Christian endurance tells us it is better not to exist at all than to exist at the price of virtue; but however this virtue has been practised by the martyrs and saints of God, it has not yet arrived at the region of governments. And Machiavelli boldly cast off the veil of hypocrisy by which the villanies of tyrants had been concealed.

Machiavelli, too, had an ideal — an ideal of a citizen, and not of a philosopher; his Italian country recovering her independence, the Italian States reconstituted under the hand of a prince — albeit a tyrant. This is his excuse; he sacrifices morality to patriotism. In accordance with this idea, and as it were to show the conclusion at which he arrived, "The Prince" concludes with an exhortation to Lorenzo de Medici to deliver Italy from the barbarians: Though formerly some sparks of virtue have appeared in some persons that might give her hopes that God had ordained them for her redemption; yet it was found afterwards that in the very height and career of their exploits they were checked and forsaken by fortune, and poor Italy left half dead, expecting who would be her Samaritan to bind up her wounds, put an end to the sackings and devastations in Lombardy, the taxes and expilations in the kingdom of Naples and Tuscany, and cure her sores which length of time had festered and imposthumated. 'Tis manifest how she prays to God daily to send some person who may redeem her from the cruelty and insolence of the barbarians. 'Tis manifest how prone and ready she is to follow the banner that any man will take up; nor is it at present to be discerned where she can repose her hopes with more probability than in your illustrious family, which, by its own courage and interest, and the favour of God and the Church (of which it is now chief), may be induced to make itself head in her redemption... This opportunity, therefore, is by no means to be slipped, that Italy after so long expectation may see some means of deliverance. Nor can it be expressed with what joy, with what impatience of revenge, with what fidelity, with what compassion, with what tears, such a champion would be received into all the provinces that have suffered by these barbarous inundations. What gates would be shut against him? What people would deny him obedience? What malice would oppose him? What true Italian would refuse to follow him? There is not anybody but abhors and nauseates this barbarous domination. Let your illustrious family then address itself to this work with as much courage and confidence as just enterprises are undertaken; that under their ensigns our country may be recovered, and under their conduct Petrarch's prophecy may be fulfilled, who has promised that —

"Virtù contr' al furore
Prendera l' arme, et fia il combatter corto,
Che l' antico valore
Ne' gl' Italici non e ancor' morto."

Frederick Schlegel believed that the object of Machiavelli was to inspire the great princes of Italy with the ambition of giving liberty to his country; and that, in tins cause, it was right to make use of those unrighteous means by which others had effected her degradation. He has also pointed out that, in his opinion, the chief fault of Machiavelli consists not in his defence of the principle that the end sanctifies the means, but in this, that he was the first who introduced into modern and Christian

Europe the fashion of reasoning and deciding on politics exactly as if Christianity had no existence. When we are impressed with a sense of the existence of God, the whole of our thoughts and principles have acquired a dignity to which we could not otherwise aspire. The visible is everywhere dependent on the unseen; and as the body is moved and regulated by the soul, so are men, nations, and states held together by the belief and the reverence of the Godhead. The moment we take away this soul, this internal and universal principle of life, the whole composition is loosened and destroyed; if we obscure its light, and obstruct its influence upon the whole, the individual members of the organic or of the political body may still preserve some power of life with them; but this life will be narrow, separate, insignificant, misdirected and destructive, rather than beneficial. It will form a principle of disunion, not a bond of harmony. When that chain of morality and religion, by which states and nations are connected together, has once fairly been broken, the destructive poisons of darkness, anarchy, and despotism begin immediately to operate, and vice is ever ready to occupy the deserted station of virtue.

But in the succeeding political works of Machiavelli we find a development of most that is good in The Prince, with some opinions directly the reverse of those portions which are censurable. The Discourses on the First Decade of Livy, were written about a year after the composition of The Prince. They give the author's views on some questions of Republican Government. After the fashion of the discourses of the Greek philosophers, these were recited to the young men of Florence in the gardens of Cosimo Rucellai. The discourses on Livy are divided into three books. In the first he treats of the internal government of the Romans, but introduces much historical learning and illustration, and discusses many political principles.

In one passage he recommends, like Cicero and Tacitus, a triple form of government. The wisest legislators, finding the defect of want of permanence in the simple forms of monarchy, aristocracy, and democracy, and avoiding every one of these kinds, thus framed a government which should consist of them all, believing it to be more permanent and stable, because prince, nobles, and people, living in the same city, and communicating in the same government, they would be all of them in sight of one another, and more capable of correction. He considered, without this, that the simple forms of government, monarchy, aristocracy, and democracy, would necessarily pass from one to another in the cycle of ages. Byron, imitating the same idea, also has said, in Childe Harold: —

> "There is the moral of all human tales,
>   'Tis but the same rehearsal of the past:
> First freedom, and then glory, when that fails,
>   Wealth, vice, corruption, barbarism at last,
> And history with all her volumes vast
>   Hath but one page."

Such were the ideas of Machiavelli. And Vico appears to have been the last great writer who predicted for every nation a decline and fall. But in the development of the representative system of government and of individual liberty there appears to be some security for permanent progress. When these do not exist there is none.

In the tenth chapter Machiavelli praises those who lay the foundations of a commonwealth. Among all excellent and illustrious men, they are the most praiseworthy who have been the chief establishing of religious and divine worship; in the second place are they who have laid the foundations of any kingdom or commonwealth; in the third those who, having the command of great armies, have enlarged their own or the dominion of their country. In the next, learned men of all sciences, according to their several studies and degrees; and last of all (as being infinitely the greater number) come the artificers and mechanics, — all to be commended as they are ingenious or skilful in their professions. On the other side, they are infamous and detestable who are contemners of religion, subverters of governments, enemies of virtue, of learning, of art, and, in short, of every thing that is useful to mankind, and of this sort are the profane, the seditious, the ignorant, the idle, the debauched, and the vile. And although Nature has so ordered it that there is neither wise man nor fool, nor good man nor bad, who, if it were proposed to him which he would choose of these two sorts of people, would not prefer that which was to be preferred, and condemn the other, yet the generality of mankind, deluded by a false impression of good and a vain notion of glory, leaving those ways which are excellent and commendable, either wilfully or ignorantly wander into those paths which will lead them into dishonour; and whereas to their immortal honour they might establish a commonwealth or kingdom as they please, they run headlong into a tyranny, not considering what fame, what glory, what affection, what security, what quiet and satisfaction of mind they part with, nor what reproach, scandal, hatred, danger, and disquiet they incur.

He proceeds to show how a people accustomed to the dominion of a prince, though by accident they may acquire their liberty, yet can maintain it with difficulty; and that a people wholly corrupted in their manners may possibly recover their liberty, but they will find insuperable difficulty to maintain it; and how much that prince or commonwealth is to be condemned that neglects to train up native soldiers.

In the fifty-eighth chapter he advances an opinion which now is held by most political writers, but certainly was then a novel one in politics, that the multitude is wiser and more constant than the prince: — I know not whether I shall not seem too bold, to undertake the defence of a thing which all the world opposes, and run myself upon a necessity of either quitting it with disgrace, or pursuing it with scandal; yet, methinks, being to maintain it with arguments, not force, it should not be so criminal. I say then, in behalf of the multitude, that what they are charged withal by most authors, may be charged upon all private persons in the world, and especially upon Princes; for whoever lives irregularly, and is not restrained by the law, is subject to the same exorbitancies, and will commit as bad faults as the most dissolute multitude in the world... And if the comparison be made betwixt mixed principalities that are circumscribed and bounded by laws and popular governments under the same ties and restrictions, the People will be found more virtuous than the Princes; but if it be betwixt loose and dissolute governments, both of the one kind and of the other, the errors on the side of the Princes will appear more great, more numerous, and more incapable of redress: for, in popular tumults, a sober man may interfere, and, by fair words, reduce them to reason; but to an enraged Prince who dares intercede, or what remedy is there to repair to, but violence and the sword? From whence we may judge and distinguish betwixt the inconvenience of the one and the other: the People are appeased with gentleness and good words; and the Prince not to be prevailed upon but by violence and force; and, if it be so, who will deny that the disease is more dangerous where the cure is most difficult? Moreover, when the People tumultuate, there is not so much fear of any present mischief that they are likely to commit as of the consequences of it, and that it may end in a tyranny. But with ill Princes it is quite contrary; the present misery is the most dreadful, because they hope when he dies their liberty may be recovered. You see, then, the difference betwixt them, — one is more dangerous for the present, and the other for the future; the cruelty of the People extends only to such as in their opinion conspire against the common good. The severity of the Prince is more against them who design against his particular interest.

He again treats of the danger of employing foreign forces. In prudence, a prince or commonwealth is to take any course rather than to bring himself into a necessity of employing auxiliaries, especially when he is to rely wholly upon them. Nor can an ambitious state or prince have a more commodious occasion to possess himself of a city or province, than when he is invited in this manner for its assistance and defence. He also insists on the necessity of constant reforms in a State. It is as clear as the day that no bodies of men are of long duration unless they be renewed. And the way to renew them is to reduce them to their first principles. For the foundations of all sects, commonwealths, and kingdoms have always something of good in them. These discourses on Livy have no regular arrangement, so that nearly the same thoughts occur in different chapters.

I may conclude my brief notice of Machiavelli with the criticism of Mr. Hallam: — Few political treatises can even now be read with more advantage than the Discourses of Machiavel; and in proportion as the course of civil society tends further towards democracy, and especially if it should lead to what seems the inevitable consequence of democracy, a considerable subdivision of independent states, they may acquire an additional value. The absence of all passion, the continual reference of every public measure to a distinct end, the disregard of vulgar associations with names or persons, render him, though too cold of heart for a generous reader, a sagacious and useful monitor for any one who can employ the necessary methods for correcting his theorems.

## 2. School of Machiavelli

Machiavelli exercised a double influence — one general, the other particular. He spread the taste for political science, and introduced the philosophy of history into the domain of politics. He also formed a school which lasted during the sixteenth century and part of the seventeenth, and which had for its principle and dogma the right to use fraud in matters of public politics.

Guicciardini, the historian of the wars of Italy, a Monarchist in politics, was opposed to the Democratic principles of Machiavelli. But he heartily concurred in those peculiar doctrines which are best known under the name of Machiavellism. Thus he lays down a rule that when a prince wishes to deceive another prince by means of an ambassador, he should commence by deceiving the ambassador, who then will pursue with much more earnestness what is confided to him, if he think that he is acting seriously than if he be obliged to feign. Candour and openness, says Guicciardini, are praised by all men. They are the marks of a generous soul, nevertheless they are sometimes inconvenient. On the contrary, fraud is useful, nevertheless it is detested, it bears with it shame; and, if it be necessary, it is only by reason of the wickedness and perfidy of others. Finally, we justly hesitate which of the two we ought to choose. Guicciardini considers that candour ought to be ordinarily used, but the other cannot be despised. In the ordinary usage of life, it is necessary to prefer the use of candour in order to obtain the reputation of a sincere man. Nevertheless, there are certain cases where dissimulation may be employed, and it will be useful to those who will cause others to believe them the more readily, because they first believed in their sincerity. Guicciardini finally blames the man who continually resorts to lies; but excuses him that does so sometimes. We recognise an age of distrust and tyranny in the words — "The man who lives under a tyranny must take care even when he speaks with his most intimate friends, not to let them see the bottom of his thoughts; for he must know that he is surrounded with all sorts of stratagems to unveil his secret sentiments."

By Machiavelli and Guicciardini fraud is discussed as a thing completely natural; and no attempt is made to exculpate or defend it. But when these doctrines were attacked, Machiavellism prepared a systematic defence. Scioppius wrote the method of Politics — Paidia Politices; Παίδια Πολιτίκης, ostensibly in defence of the doctrines of Aristotle and St. Thomas Aquinas. But he selects from their writings some passages, which, separated from the rest, appear to contain the doctrines of the Prince. Scioppius pretends to demonstrate this thesis, that Politics are distinct from Morals, that each science has its own principles, and that to introduce the principles of Morality into Politics is to confound the limits of the sciences, and to violate the laws of method. The errors of his adversaries came from their ignorance of Logic. Logic teaches the method of proof. The method of a science consists only in employing the principles proper to it, and in rejecting those that are foreign. The end of politics is the happiness of the State. Such being the case, it must be occupied not only with the best form of government, but also with the best in a given situation. As the science of medicine not only occupies itself with a state of perfect health, but also with all possible degrees of health, so Politics should treat not only of a perfect government, but of all governments. It is also more important that politics should treat of bad forms of government than of good. Good governments are like good vessels which support themselves. The bad are those which have need of assistance. Such is the opinion of St. Thomas: "Those which are the best ordered according to reason can sustain many and great shocks. But the badly ordered are destroyed by trifling shocks, and therefore need greater caution." — Illæ quæ optimè ordinatæ sunt secundum rationem, multos impulsus et magnos sustinere possunt. Malè autem ordinatæ a modicis corrumpuntur, et ideo majori indigent cautelâ. Hence arises the error of Plato who treats only of the best form of government. His doctrine has no utility, men being incapable of supporting this perfect form. The business of politics is to treat of those things which are really useful and practicable. Unhappily evil forms of government are more conformable to human nature than the good. It results, says Scioppius, from these principles, that to treat of tyranny and of the means of preserving it is to remain faithful to the objects of politics, and those who reproach a publicist with having spoken of tyranny, reproach him with having treated of the subject matter of his science. Another error is to reproach publicists with not introducing into politics principles that are wholly strange. The wicked and the base are ideas that belong to morals, not to politics. Morality has two parts, one general, one particular. The first gives principles, the second precepts. The science of politics studies what is; morals, what ought to be. Still Scioppius acknowledges that the separation could not be absolute. Consequently, even although logic should desire, that politics should speak of tyranny as of a fact without examining whether it be good or bad, prudence exacts that we should blame tyranny, and turn men aside from it. For the object of politics is the happiness of the State, and tyranny neither produces the happiness of him that exercises it, or of him that suffers.

Such is a brief sketch of the little book of Scioppius, which plainly was written in defence of Machiavelli, although he is not named. Machiavellism, in the sixteenth century, influenced even the writings of its opponents. Thus Justus Lipsius appears to make Politics rest on Morality. His first book is entirely consecrated to the enumeration of the virtues of the prince. The prince should not be a Lord over serfs, but a governor over citizens. The prince should be content with repentance rather than punishment. If contracts and conventions be violated there is no longer commerce amongst men. The covenants of peace should never be violated, nor should good faith be postponed to sovereignty. Such are the maxims of Lipsius; but they are not his only maxims. He admits deceit into politics. He does not go quite so far as Machiavelli, and sets boundaries to the domain of fraud. There are, according to him, three species of fraud, the trivial, the mean, and the great. The first is not too far removed from virtue, and is bedewed only with some drops of malice; it is defiance and dissimulation. The second touches on the borders of vice; it is conciliation and corruption. The third is separated not only from virtue, but from laws; it is perfidy and injustice. He advises the first, endures the second, and condemns the third. He approves and permits certain frauds, and what he calls little corruptions and finesse.

To complete a notice of the school of Machiavelli, we must pass the confines of the sixteenth century. The celebrated Fra Paolo Sarpi[21] was the servant, councillor, and secretary of Ven-

---

[21] B. 1552, d. 1623; Opinione del Padre Paolo servita, come debba govenarsi la Republica Veneziana per havere il perpetuo dominio. Venice, 1681. Traduit en Français, par l'Abbè de Marsy, Berlin, 1751.

ice. His book, written in 1615, exposes to us the means of preserving and maintaining Venice in her ancient power, and is inspired as well by Machiavelli as by the traditions of the Council of Ten. He starts with the principle that the Republic will last as long as it does justice. But what is justice? The first justice for the Sovereign is to maintain himself Sovereign. He soon tells us what he means by justice. No nobleman ought to be punished with death, however criminal he may be, because the order of nobility loses more in respect by the humiliation of one of its members than it gains in honour by an act of justice. At least there should be no public execution. Therefore, in such a case, the criminal should either terminate his life in prison, or be delivered from it in a secret manner. In quarrels between nobles, or between nobles and subjects, there should be two weights and two measures. If a noble without credit and without power maltreat a great man, great severity should be used. If a noble has maltreated a subject, all imaginable means must be sought to put him in the right. If a subject has injured a noble, chastisement must be inflicted to excess. At all price the custom must not be introduced of raising a hand against a Patrician, and the people must be nourished in the idea that a Patrician's blood is sacred. Such were the secret politics of Venice. But if inequality was to be the rule in matters of criminal justice, equality was to be the rule in matters of civil justice. In civil justice, says Fra Paolo, a perfect impartiality must be displayed, and the dangerous opinion must be put down that the balance inclines always to the side of the rich and noble. For all that concerns this civil justice, exactness cannot be pushed too far. In effect, when a citizen is assured of having justice whenever he deserves it, he can be brought to endure much. But, however favourable to the nobles Fra Paolo displays himself, he is not a partisan of aristocracy. His political scheme was this, to transform the aristocracy of Venice into an oligarchy, and to concentrate power into a small number of hands. The government was composed at Venice of three institutions — the great council, or general assembly of the nobles, the democratic element in the constitution; the Senate of Three Hundred, the aristocratic element; the Council of Ten, the oligarchical element. Paolo's plan was to annihilate the Great Council, because it savoured too much of the people. "We ought," says he, "by every species of artifice, procure the Great

Council to delegate to the Senate, and to the Council of Ten all authority; but this should be done by secret ways, the mystery of which cannot be discovered until after the event." The laws and constitution of Venice had for defender a species of tribune of the people called avogador. Fra Paolo does not propose to abolish the office, but designs to intrust it to a man of high birth, more or less bound up with the usurpations of the aristocracy. To Fra Paolo the government of Venice did not appear sufficiently despotic. He has no less contempt for the people than for the small.nobility, whom he counsels to keep in poverty. "For they are," says he, "like vipers who cannot use their venom in the cold." His internal policy is secret cunning, concealed partiality in favour of the nobles, mysterious oppression of the people. With respect to external policy, he advises that the people of the kingdom of Candia should be kept with the same precautions as ferocious beasts. They are like convicts who repay indulgence with revolt. Even in the territory of Venice his policy has always the same end — the sacrifice of the interests of the people to the interest of the sovereign. The inhabitants of Brescia, says Fra Paolo, should be deprived of the privilege which they enjoy, that property in their territory can be purchased only by Brescians; for if the Venetians could extend into that happy country, the same result would be seen as in Padua, where scarcely a third of the territory has remained the property of the inhabitants. If there be rich heiresses in the country they should be married to Venetian nobles; whence results two advantages — the enriching of the capital, and impoverishment of the province. If any inhabitant of a province be raised to offices of state, this should be done, because it turns to his particular advantage, and not to the advantage of the country. If he prove the chief of a party he must be exterminated at all hazard; but, if he be powerful, ordinary justice will not serve; let poison do the work of the axe. Piuttosto faccia il veneno l'uffizio di man-igeldo. Such were the politics of Fra Paolo, and in a great measure of the Republic of Venice.

There is a certain difficulty in clearly refuting the sophistry of Machiavellism. Is it ever right to do a thing in itself injurious apart from motive? It clearly is. It is right to oppose violence against a wrong doer; to slay the man who wrongfully attempts to slay his neighbour. The school of Machiavelli carries this principle one step further, and says it is right to oppose fraud against a wrong doer, and to commit crimes for the sake of the welfare of the state. The idea of complete reciprocity, which is the original idea of justice, an eye for an eye, a tooth for a tooth, is at the root of Machiavellism But the right to use fraud is not the same with the right of defence. The attack being repulsed all is as before; no injury has been done to the laws of honour, justice, and morality. Honesty is the best policy in politics as well as in commerce. He who deceives gains in detail, but loses in the whole. If a merchant lose his credit he loses his capital. Honour is the credit of governments.

## 3. Sir Thomas More, 1480 — 1535

De optimo reipublicæ statu deque novâ Insulâ Utopia libri duo, auctore Thomâ Moro, 1516.

Whilst Machiavelli wrote the code of experimental, pagan, and materialist politics, speculative politics inspired by spiritualism, were displayed in England in the writings of another great intellect. The Prince was written in 1513, though not published until 1532. The Utopia was written in 1516; it is the counterpart of the Prince, and represents the opposite extreme of the human mind. In place of the purely practical statesman who gives to a state self-preservation as the sole end, we see the reformer who dreams of a new phase of society. With Machiavelli politics were intellect without a heart. Sir Thomas More infused into politics the genius of Christianity. The Utopia is the first great work written by an Englishman in the nature of an essay on Jurisprudence. This celebrated man was successful in most of the public departments of life. His fame as a scholar was spread through Europe. He was an able lawyer, a refined courtier, an enlightened statesman, a diplomatic ambassador. He was the first layman that was made Lord Chancellor of England, who was not of noble birth, or had not previously filled some high judicial office. In his practice at the bar he was famous for his skill in International Law.

But the authorship of the Utopia alone would have immortalised his name. And with reference to this work it is only to be regretted that the genius which in such an age could develop the principles of the Utopia was not resident in some other person than the Lord Chancellor of Henry VIII. For the extravagances and absurdities of the Utopia, and its very form, were plainly designed by him to soften the severity of his condemnation upon the then government and laws of England. If he had been some obscure scholar, instead of one of the first amongst English statesmen, the principles inculcated in the Utopia would have appeared in a scientific form, and in a regular treatise upon laws and government.

The truly original element introduced by Sir Thomas More into political science is the spirit of justice and charity revealed by the Gospel, and which the grand action of Christianity had caused to be felt in the heart, and often manifested in outward actions. Inspired by the same sentiments in their pathetic exhortations to the great ones of the earth, the Fathers of the Church had not always avoided the errors of Communism. An ardent Christian from conviction, as his religious life and death of martyrdom attest, the author of the Utopia, at sight of the unjust inequalities resulting from feudalism, at the spectacle of the misery of the bulk of the population, embraced the idea of Communism as a consolation, as a recollection also, purified by a holy influence, of the Republic of Plato, as a romantic theme of which he was not the dupe. When, drawing a harrowing picture of the sufferings endured by the immense majority of the people of his time, he declaims on the millions of children abandoned to the ravages of a vicious education — on the corruption that withers, beneath the very eyes of the prince, the young plants that ought to flourish for virtue — when he adds: — "And you punish them with death, when grown to manhood they commit the crimes which were planted in their hearts from their cradle;" when he condemns excessive punishment, and raises his voice against the punishment of death, for which he substitutes hard labour, we see not only the philosophic presentiment of modern philanthropy, but also the outpourings of a truly Christian spirit.

Utopia [ὀυ, τόπος, or "No where"] is an island where perfect happiness arising from perfect government exists. There the Law is the Law of Nature; Religion is love and charity; Peace reigns; Money is unknown.

Some have pretended to discover in the Utopia most of the principles of laws and government in later times illustrated by Adam Smith, Sir James Mackintosh, Sir Samuel Romilly, and Jeremy Bentham. But it is at least singular to find the Chancellor of Henry VIII. advocating the ballot, annual parliaments, a complete form of representative government, and the reform of the barbarous Penal Code of England. In the second book of the Utopia he describes the method of election in the imaginary republic. They take an oath before they proceed to an election that they will choose him whom they think fittest for the office. They give their voices secretly, so that it is not known for whom every one gives his suffrage. The prince is for life, unless he is removed upon suspicion of some design to enslave the people. The Tranibors[22] are newly chosen every year, but they are for the most part still continued. All their other magistrates are only annual.

Sir Thomas More also clearly saw and censured the iniquitous severity of the Criminal Law of England. In the first book, Raphael Hythloday, his great traveller, who had seen Utopia, says, "One day when I was dining with him [the King of England,] there happened to be at table one of the English lawyers, who took occasion to run out in a high commendation of the severe execution of justice upon thieves, who, as he said, were then hanged so fast that there were sometimes twenty upon one gibbet. Nevertheless, it puzzled him to understand, since so few escaped, that there were yet so many thieves who were still found robbing in all places. Upon this, I said with boldness, there was no reason to wonder, since this way of punishing thieves was neither just in itself, nor for the public good; for, as the severity was too great, so the remedy was not effectual, simple theft not being so great a crime that it ought to cost a man his life, and no punishment, how severe soever, being able to restrain those from robbing who can find out no other means of livelihood. In this not only you, but a great part of the world, imitate ignorant and cruel schoolmasters, who are readier to flog their pupils than to teach them. There are dreadful punishments enacted against thieves, but it were much better to make such good provisions by which every man might be put in a method how to live, and so be preserved from the fatal necessity of stealing and dying for it."

Sir Thomas More in that intolerant age was still a warm advocate of religious toleration. The following extract is taken from the conclusion of the second book: — At the first constitu-

---

[22] Scil. Members of Parliament.

tion of their Government, Utopus having understood that before his coming among them, the old inhabitants had been engaged in great quarrels concerning religion, by which they were so broken amongst themselves, that he found it an easy thing to conquer them, since they did not unite their forces against him, but every different party in religion fought by themselves; — upon that, after he had subdued them, he made a law, so that every man might be what religion he pleased, and might endeavour to draw others to it by the force of argument, and by amiable and modest ways, but without bitterness against those of other opinions, so that he ought to use no other force but that of persuasion, and was neither to mix reproaches nor violence with it; and such as did otherwise were to be condemned to banishment or slavery. This law was made by Utopus not only for preserving the public peace, which he saw suffered much by daily contentions and irreconcilable harts in these matters, but because he thought the interests of religion itself required it. Such was Sir Thomas More's noble views on the subject of Toleration.

If, again, we examine the constitution of the family planned by this imitator of Plato, we perceive still more the influence of Christianity. Woman, sacrificed by the ancient legislature and by Plato, assumes her natural rank and dignity. A severe legislation presides in respect of marriage. The chastity of woman is honoured; her modesty respected. Add to this the abolition of castes, and the organization of material labour, even by the injudicious clause which imposes it on all, and we perceive the progress of humanity from the days of Plato.

The Utopia has been by far the most successful of the works which have imagined an ideal perfect state of society and manners. The Oceana of Harrington, the Civitas Solis of Campanella, and the New Atlantis of Lord Bacon, have been comparatively failures. Dean Swift, in his treatises of a similar nature, has sacrificed philosophy to Satire.

## 4. The Spanish Ecclesiastical Jurists, 1500 — 1600

Hitherto, amongst works strictly juridical, few have appeared except upon the details of the Roman Law. We have now to consider a series in which the principles of morals, justice, and polity are discussed.

Vasquez, who flourished between 1509 and 1566, in his Controversiæ Illustres, first divided the law of nations into primary and secondary. By the former he understood the mere law of nature, by the latter the civil laws, institutions, and ordinances adopted by the greater part of nations. According to Vasquez, the secondary law of nations is not so much natural as positive, for all those things which belong to the law of nations were first only matters of civil law, but by degrees spread to other nations and states; and thus as soon as any thing was invented and accepted by any one man or region, it then was only a matter of civil law not of the law of nations. On the contrary, also if whatever now be the law of nations — *Jus Gentium* — were to come into disuse so as to remain almost with only one province, it would almost unquestionably cease to belong to the Jus Gentium, and be only a matter of civil law. This is a most confused idea of the law of nations.

The *Relectiones Theologicœ*[23] of Francis de Victoria is a book which has become remarkably scarce, although it passed through at least six editions, from the first edition published at Lyons in 1557, to the latest published at Venice in 1626. It consists of thirteen *relections,* as the author calls them, or dissertations on different subjects treated as questions of casuistry. Two of these, the fifth entitled *De Indis,* and the sixth *De Jure Belli,* relate to subjects of international law.

The fifth relection enumerates the various titles by which the Spanish assumption of sovereignty over the new world and its inhabitants has been vindicated. The author asserts the natural right of the Indians to dominion over their own monarchy, and to sovereignty over their own country. He denies the assertion of Bartolus, and the other civilians of the school of Bologna, that "the Emperor is Lord of the whole world," or that the Pope could confer dominion on the Kings of Spain over those parts inhabited by infidel barbarians. He rests their title, or what he calls the right of natural society and intercourse, as authorizing the Spaniards to sojourn and trade in those parts of the world, without injuring the native inhabitants. The refusal of hospitality and

---

[23] This analysis of Victoria is taken from Wheaton's Law of Nations. I have not been able to procure a copy of the *Relectiones.* Mr. Hallam states there are only two copies in England.

permission to trade he holds to be a just ground of war, which again might lead to the acquisition of sovereignty, through the right of conquest, confirmed by voluntary cession. He denies the right of making war upon the infidel natives for refusing to receive the gospel, but asserts that they might beacon-strained to allow its being preached to those who wished to hear, and prevented from persecuting the new converts. At the same time he seems conscious that his license might be abused by his countrymen, and therefore strives to limit it by tempering their zeal with mercy, and prohibiting all violence which, under the pretext of religion, might minister to their avarice and other worldly passions.

The sixth relection treats exclusively of the laws of war, and examines the four following questions: — 1. Whether Christians may lawfully engage in war? 2. In whom the authority of declaring and carrying on war resides? 3. What are causes of just war? 4. What may lawfully be done against an enemy in a just war?

Upon the fourth question Victoria holds that Christians may lawfully engage in defensive war, repel force by force, and recapture their property taken by the enemy. They may even engage in offensive war, which he defines to be that in which compensation is sought for injuries received. These propositions of natural law he supports by quotations from the sacred Scriptures, and the authority of the Fathers of the Church.

He answers the second question by stating that since it is lawful to repel force by force, war merely defensive may be waged by the private authority of the party injured for the defence of his person or property. But there is this difference between a private person and the State, that the right of the former is confined to mere self-defence, and does not extend to the redress of injuries or even to the recapture of things unjustly taken after an interval of time has subsequently elapsed. The resort to force in self-defence must be against a present danger, or as the civilians express it, *in incontinenti.* The State on the other hand has not only the right of defending itself, but of seeking the redress of injuries done to itself or its subjects. The authority of making war for the latter purpose therefore, resides exclusively in the Sovereign or State. But the question recurs what constitutes a State? The answer is, that it is a perfect community —

that is, such as does not form a part of any other State, but which has its own laws, its own legislature, and its own magistrates; such, for example, as the kingdom of Castile and Arragon, the Republic of Venice and the like. There may even be several perfect communities or States under the dominion of the same Prince, in whom alone is vested the right of declaring and carrying on war, but this right cannot lawfully be exercised by vassal principalities which form members of an Imperial State.

The third question he answers, in the first place, negatively, that diversity of religious faith is not a cause of just war, nor as against an infidel nation, that they refuse to embrace Christianity, nor the extension of dominion, nor the glory and private advantage of the prince who ought in all things to rule with a sole view to the public interest of the State. The difference between a lawful king and a tyrant consists in this, that the former rules for the good of his people, the latter for his own private advantage. It is to make slaves of citizens, to compel them to bear the burthens of war, not for the public interest, but for the mere private advantage of the prince. Injury received is the sole just cause of war. Natural law prohibits killing the innocent, and it is, therefore, unlawful to draw the sword against those who have done us no injury. Victoria omits the consideration of the question, whether God may not have otherwise ordained on some special occasions; for He is the Lord of life and death, and may otherwise dispose in vindication of his own cause. Nor is every degree of injury sufficient to justify a resort to war. As in civil society every crime is not to be visited by the severest punishments, such as death, exile, and confiscation, so neither in the great society of nations is it allowable to resist slight injuries with the slaughter and devastation which war brings in its train.

The fourth question he answers, that it is lawful in war to do every thing which is necessary for the defence and preservation of the State; it is lawful to recapture things taken by the enemy, or to recover their value, to seize on so much of his property as may be necessary to defray the expenses of the war, and to compensate all damages unjustly sustained. In a just war we may even go farther, and occupy the enemy's territory and his fortresses, so as to punish him for injuries inflicted, and obtain peace and security against his hostile designs.

Such are the belligerent rights incident to a just war. But the author inquires, in order to constitute a just war, is it sufficient that the belligerent believes it to be just? To which he answers, not in all cases. It must be referred to the judgment of wise men to determine whether the war be founded on a just cause. The greatest care and diligence ought to be used in this inquiry, and the reasons urged even by the adverse party ought to be well waged. A war may be just on both sides, each party believing himself to be justified. Even the Turks and Saracens may be said to wage just war against Christians, since they believe that they are thereby serving God. Subjects are not bound to serve their prince in a war manifestly unjust, since no temporal authority can justify us in slaying the innocent. At the same time the duty of examining the question of the justice or injustice of the war devolves principally on the chief men of the nation, who ought to be consulted by the sovereign on such momentous occasion. Those inferior members of the State who are not called to the public council, may lawfully abide by the decision of their superiors as to the justice of the war. In a doubtful case the subjects are bound to obey the orders of their sovereign.

Returning again to the question, what acts of hostility are lawful, he inquires whether it is lawful to kill the innocent? which question he answers in the negative. Women and children are presumed to be innocent even in war against the Turks. The presumption is also extended by the usage among Christians to husbandmen, and in general to all persons engaged in civil or religious life, and to strangers sojourning in an enemy's country. Still these persons among the enemy may lawfully be despoiled of their goods, such as ships, arms, and money, which are the sinews of war; but if the war may otherwise be prosecuted successfully, the property of husbandmen and other innocent persons ought not to be destroyed or carried away. The property of both innocent and guilty is subject to reprisals in case restitution is refused of things unjustly captured: thus, if French subjects make incursions into Spain and plunder the inhabitants, and redress is refused by the King of France, the Spaniards may, by authority from their prince, despoil innocent French merchants or husbandmen. The letters of marque and reprisal which are granted in such cases are not unjust, since it is owing to the neglect and fault of the other prince that this license is granted to despoil his innocent subjects. But they are perilous and give occasion to indiscriminate plunder.

As it is unlawful to kill children and other innocent persons, so neither is it lawful to carry them into captivity. But in a war against Pagans, which may be said to be perpetual and without hope of obtaining satisfaction, doubtless the women and children of the Saracens taken prisoners may be detained as slaves. By the law of nations prevailing among Christians, it is not lawful to make slaves of captives taken in war, but they may be retained until redeemed by the payment of a ransom which is not to be extended beyond what the necessity of war and the usage of belligerents may require.

Victoria then puts the question, whether hostages for the observance of a truce or other compact between enemies may lawfully be put to death on the infraction of the compact? which he answers by a distinction between the hostages who have borne arms and innocent persons such as women and children. The former may, the latter may not, be put to death in the case supposed. As to the question whether all persons who take arms against us may lawfully be slain, he answers that in the heat of battle, or in the attack and defence of a besieged place, whilst the conflict is still in *periculo,* all who continue to resist may be put to death.

The only doubt is in the case where victory is already secured, and no danger is to be apprehended from the enemy, whether those who have taken up arms against us may lawfully be slain. This doubt he solves by quoting the command of Jehovah to the Jews, in the twentieth chapter of Deuteronomy, forgetting what he had before said as to such special precepts being applicable only to the particular occasion. Not altogether satisfied with this indiscriminate licence to slaughter enemies no longer resisting, he limits it to the necessity of striking terror into the survivors, and then obtaining security against their hostile designs. He, therefore, concludes that it is not always lawful to slay all who have taken up arms. But this mitigation of the extreme rights of war is not applicable to infidels with whom there can be no hope of obtaining just terms of peace. And he understands the precept in Deuteronomy as being directed against such, so that he at least comes to the conclusion that as between Christian enemies those who no longer resist cannot lawfully be slain, especially as subjects are not bound to inquire minutely into the justice of the war, but may take up arms at the command of their prince, and, therefore, may be considered in this sense as innocent persons. And even though by the law of nature, military persons who surrender or are taken prisoners might lawfully be slain, the usage and custom of war which had become a part of the law of nations had ordained otherwise. But Victoria states that he had never heard that the usage and custom extended to the case of the garrison of a fortified place which surrendered at discretion. Where there is no capitulation expressly securing the lives of the prisoners, they may lawfully be put to death.

As to the question whether things taken in a just war become the property of the captors, he answers, that as the object of such a war is to obtain satisfaction for injuries done by the enemy, the things taken from him may be confiscated for that purpose. But it is necessary to distinguish among those things taken in war. These are either movables, such as money, clothing, silver, and gold; or immovables, such as lands, cities, and fortresses. As to movables, they become by the law of nations the property of the captor, even if they exceed in value the amount of the injury inflicted by the enemy.

For this position he cites the I *si quid in bello,* and I *hostes,* ff *de capti,* and c *jus gentium* I, and Inst *de. rer. divs,* § *itemque ab hostibus,* where it is expressly said, "quod jure gentium quæ ab hostibus capiuntur, statim nostra fiunt." He fortifies the authority of the Roman law in this respect by that of the sacred Scriptures and the writings of the Casuists. Admitting that a captured city may be given up to plunder, he restrains this concession to cases of dire necessity, which can alone justify a resort to this cruel extremity. As to immovables, he states that the lands, cities, and fortresses may be occupied and held until adequate satisfaction is made for the injuries inflicted by the enemy. But the exercise of the right is not to be extended beyond what equity and humanity may justify, in order to obtain indemnity for the past and security for the future. On the settlement of the term of peace, only so much of the enemy's territory can justly be retained as is necessary for these purposes. The right of conquest gives a just title to this extent to the acquisitions made in war, and finally confirmed by the treaty of peace. Contributions may also be levied on the enemy, and that not only to the extent of an adequate indemnity, but by way of punishment proportioned to the offence. In extreme cases where the amount of injury is very great, and no other security can be obtained for the faithful observance of the peace, the existing Government of the conquered country may be subverted and the sovereignty united to that of the conqueror. All these extreme rights of war are to be tempered in their exercise by the consideration that the justice or injustice of the war may be doubtful, and the enemy's sovereign may act bona fide in carrying it on after having carefully examined the question through the investigations of wise and good men.

Victoria concludes this dissertation by laying down three canons or rules of conscience relating to the subject. 1. That the sovereign in whom is vested the right of making war, not only ought not to seek for occasions of hostility, but as far as in him lies to live at peace with all men according to the precept of St. Paul to the Romans; all men being our neighbours, whom we are bound to love in the same degree as ourselves, and inasmuch as we have a common Lord at whose tribunal we must render an account. Nothing, therefore, but the strongest necessity can justify a resort to arms in order to obtain the redress of injuries.

2. War being undertaken for a just cause is to be prosecuted not to the utter destruction of the enemy, but in order to inflict upon him such an amount of evil as may be necessary for the defence of the State and obtaining a secure peace.

3. Victory being once obtained is to be used with moderation and Christian modesty. The conqueror is bound in determining the amount of satisfaction due to his own nation, to consider himself as an impartial judge between the two belligerent States. He is the more bound to this rule of moderation, inasmuch as wars among Christians are generally to be attributed to the misconduct of rulers. Subjects take up arms for their prince, confiding to the justice of his cause, and most unjustly suffer for the faults of their superiors, as says the poet: —

"Quicquid delirant reges, plectuntur Achivi."

Dominic Soto, a Spanish Dominican, and the pupil of Victoria, published his treatise De Justitia et Jure, in 1580. This is characterized by Mr. Hallam as the first original work of any reputation in ethical philosophy since the revival of letters. The laborious folio inspires us with great admiration for the author's zeal; but it is now forgotten. The following eulogium on Justice gives an idea of his style: — Illustrissima Justitiæ virtus, fidei nostræ legitima proles, spei robur, charitatis pedissequa, caterarumque virtutum clarissimum jubar, quamcum profana tum cum primis Divina oracula super æthera tollunt: ut pote quæ homines, civile animal, in unum congregat, ab injuriis vindicat, amore conciliat, in pace retinet, virtutibus ornat, ad æternam denique felicitatem divino munere subvehit.

Soto was distinguished for the active part which he took in the Council of Trent. He was consulted by the Emperor Charles V. on the occasion of a conference held before him at Valladolid in 1542, at which Sepulveda appeared as the champion for the Spanish colonists, and the great Las Casas as an advocate for the oppressed American Indians. The opinion of Soto was founded on reason, truth, and the Christian religion, — "Neque discrepantia ut reor est inter Christianos et infideles; quoniam jus gentium cunctis gentibus æquale est." Soto, too, in bold and energetic language, condemned the atrocities of the slave trade.

Amongst the Spanish Doctors of the sixteenth century, not the least was Franciscus Suarez.[24] Grotius says of Suarez that he had hardly an equal, in point of acuteness, amongst philosophers and theologians; and Suarez has had the merit, even in that age, of having clearly observed the distinction between what is commonly called the Law of Nature and the conventional rules of intercourse observed between nations. He first saw, as Sir James Mackintosh has said, that International Law was composed, not only of the simple principles of justice applied to the intercourse between states, but also of those usages long observed in that intercourse by the European race, which have since been more exactly distinguished as the Consuetudinary Law of the Christian Nations of Europe and America. For the basis of his works he took the philosophy of Saint Thomas Aquinas. For him syllogism and authority are always decisive arguments; his principles are elevated and profound; he represents the great traditions of the Middle Ages; he is a worthy disciple of Saint Thomas Aquinas, and is the latest representative of the Scholastic philosophy. The most remarkable work of Suarez is his treatise on Laws, based on the "Laws" of Saint Thomas, whose doctrines in a great measure he reproduces with certain modifications of detail. It is

[24] Born 1548, died 1617.

a treatise on Natural Law according to the principles of the philosophy of the Middle Ages. In all the schools there was a treatise on the Just and Eight or a treatise on Laws. Suarez has thus composed a considerable book, in which all the opinions of the doctors are collected, condensed, and compared together, so that whoever thoroughly knows the treatise on Laws by Suarez, knows to the bottom all the ethics, all the natural law, and all the politics of the Middle Ages.

The laborious treatise of Suarez, "De Legibus ac Deo Legislatore," is divided into ten books. It is a digest of all the discussions of the Christian Fathers on the subject of justice, interspersed with numerous illustrations from Plato, Cicero, and other pagan philosophers. In the preface he says the science of Civil Right — Juris Civilis Prudentia — is nothing more than a certain application or extension of moral philosophy to regulate and govern the political morals of the state. In the first book he discusses the nature of Law, and analyzes the divisions and definitions of former authors. Plato, in the Timæus and Phædrus, divided Law into divine, celestial, natural, and human; of which terms the second is not admitted by theologians; either because it is superfluous, or contains an erroneous doctrine. For by the celestial law Plato understood Fate. Now, if he understood that this law was such as not to be subject to Divine Providence, or to all things, even to men, to the extent of imposing necessity upon the peculiar operations of the soul, the opinion was false, and contrary to the Divine Government and to Free Will. But if he understood by the celestial law only what Aristotle said — that this inferior world was united with the celestial spheres, and thence governed by natural influences and chances, which always depend from God, and change bodies, not souls, then it is not proper to make such a division; because in this sense it is comprehended under natural law. Omitting, therefore, the second term — celestial — the other three are in use amongst theologians, but in a sense somewhat different. The Divine Law, with Plato, is governing reason existing in the mind of the Universal Deity; which law theologians also acknowledge, but call it the Eternal Law. For the law may be called divine in two ways: in one, because it is in God himself; in the other, because it is promulgated immediately by God himself. Plato used the term Divine Law according to the former sense; but the theologians, with St. Augustine, call it Eternal, to distinguish it from that law which the Deity promulgates. The first division of Law is into temporal and eternal; the next is into natural and positive. This second division is recognised by theologians, and the phrases *lex positiva* and *jus positivum* occur frequently amongst the Fathers. The phrase Natural Law has been used in various ways by philosophers, theologians, and jurists. Plato uses the term Natural Law to include every natural inclination placed in things by their Creator, by means of which they are directed to their peculiar acts and ends. So, according to the Fathers, all things which are governed by Divine Providence participate in some eternal law; whilst, according to the Institutes, natural law is common, not only to men, but also to the other animals. But the proper natural law which pertains to moral philosophy and theology is that which is inherent in the human mind to distinguish the good from the base — "Lex ergo naturalis propria, quæ ad moralem doctrinam et theologiam pertinet, est illa quæ humanæ menti inisidet ad discernendum honestum a turpi."

In such a definition of Natural Law Suarez plainly confounds Ethics with Jurisprudence; and implies simply the Moral Sense of right and wrong. Nor is he more correct in his definition of Positive Law, which he states is so called because it is added to Natural Law, and does not necessarily flow from it — Inde enim positiva dicta est, non ex illâ necessario manans. Natural Law is now understood to be the theory of that part of our duties which is capable of being enforced; whilst Positive Law, so called as existing by position, has been shown by Savigny to arise naturally and necessarily from the internal nature of man, and the external circumstances in which he is placed.

In the seventh chapter of the first book it is maintained, and illustrated with numerous authorities, that it is the essence of a law that it be passed for the public good. The second book is entitled "De Lege Æternâ Naturali, ac Jure Gentium." After illustrating further the doctrine that natural law is natural reason, he distinguishes it from conscience. For the law lays down a general rule about actions, but conscience gives a practical dictation in a particular case; whence, rather, it is, as it were, the application of the law to a particular occurrence. According to the Civil Jurists, Jus Naturale is distinguished from the Jus Gentium, inasmuch as the former is common to man with the brutes, but the latter peculiar to man alone. After discussing the various nice distinctions of the theologians, Suarez finally adopts the definition of the Institutes as to the Jus Gentium; and lays down that the Jus Gentium differs in its precepts from the Jus Civile; because it is established not in what is written, but in custom; and not merely that of one state, but of many. He then, in the following noble language, explains the reason for the Law of Nations: The reason of this law is, that the human race, although divided into various nations and kingdoms, always has some unity, not only specific, but also political and moral, indicated by the natural precept of natural love and charity, which is extended to all, even strangers, of whatsoever nation they may be. Wherefore, although every state, republic, or kingdom, be in itself perfect, nevertheless, each of them is also a member of the universal human race. For these communities are never so self-consistent in themselves as not to stand in need of mutual aid, and alliance, and communication; sometimes for their amelioration and greater advantage, sometimes by moral necessity. Wherefore, they need in some manner to be rightly directed in this species of communication and alliance. And although, in a great measure, this may be done by natural reason, still not sufficiently and immediately for all; and hence special laws have been introduced by the practice of the nations themselves.

The remaining books of the treatise De Legibus are, III. De Lege Positivâ Humanâ; IV. De Lege Positivâ Canonicâ; V. De Varietate Legum Humanarum; VI. De Interpretatione, Mutatione, et Cessatione Legum Humanarum; VII De Lege non scriptâ, quæ Consuetudo appellatur; VIII. De Lege Humanâ favorabili, seu Privilegio; IX. De Lege Divinâ Positivâ veteri; X. De Lege novâ Divinâ.

In the sixteenth century the doctrine of Tyrannicide appeared in the political writings of all parties. Languet, Buchanan, Bodin, and Mariana, all enforce it as lawful. And the execution of Charles I. appears as the result of the studies of the advanced republicans who lived in that age.

Mariana's book was published in the year 1603, but still has been generally classed amongst the works of the sixteenth century. It commences with an introduction written in imitation of a dialogue of Plato or Cicero. Mariana has described a mountain near Toledo, where, under great trees which the rays of the moon shone through, he used to repose from the labours of the day with a friend. There they paid homage to God, singing alternately sacred psalms; or distracted their leisure by interesting conversations on letters and philosophy. It was from one of these interviews that the treatise Do Rege had its origin.

Mariana, like Bellarmin, is the partizan of the government; but he is also the friend of liberty. He demonstrates the superiority of monarchy; but he develops with all their force the contrary reasons. For the rest, he subordinates monarchy to the power of the people. And when he is asked which is superior to the other, he adopts the principles of Languet and of Bouchier. Mariana does not hesitate to declare the prince is inferior to the state; in other words, that the monarchical power has something beyond it — the people, the nation, society; that there is a sovereign beyond the sovereign; that the authority of kings owes its origin to the people, and is not legitimate without its consent. The government of a family must be distinguished from that of the state. The chief of the family commands slaves; the chief of the state, freemen. It is for the essential interest of the state, for taxes, for the abrogation of laws, for the change in the order of succession, that the will of the people is superior to that of the prince. There is another and a graver reason: the republic must always reserve the right of punishing a wicked prince. But if the people were completely despoiled, what resources would they have to overwhelm a tyrant who dishonoured them by his vices? One chastisement is necessary for perverse princes — this is, tyrannicide. A tyrant is a public enemy; he must be treated as an implacable enemy. If such an action were criminal, the human race would hold in horror the names of those, who, at the peril of their lives, saved liberty, and delivered their country from their oppressors. On the contrary, the names of Harmodius, Aristogiton, and Brutus, have always been cited with honour. From the admission of all philosophers, the right to assassinate a tyrant is not doubtful, when he has acquired the empire by violence; then this right belongs to an individual person, without any deliberation of the citizens. But if the throne is in the hands of a prince, caution is required, and we must hesitate to drive him from it rashly; we must try at first to correct him, but if he resists all remonstrances, the republic or the people has the right of taking power from him, of proclaiming him a public enemy of declaring war against him, and finally putting him to death; and once war is declared, the right of executing the sentence belongs to every private individual who does not fear, at the risk of his life, to save the state. In default of the legal meeting of the assemblies of the people, the people can and ought themselves rise against the tyrant; and the right of life and death belongs to them always; only it is not the province of a private individual to decide if the prince be a tyrant, but it is suitable to wait for the decision of grave and wise men, at least as long as the public voice is not pronounced. Thus the right to kill a tyrant is absolute. Finally, Mariana decides it is not lawful to use poison.

## 5. Balthazar Ayala, 1548 — 1584

Besides the works connected with the casuistry of the schoolmen, numbers of practical treatises were also published in the sixteenth century by Spanish and Italian writers. Spain, under Charles V. and Philip II., was the first military and political power in Europe maintaining large armies and carrying on long wars. Spain was also the first, nation that felt the want of that more practical part of the law of nations, which reduces war to some regularity. Among the earliest of these works is a treatise by Balthazar Ayala, Judge-Advocate to the Spanish army in the Netherlands, under the Prince of Parma, in 1581. This work is divided into three books, the second of which relates exclusively to military policy, and the third to martial law. In the first the author treats of the laws of war as a branch of the law of nations, with a continual reference to examples drawn from Roman law and Roman history. The first chapter expounds the received forms of declaring war, and other belligerent ceremonies, which the author deduces from the Roman fecial law, and without, the observance of which no war was deemed just by that people. The second chapter treats of the just causes of war. Ayala concurs with Victoria in attributing the authority of declaring and carrying on war to the supreme power of the state. War is just when undertaken for the power of the state, its subjects, its property, its allies, and for the recovery of persons or things unjustly taken by the enemy. Neither rebels nor pirates are considered as public enemies; they are not entitled to the rights of war in respect to captures and postliminium; property in things taken by them is not lost to the original owners; but things taken from them become the property of the captors, as if taken from a public enemy.

In all these cases the subject is bound to submit his judgment to that of the sovereign, who alone is responsible for the justice or injustice of the war. A war may be just in a legal sense, even when not founded on a just cause, since there is no sovereign arbiter between states. That war may be called just which is declared and carried on by the lawful war-making power. Thus, Ulpian says: "Hostes sunt quibus publice populus Romanus bellum decrevit, vel ipsi populo Romano ceteri vero latrunculi vel predones appellantur." A war thus declared entitles both belligerent parties to all the rights of war.

The third chapter contains a digression upon duels or private combats, which the author condemns as a violation of all laws, human and divine. The fourth treats of reprisals against the property of the offending nation, which can only be granted by the supreme authority of the state in which the war-making power is vested. The fifth chapter treats of things taken in war, and of the jus postliminii. Things taken from the enemy in a just war become the property of the captors. But a distinction is to be made between movables and immovables, such as lands and houses, which last are confiscated to the use of the state. And by the laws of Spain, not only lands and houses, but ships of war taken from the enemy become the property of the crown. Even as to other movables, the right of the captors to appropriate them as booty is restrained by that of the state to regulate the division, reserving to itself a certain share, and distributing the rest according to the respective rank of the captors. Ayala cites the texts of the Roman law, showing that not only things, but persons, taken in war, become the property of the captors, and that slavery, which did not exist by the law of nature, was thus introduced through the law of nations. Among Christian nations, however, an ancient and laudable custom had substituted the practice of ransoming prisoners of war for that of making them slaves. The more ancient usage of reducing prisoners of war to servitude still subsisted at the time when he wrote as between Christian and infidel nations, such as the Turks and Saracens. Persons reduced to slavery in this manner recover their liberty on their return to their own country jure postliminii. The original owner is likewise entitled to the restitution of lands and other immovable property from which the enemy is expelled. The same legal fiction is also applicable to the case of ships and other movables recaptured from the enemy. As to these last, our author adopts the distinction of Labeo, — "Si quid bello captum est in præda est, nec postliminio redit." Such movables as are recaptured before they have been carried intra præsidia hostium, are consequently to be restored to the original proprietor, because they have not been appropriated as booty. Things recaptured from pirates are to be restored, whether they have been carried intra præsidia or not, because a capture by them is wholly void.

The sixth chapter relates to the duty of keeping faith with enemies. This duty is enforced, as usual, by examples taken from Roman history and the precepts of Roman philosophers, such as Cicero, Seneca, and others, who taught that the performance of contracts made with an enemy was not to be eluded under the pretext of duress, or by subtle interpretation of the words, in order to defeat the real intention of the parties. Such was the quibble of Q. Fabius Labeo, by whom Antiochus, having been defeated, had stipulated to deliver up half his fleet, which treaty the Roman general executed by sawing each galley in halves, and thus depriving the king of the whole navy. So also the Romans destroyed Carthage, which they had stipulated to preserve, alleging that the promise was to spare the citizens, not the city.

Our author also mentions the case of the ten Romans captured by Hannibal at the battle of Cannæ, and sent to Rome to negotiate an exchange of prisoners, under a promise confirmed by oath to return if they failed in effecting that object. One of them sought to elude his engagement, by going back to the Carthagenian camp under pretext of having forgotten something, and then pursued his way to Rome. According to Polybius, the senate ordered him to be bound and delivered up to Hannibal; for as Cicero justly observes, "Fraud does not absolve, but only aggravates perjury."

What has been said refers only to public enemies engaging in lawful war, and not to pirates and robbers, with whom there can be neither faith nor compact. This brings him to consider the nicer case of compacts with rebels, which, as might naturally be expected from a Spanish civilian writing in the camp of the Prince of Parma in the Netherlands, he declares to be absolutely void, as well as those made with tyrants; by which term he means usurpers, since he had before enforced the duty of passive obedience to lawful princes, however cruel and oppressive their conduct. Promises extorted by tyrants are not binding, since they lack the essential ingredient of free consent. The same may be said of those compacts which a people in rebellion unjustly extort from their prince. Nor is faith to be kept with public enemies in all cases; that is to say, in those cases referred to by Cicero, where the circumstances have so changed that the performance of the promise would be injurious to the party to whom it is made; as where it is contrary to the divine law, or where made by an unauthorized individual to the prejudice of the state, or where the enemy himself is guilty of a breach of faith. It is not lawful to avenge perfidy by perfidy, but a convention, whether of alliance, peace, or truce, which is infected by fraud, is void ab initio.

The seventh chapter relates to treaties and conventions. These were stated by the Roman ambassadors to Antiochus to be of three kinds: — 1st. Where the victorious party dictates laws to the conquered people, of which there are so many examples in the Roman history. 2nd. Treaties of peace and friendship founded on the basis of equal reciprocity, such as that concluded between the Romans and Sabines. 3rd. Treaties of friendship and alliance between nations who had never been engaged in war with each other. This class may again be divided into treaties of defensive alliance, and those which are both offensive and defensive. To these may also be added treaties of commerce. Our author here explains the difference between a fœdus and a sponsio, according to the Roman law. The commander of an army has power to make a temporary truce, but not a perpetual peace, without special authority from his sovereign.

The eighth chapter treats of stratagems and frauds in war. It is allowable to attack an enemy by force or fraud, and any kind of deceit or stratagem may be practised against him provided good faith is observed in respect to the performance of promises. The Greeks and Carthagenians boasted of their skill in deceiving the enemy; but the Romans, in the earlier days of the Republic, magnanimously disdained such acts. If they subsequently adopted them, it was not without strong opposition on the part of those senators who appealed to the better example of their ancestors.

The ninth chapter concerns the rights of legation. Our author asserts that the character of ambassadors had ever been considered sacred and inviolable among all nations, and quotes several examples where the judgment of the fecial college determined the Romans to deliver up to the enemy those who had violated the jus gentium in this respect. He refers to the conduct of the Dictator Posthumius, who carried his scruples so far as to liberate certain Volscians who had been clothed with the office of legati in order to mask their real character of spies who came to examine the Roman camp. But Ayala doubts whether the immunity of ambassadors extends to a case where they act in a manner so inconsistent with their official character.

The rights of legation belong only to public enemies, not to pirates, robbers, and rebels. Traitors who take refuge in the enemy's country cannot protect themselves by assuming the character of ambassadors. Our author applies this to the famous case of the ambassadors of Francis I., native subjects of Charles V., who were assassinated on their way through the Milanese to Venice and Turkey, and whose murderers the emperor refused to deliver up.

## 6. Albericus Gentilis, 1551 — 1611

Albericus Gentilis was born in the March of Ancona about the year 1551, of an ancient and illustrious family. He was an Italian Protestant, who, through the influence of the Earl of Leicester, was elected to fill the chair of Civil Law at the University of Oxford in 1582. He did not confine his attention to the Roman law, the only system then thought worthy of being taught in a scientific manner, but investigated the principles of natural Jurisprudence and of the consuetudinary law governing the intercourse of Christian nations. His attention was especially directed to this last by the circumstance of his being retained as the advocate of Spanish claimants in the English prize courts. The fruits of his professional labours were given to the world in the earliest reports of judicial decisions on maritime law published in any part of Europe. His more scholastic and academical studies produced one of the earliest regular treatises upon the laws of war — De Jure Belli — published in 1589, and dedicated to the Earl of Essex. Grotius acknowledges his obligations to Gentilis, and Mr.Hallam remarks, "that this comparatively obscure writer was of some use to the eminent founder, as he has been deemed, of international Jurisprudence, were it only for mapping his subject, will be evident from the titles of his chapters which run almost parallel to those of the first and third books of Grotius." His title to be considered as the father of the modern science of public law, is asserted by his countryman Lampredi: "He first explained the rules of war and peace, which probably suggested to Grotius the idea of writing his own work; worthy to be remembered, among other things, for having contributed to augment the glory of his native Italy, whence he drew his knowledge of the Roman law, and proved her to be the earliest teacher of natural Jurisprudence, as she had been the restorer and patroness of all liberal arts and learning."

Gentilis also published, in 1583, a treatise on embassies — De Legationibus — which he dedicated to his friend and patron, Sir Philip Sydney. The first book of this work contains a historical deduction as to the origin of the different kinds of embassies, and the ceremonies anciently connected with them by the Roman fecial law. The second book treats more specially of the rights and immunities of public ministers. He examines the question, whether they are entitled to a privileged character in respect to any other power than that to which they may be accredited. In strict law he concludes they are not; but it ought to be considered that ambassadors are the ministers of peace representing the person of their sovereign, charged with the business of the state, and universally considered, even by enemies, as possessing a sacred and inviolable character. The rights of legation do not extend to pirates and rebels; such criminal associations of men do not constitute a state; they are not public enemies. The case of a civil war is more doubtful. Here both parties claim to be the state, and each treats its adversary as guilty of treasonable resistance. The question must depend upon the respective factions being so evenly balanced as to make it for the interest of each to treat the other as if entitled to all the rights of public war. Whatever may be the effect of civil dissensions, difference of religion, at least, cannot be held to deprive the respective parties of the rights of legation. They may affect to treat each other as heretics and schismatics, but they are not therefore absolved from the obligations of public law. The immunity of the ambassador from the local jurisdiction of the country where he resides extends to the persons of his suite, to his property, and to his dwelling. But

Gentilis very inconsistently holds that the ambassador is subject to the ordinary jurisdiction of the civil tribunals of the place where he resides in respect to contracts made during the continuance of the embassy. This anomalous opinion is not confirmed by any other public jurist, and appears to be founded upon a misapplication of the Roman law, in respect to the legatus representing his province or city at the capital of the empire, or the legatus sent from Rome into the provinces on a special mission, who, of course, would be amenable as a subject to the local tribunals of the place where he temporarily resided, and where the contract was made. Yet, he not very consistently maintains that a foreign ambassador cannot be punished by the tribunals of the state where he resides for a crime committed by him, but even in the case of a conspiracy against the government must be sent out of the country.

The third book relates almost exclusively to the qualifications required in a good ambassador, which, according to our author, are almost as numerous as those required by Cicero to form his perfect orator. Besides the gifts of natural genius and peculiar aptitudes for this vocation, Gentilis requires eloquence, an extensive knowledge of history and political philosophy, dignity of manners, and high courtly breeding, temperance, fortitude, prudence, and a sacred regard to truth and rectitude; in short, all those attainments, qualities, and virtues which, according to him, were found united in his illustrious friend and patron, Sir Philip Sydney.[25]

From what has been shown of the discoveries of Suarez and Gentilis, it will have been seen that Grotius has no right to be considered as the inventor of the science of International Law.

## 7. The Dutch and German Schools

In the cultivation of the Civil Law France took decidedly the lead for nearly two centuries, until she found a rival in Holland. The Dutch School may be considered to have commenced with the founding of the University of Leyden in 1575, to which place Donellus was invited about that time, he being obliged to leave France on account of having embraced the Protestant religion. It was he who gave the first great impulse to the study of the Civil

[25] This analysis is taken from Wheaton.

Law in Holland. Other universities were subsequently founded, each of which had its law professors. Grotius and Vinnius flourished about the middle of the seventeenth century, Van Leeuwen and Huber towards its close. In the following century we have the names of Voet, Westenberg, Schulting, Noodt, and Bynkershoek. These raised the reputation of the Dutch schools so high that students in general repaired to Leyden and Utrecht, instead of to Bourges and Toulouse. In the political changes and revolutions which afterwards took place, the universities and law schools of Holland suffered, and though these afterwards partially recovered, Holland has not regained its former position. It has now a respectable school of law, but it cannot pretend to vie with the schools of Germany.

Zasius was the founder of the German School. For a long time the voluminous works of the civilians of that country were extremely heavy and barbarous in their style, though exhibiting much industry and research. Halvander, who died in 1531, is one of the first names really deserving of notice. He was distinguished chiefly for his learned edition of the Corpus Juris Civilis, in which the Greek novels, hitherto known through a Latin translation, were for the first time given in the original. During the latter part of the same century many professors of distinguished merit appeared. Most of them however were foreigners, as Giphanius, "the boast of Germany," Donellus, already noticed as adorning the Jurisprudence of France and Holland, Balduinus and Gothofredus the elder, whose edition of the Corpus Juris Civilis makes an epoch in Jurisprudence, it being the text-book generally received. In the seventeenth century this school degenerated, but towards the close of the same century the historical study of the Roman law began to make progress. The most conspicuous German civilian of the eighteenth century was Heineccus, whom Sir James Mackintosh designates as the best writer of elementary books with whom he was acquainted, on any subject. At present Germany is unrivalled in this branch of learning. A new school of historical Jurisprudence, founded several years ago by Professor Hugo, has firmly established itself there, and is extending its branches to other countries. A conspicuous ornament of the same school, Haubold, died a few years ago. The works of these two authors are extremely valuable. But the acknowledged chief of the historical school of Jurisprudence is

Savigny, of Berlin, the learned historian of the Roman law. The field of historical Jurisprudence is comparatively new, for none of the French Cujacian school undertook a work strictly historical, unless Gruchy and a few others can be considered as exceptions. And although something was formerly done in Germany and Italy in this department of knowledge, much yet remains to be explored.

## 8. Bodin, 1550 — 1627

Joan. Bodini Andegavensis De Republicâ libri sex Latinè ab auctore redditi, multo quam antea locupletiores, cum indice copiosissimo. Lugduni 1586; Frankfort, 1591. (Translated into English by Knolles). J. Bodin et son temps par Baudrillart: Paris, Guillaumin, 1853. Thierry: Introduction aux documents inedits pour l'histoire du Tiers-etat. Bayle's Dictionary, Art. Bodin.

Among the political writers of the sixteenth century Bodin, although now almost unknown, is confessedly the first, both, in the elucidation of correct principles, and the honest boldness with which he states them. Machiavelli scientifically analyzed villany. Sir Thomas More was afraid to state his political opinions except under the veil of a fable. Of Bodin, Dugald Stewart has said, "I know of no political writer of the same period whose extensive, and various, and discriminating reading appear to me to have contributed more to facilitate and guide the researches of his successors, or whose references to ancient learning have been more frequently transcribed without acknowledgment." The Republic of Bodin was originally published in French in 1577. It was afterwards enlarged by himself, and published in Latin in 1586.

Bodin himself indicates in his preface the object which he proposes in writing the Six Books of the Republic. This object is two-fold, practical and theoretical. In the former, he seeks to defend the principle of authority so strongly shaken by the civil wars; in the latter, he endeavours to point out the functions of the State — to determine its ideal. He proceeds farther, he wishes to write a treatise embracing all political science, with the different orders of facts which it comprehends, and with the laws which preside over it. He cites ancient writers, not as authorities, but on account of the truth to be round in them — to enlighten his work by their reasoning and examples. He reproves those who have discoursed upon politics without possessing a knowledge of the laws — never himself separating the historian, the philosopher, and the lawyer. To write upon matters of state without an acquaintance with public law, he pronounces to be a profanation of the mysteries of political philosophy — profaner les mystères de la philosophie politique.

Machiavelli is the adversary almost always present to Bodin; it is against him that he has written, even more than against the anti-monarchical pamphleteers. Bodin refuses to separate Morals from Politics. And on the subject of the great idea of Justice, the author of the Republic opposes Plato to Machiavelli, as, upon the other questions, he opposes the practical wisdom of Aristotle to the Platonic speculations. He declares that he pursues a double war — one against political immorality serving as a cloak to tyranny; the other against anarchy, placing itself under the invocation of Eternal Right. The first chapter of the De Republicâ is entitled, "Quis optimus sit Reipublicæ finis." A state is defined to be a number of families, and of the things common amongst them, governed by supreme power and reason. And the end of government is the greatest good of every citizen. The words Republic and State are used as synonymes by Bodin. The state for him signifies the sovereign power with the fundamental law which serves as its rule, and with the different powers which emanate from it. The sense of the word republic is more extended in containing and recalling, in a manner, more immediate the idea of society and of community (res publica). La Republique est un droit gouvernement de plusieurs menages et de ce qui leur est commun avec puissance souveraine. Upon this definition he builds his system. He uses the expression "droit gouvernement" to distinguish republics or societies from bands of robbers and pirates, who possess governments, but governments whose object is the destruction of justice.

The good — le bonheur — is not the sole, or even the principal end of the well-ordered republic, according to Bodin. It is in this respect that the definitions of Aristotle, and almost all the ancient definitions, appear to him faulty and incomplete. He would not fashion a republic in idea and without effect, such as Plato and Sir Thomas More have imagined. The Republic of Boden is the first sincere effort of an alliance between idea and fact — between the rational and experimental methods.

Bodin, in his preface, founds the state upon justice. His principle is the identity of nature, and of the end of man and the state. The sovereign good of the one is consequently the sovereign good of the other. He places the sovereign good of man in contemplation and action, which relate to the soul and the body. The good of the body consists in the health, strength, beauty, and proportion of the members; the good of the soul, in the moral virtues, in the intellectual faculties. The Republic of Bodin has a body and a soul, it acts and contemplates, it pursues a material destiny, and a moral end. Its body is its territory, more or less fertile — its good is composed of the natural advantages, such as a good climate, soil, position. The good — les bons — of the soul is the chief end of society, which cannot be developed without a previous security, and a certain satisfaction of the body's wants. Bodin concludes by affirming that the more republics, once their first wants have been satisfied and secured, will advance in their moral and intellectual development, the nearer they will approach the ideal, and will consequently become well constituted — bien ordonnées. Bodin, in his moral philosophy, follows Plato, as in politics he prefers Aristotle. The ancients defined a Republic as a society of men assembled together to live well and happily. But the word happily is unnecessary, for a Republic may be well ruled and yet afflicted with poverty, abandoned by friends, beset by enemies.

He next treats of the Family. If the end of society is the inquiry after the good, its rule is justice, its foundation is the family which Bodin regards as the true source and origin of every republic. The family appeared to him a state in miniature — en abrégé. Bodin considers as necessary to constitute a family, the head of the family, the mistress, children, and servants, whether slaves or free. Three families suffice to form a Republic. The totality of families constitute the people. The object of sovereign power is to unite; in it reposes the unity of nations, as the succession of families creates their perpetuity. Familia est plurium sub unius ac ejusdem patrisfamilias imperium subditorum, earumque rerum quæ ipsius propria sunt recta moderatio. The family is the beginning and rudiment of the state. Bodin upholds the patriarchal authority, both mental and paternal, with a high hand. "The true discipline," he says, "of the father and children depends on the paternal power, which either nature or God himself hath given to every one over his children. The word power is common to all who have either publicly or privately the right of government. 'A prince,' says Seneca, 'has power over his subjects; a magistrate over citizens; a father over children; a schoolmaster over scholars; a general over soldiers; a master over slaves.' But out of all these the right of government has been given by nature to none except to the father."

Bodin then proceeds to refute communism: for, if the family and the city — things private and public, the common and particular — are confounded, there can exist neither state or family. There must, however, be some things common to the state, as the public demesnes and treasure.

Persons and things used in common will be less carefully treated, because love, shared amongst a variety of persons or things, loses in intensity and purity. However, it never has received a complete application, as it is so repugnant to human nature. To the family should be left as much liberty as is compatible with the laws made with a view to common right. The individual makes part of the general good. The authorities which he cites to establish the divine and human authority of the husband over the wife, of the father over his children, are, the Bible, ancient philosophy, the Roman law, the traditions of all peoples. The command over the family is divided into four principal branches: that of the husband over the wife; of the father over his children; of the master over his slaves; of the master over his servants. He regards divorce as a barrier against the passions and the crimes which concern the family. He claims for the father the right of life and death over his children. He does not admit what we call the right of the children to the inheritance.

In the fifth chapter is discussed the question, "An servitia ferenda sint in republicâ bene constitutâ?" This is illustrated with much learning; but he comes to no very exact conclusion. "In whatever places slaves may exist, they ought not to be manumitted at once and together; but this must be done by degrees, and a commencement must be made with those who have learned in mature age some art by which they can support themselves. Otherwise they must perish, as befell those whom the Emperor Charles V. commanded to be manumitted at once in Spain."

This observation would be usefully borne in mind by those

who advocate the immediate emancipation of the slaves in the United States of North America. There can be no doubt but that the sudden change from slavery to freedom of those unhappy negroes would be accompanied with most disastrous consequences to themselves, and to the countries where they are located. In the enfranchisement of the negroes, it appears necessary to consult the historical example of the abolishment of slavery in Western Europe. The first step was to make the slaves bound to the estates upon which they were born: they became adscripti glebæ. By this, one of the most harrowing evils of slavery, the separation of families, with its consequent demoralization of mind and body, wag, in a measure, prevented. Besides, the slave resident on the estate, or in the house, was entitled to acquire and secrete a small portion of property, which finally became legally his own under the name of peculium. And lastly, the masters, in the course of time, became imbued with somewhat more kindly feelings towards those whose ancestors had laboured on the same property, increasing its fruits for a number of years. These three circumstances arising directly from the fixing the slaves upon the estates where they were born, together with the doctrine preached by the Catholic Church, that all men were equal in the sight of God, are the principal elements in the abolition of slavery through Europe.

In the conclusion of the chapter, Bodin says, that if it be true there is always room for the Divine Law, and that it is not confined within the boundaries of Palestine, why should not that law, so usefully and wisely promulgated by God, concerning slavery and liberty, prevail rather than the laws excogitated by the minds of men?

In this chapter Bodin, following Aristotle, regards servitude as a constituent element of the family. He considers the question under two points of view: as to its justice, as to its utility. With respect to slaves, there are two difficulties which have not yet been solved. The first is to determine if the servitude of slaves is natural and useful, or against nature; the second, what power the master ought to have over the slave. To say that there is a praiseworthy charity in preserving the life of a wounded prisoner, which is considered by some to be the origin of slavery, is to say that it is the charity of robbers or pirates who boast in having given life to those whom they have not killed. He asks is it pity which preserves captives for the purpose of making a profit by them as with beasts. His servitude can never be useful to the slave; in all cases it is prejudicial to him, without being ever to his advantage, a circumstance opposed to the fundamental principle of every society. Nor is its universality any argument in its favour; nor its mildness. Bodin considers that it was fear which principally led to the emancipation of the slaves in Modern Europe. In 1250 the last traces of slavery disappeared in Italy. He concludes by saying that moral law and reason demand as much as utility the freedom of the slave. As to the means, he recommends a previous instruction in some trade or other before at once emancipating them.

The sixth chapter discusses the Citizen. "Est autem civis nihil aliud quam liber homo, qui summæ alterius potestati obligatur." For before any citizen or form of state existed, every father of a family had supreme power of life and death over his children and wife. But after that violence, and ambition, and avarice, and revenge, had supplied them with arms against one another, the issues of wars made the conquerors enslave the conquered. And he who had fought bravely as a general, governed not only his family, but also his enemies, as well as his companions: but the latter as friends, the former as slaves. Then that full and complete liberty given by nature to every man, to live as he pleased, was altogether taken from the vanquished, and even lessened to the conquerors, by him whom they had chosen as their leader; because it was necessary for each man, in private, to acknowledge the supreme authority of another. Hence was the first origin of slavery and subjects, of citizens and strangers, of prince and tyrant. To this conclusion reason itself conducts us, that empires and commonwealths were first united by force, even if we were deserted by history.

The second book treats of the different species of government in a state. These are Monarchy, Aristocracy, and Democracy. "Rex est qui in summâ potestate constitutus naturæ legibus non minus obsequentem se præbet, quam sibi subditos quorum libertatem ac rerum dominium æque ac sua tuetur fore confidit." This definition is defective, in making no distinction between monarchy and tyranny, inasmuch as Bodin thus places no restraint upon the will of the Prince. "Aristocratia Reipublicæ forma quædam est in quâ minor pars civium in universos ac singulos cives summæ potestatis jus habet." This definition is also erroneous. It arises from the principle of the division of labour, that a small number of the citizens must exercise the functions of the government. But perhaps Bodin intended to define that state in which the majority were without political rights. 'Respublica popularis est, in quâ cives universi, aut maxima pars civium, cæteris omnibus non tantum singulatim, sed etiarn simul coacervatis et collectis, imperandi jus habent."

The third book is principally on Councils of State and Magistrates. The first chapter of the fourth book is entitled "De Ortu, Incremento, Statu, Conversione, Inclinatione, Occasu Rerum Publicarum." A revolution ensues when the form of polity is changed; but this ensues when the popular power is transferred to one, or the power of the law to all citizens. The power of the people goes to the aristocracy either when the strength of the commonwealth has been crushed by enemies, or on the slaughter of a great army of citizens: but, on the other hand, the popular power receives a great increase when victory has been obtained. Often, however, the popular power changes into monarchy; and this most frequently from civil sedition, or if unbounded authority be given to the supreme magistrate. Cicero says, "Ex victoria cum multa, tum certe tyrannis exsistit." On the other hand, tyrannies frequently end in popular states; because the people who cannot endure moderation, when the tyrant is once removed, desiring to communicate supreme power to all, pursue all the friends of the tyrant with such hatred as to desire to leave not one. Hence are the destructions, exiles, proscriptions of the nobles. But aristocratic states cannot be changed into popular without external or domestic violence. However, the popular authority is often transferred quietly to the nobles. And this happens in two ways: either when humble rustics, workmen, or merchants, intent on their domestic affairs, spontaneously abandon public business; or when the number of citizens having been diminished by pestilence or war, the number of strangers to whom residence is permitted without the right of suffrage or government is increased. But this is most to be feared in an aristocratic government when the plebeians are excluded from all honours and offices; which, although it is difficult to bear with content, still must be borne if the reins of power be given to the best; but when they are given to wicked and unworthy men, each one the boldest will seduce, on opportunity, the people from the aristocracy; and this the more easily the less the aristocracy are unanimous amongst themselves, which is dangerous to all states, but mostly to an aristocracy.

Chapter V. is on the State and the City. The citizen is, as it were, a subject; he pays obedience to a power which has been in almost all cases established by conquest or violence. The citizen is a free man obedient to the sovereign power. Several citizens, natural or naturalized, or enfranchised slaves, constitute a republic when governed by the sovereign power of one or more rulers. Aristotle considers that to entitle a man to citizenship, he must be qualified to take part in the making of, or carrying into execution the laws of the city. The idea of sovereignty forms, as it were, the keystone in the political system of Bodin.

Chapter VI. is on Sovereignty. One of the characters of sovereignty with Bodin is permanence or perpetuity. It does not consist in absolute power, such as has been vested in a dictator for a stated period. This is simply a commission. The people or rulers of a republic can bestow or transmit, simply and purely, the sovereign and perpetual power to any one. Limits are placed to sovereignty. The prince should scrupulously observe his engagements; should not capriciously change laws; individual property should be maintained — Si la justice est la fin de la loi, la loi l'œuvre du prince, le prince est l'image de Dieu; il faut, par même suite de raison, que la loi du prince soit faite au modèle de la loi de Dieu. The first mark of sovereignty is the power of giving law to all in general, and to each in particular. Ancillary to this the law can put an end to custom. The other indications are the power of making war and peace; the power of appointing the chief officers; the power of pardoning those condemned by the laws.

Chapter VII. is concerning the forms of the State. The sovereign power may reside in a single prince, in an aristocracy, or in the entire people, or in a body composed of the first three. Lawful monarchy — loyale ou legitime — is that in which the subjects obey the laws of the monarch, and the monarch the laws of nature. Feudal monarchy — seigneuriale — is that in which the prince is made master of the lives and properties of a people by the right of arms and conquest — governing his subjects as a good father his slaves. Despotic monarchy — tyrannique — is that in which the monarch, contemning the laws of nature, abuses the free persons as if they were slaves; abuses the property of his subjects as his own. The prince is not born a legitimate king; he becomes such; it is a quality which he acquires, not a gift of nature.

Aristocracy may be feudal, legitimate, or factious — seigneuriale, legitime, ou factieuse. The German Empire Bodin asserts to be a great aristocracy, though generally considered as a monarchy.

Chapter XI. is on the Senate and Parliament. The senate is the legitimate assembly of the councillors of the state, in order to give advice to those who possess the sovereign power in every republic. Age and experience are the qualities required in the composition of the senate as well as sound judgment and counsel. The right of proposing ought to belong to each member, with a complete independence. He considers the office should continue for life.

Chapter XII. is on the office of Magistrate in its relation with the ruling and the ruled. A magistrate is an officer who has the power of commanding in the state. An officer is a public person who has an ordinary charge limited by law. The magistrate should cause the enormity of offences to be understood, in order that the guilty may perceive what they have merited, so as to induce them to repentance; and, in doing this, the penalty has less of bitterness, and more of profit. There are three ranks of magistrates. The first recognise only the supreme majesty; the second obey the one and command the other; the last have command only over particular subjects. In the presence of the sovereign the whole power of the magistrate is held in complete subjection.

Chapter XIV. is on the Theory of Revolutions. The essence of a revolution consists in a change or displacing of sovereignty. The causes of revolutions are a contest arising between the claimants on the failure of the posterity of the princes, inequalities in wealth, oppression, ambition of a commander, alterations in laws. The first monarchies had their origin in violence. In the hereditary descent of monarchies there is an advantage which contributes to preserve monarchies from revolutions, which is, that the people have a certain inclination which induces them to respect, even in wicked princes, the virtue which shone in their ancestors. Revolutions in aristocratic and popular states could be prevented by abstaining from giving to the same man, with the supreme dignity, the supreme command. Sedition or division amongst its leading men is the great bane of an aristocracy. The admission of unworthy men into high offices has more than once caused a revolution in an aristocracy. The same consequence arises from the banishment of some powerful citizen. Another cause of revolution, already noticed by Aristotle, is the absence of a middle class, whose presence is necessary in all well established states. Changes of government are most desirable when least felt. The change which goes on gradually is more tolerable, whether it be from evil to good, or good to better. This analysis of political causes incentive to revolution, leads Bodin to treat of the means of obviating them. In theory, as in practice, Bodin declares in favour of monarchy, though he wishes to see existing governments modified, rectified, and purified. The natural causes of revolutions are human liberty — the action of Providence — the world itself. By wisdom and prudence, which God has given to men, revolutions can be avoided. Changes in the state or laws should never be made all at once, but slowly, conformably to nature in her marvellous works. The first rule for maintaining states is to well understand the nature of the state, and the causes of the maladies peculiar to it. If it be dangerous to change laws frequently, it is in like manner dangerous to change magistrates, whose appointments should continue for life. The first point which ought to influence legislators is to place conditions, offices, and all other rewards of virtue, in public view, and to share them amongst the subjects according to the merits of each; this cannot be done by bestowing them in perpetuity. He who distributes honours and offices amongst a small number of individuals, which is inevitable when they are conferred for life, kindles jealousies in one towards another. Another objection to the irremovability of magistrates is the impunity acquired by any holding office for life. This question, respecting the duration of office, depends almost entirely upon the form of the state. It is a question whether influence, authority, respect, which the people ought to possess for their magistrates, are reconcilable with a short duration of office.

In order to assure the good order of the state; in order to prevent the revolutions which threaten to overthrow it, a harmonious concord amongst the magistrates appears an indispensable condition. One of the causes of the inferiority of democracy and aristocracy is that the contending factions have nointervening party to reconcile them. The inducing principles of revolution are not pure accidents; they are connected with the profoundest political and social causes. He proceeds to enumerate some of them: — The denial of justice; oppression of the vulgar; the unequal distribution of penalties and rewards; the excessive wealth of a few; the extreme poverty of the many; the too great indolence of the subjects; impunity for crime. Faith is the best foundation for a republic. The object of Bodin in this chapter is to reform the society and the state, to infuse more of reason, more of justice, into some of the essential laws, to prevent inequality from advancing to an excessive degree.

Chapter XV. is on the Theory of Climate. It is indisputable that the economical progress of a nation depends not only upon the resources presented by the climate, but by the wants which it calls forth, and the efforts which it demands. Bodin naturally prefers middle and temperate regions, the advantages of which he points out. His maxim on this question is that "the good architect accommodates his building to the nature of the material which he meets upon the place." The people of the south are subject, so far as the body is concerned, to great maladies, and, so far as the mind is concerned, to the greatest vices; and, on the contrary, there is no people who possess bodies more adapted for living long, and minds more awake to the greatest virtues. The nations of the climates intervening between the north and south being more rational and less violent, have recourse to reason, to judges, and to the tribunals. The people of the south appear created for the investigation of the most abstruse sciences, in order to instruct other people; those of the north for labour and mechanical arts; those of the temperate zone for commerce, trafficking, judging, commanding, establishing republics, composing laws for other peoples. With respect to those inhabiting maritime places and large mercantile cities, they are more wily, cunning, and complaisant, than such as are removed from the sea and commerce. Men are more grave and settled where the air is mild and sweet, than they are where it is tempestuous. How far discipline, laws, customs, have the power of changing nature, is well illustrated in the case of Germany. Self-love being one of the strongest motives of man, and emulation one of the most powerful means of the progress of society, the question of rewards occupies a principal place in the state. In the popular state the rewards are more honourable than profitable, for the mob look only to their own advantage; the contrary occurs in a monarchy, in which the prince who distributes the rewards is more jealous of his honour than profit. The well-being of the state depends on the way in which the rewards and punishments are distributed. To confer ranks of honour appears to him one of the most precious attributes of sovereignty.

Bodin argues for the separation of the judicial and political powers. He maintains that justice ought never be subject to the vices of princes, and to the fancies of the people. He affirms that the more sovereignty augments its prerogatives, the more it diminishes its power. The state cannot fail to prosper when the sovereign retains the prerogatives which concern his sovereignty; the senate guards its authority, the magistrates exercise their power, and justice preserves its ordinary course.

Chapter XVII. is on Internal Security and Alliances Bodin holds that in the popular state it is expedient to train up to war the subjects, in order to avoid the inconveniences to which such a state is naturally subject. With respect to monarchies, if they are of great extent, it is not expedient that the prince should erect citadels nor strong places except on the frontiers, that the people may not presume that there is an intention to overawe them.

Chapter XVIII. is on Taxes and Finance. The first rule which Bodin lays down in matters of finance is probity. Three points engage alternately our attention. 1. To provide resources for the state. 2. To use them to the profit and honour of the state. 3. To spare and keep some part for any want. He says that in general there are seven methods of supplying the resources of the state. 1. The demesne of the state. 2. Conquest. 3. Gift of friends. 4. Trade. 5. The tribute of allies. 6. Levies from merchants. 7. The taxes of the subjects. The taxes should fall equally upon all.

Bodin published also, in 1591, a work entitled Juris Universi Distributio. In it Jurisprudence is thus described and divided: Ars tribuendi suum cuique, ad tuendam hominum societatem; hæc ad quatuor causas, ac totidem quæstiones, referri potest. An sit, quid sit, qualis sit, cur sit? Eadem quatuor partibus constat lege, æquitate, legis actione, judicis officio." Further according to Bodin, law is twofold, natural and human; natural law is inculcated by our reason; human law is the work of man, and is divided into jus gentium and jus civile. However, Bodin adopted the faulty classification of the Roman law: "Materia, circa quam omnis de jure quæstio versatur, in personis est aut in rebus aut in factis et dictis personarum."

## 9. Hooker, 1553 — 1600

Although no great writers on Jurisprudence had hitherto appeared in England, the principles of civil and political liberty had been well understood from an early age. Nor did the progress of these principles appear much endangered until the accession of the Tudor line of Sovereigns. The Great Charter of the liberties of England through some of its chapters asserts the natural freedom of man in language to which the experience of six centuries and of far more advanced civilization can add but little. The twenty-ninth chapter of Magna Charta says: — "Nullus Liber Homo capiatur, vel im-prisonetur, aut disseisietur de libero tenemento suo, vel libertatibus, vel liberis consuetudinibus suis, aut utiagetur, aut exuletur, aut aliquo modo destruatur, nec super eum ibimus, nec super eum mittemus nisi per legale judicium parium suorum, vel per legem terræ. Nulli vendemus, nulli negabimus aut differemus justitiam, vel rectum." So the thirteenth Chapter of Magna Charta provided that all merchants should have their safe and sure conduct to depart out of England, to come into England, to tarry in and go through England, to buy and sell without any manner of civil tolls, by the old and rightful customs, except in time of war. So Bracton, in his treatise "De Legibus Angliæ," boldly laid down that the king could do only what the law allows. His power is to do justice and not injustice. While he does justice, he is the minister of the Eternal King; but when he falls into injustice, he is the minister of the devil: for he is called king, *rex,* from well-governing, not from reigning, — "a bene regendo, et non a regnando." For he is king when he governs rightly, — a tyrant when he oppresses the people intrusted to him.

John Poynet, Bishop of Winchester, under Edward VI., wrote "A short treatise of Political Power, and of the true obedience which Subjectes owe to Kynges." It was published in 1556. Strype says: — "This book was not favourable to princes. Their rigour and persecutions puts their subjects upon examining the extent of the royal power, which some were willing to curtail and straiten as much as they could. The book was printed again in 1642 to serve the turn of those times." Poynet's work is divided into seven chapters, entitled thus: — I. Whereof politique power groweth, where of it was ordained, and the right use and duty of the same. II. Whether kings, princes, and other governors, have an absolute power and authority over their subjects. III. Whether kings, princes, and all other politique governors be subject to God's laws, or the positive laws of the country. IV. In what things and how far subjects are bound to obey their princes and governors. V. Whether all the subject's goods be the emperor's or king's own, and that they may lawfully take them for their own. VI. Whether it be lawful to depose an evil governor, and kill a tyrant. VII. What confidence is to be given to princes and potentates. On the doctrine of deposing kings, Poynet says: — "The manifold and continual examples that have been from time to time of the deposing of kings and killing of tyrants do most certainly conform to be most true, just, and consonant to God's judgment. The history of Kings in the Old Testament is full of it... The reasons, arguments, and laws that serve for the deposing and displacing of an evil governor will do as much for the proof that it is lawful to kill a tyrant, if they may be indifferently heard. As God hath ordained magistrates to hear and to determine private men's matters and to punish their vices, so also he willeth that the magistrate's doing be called to account and reckoning, and their vices corrected and punished by the body of the whole congregation or commonwealth."

The reigns of the Tudors were so unfavourable to popular liberty, and the high ideas of prerogative were so boldly advanced by the ministers of power, that it is remarkable to find the assertion of the true principles *of* civil government in a work displaying so much eloquence and erudition as the Ecclesiastical Polity, Richard Hooker published the first four books of his Ecclesiastical Polity in 1594; the fifth in 1597. He died in 1600; and the remaining three books were not published until 1647. His works are remarkable for the bold exposition of constitutional principles under the then despotic government of the Tudors. Hooker laid down fundamental ideas of the greatest importance, — the mutability of Positive Law and the eternal obligation of the Divine Law. The assertion of this doctrine in the reign of Elizabeth was a matter of greater consequence than it is in the reign of Victoria. The recent geographical discoveries had introduced a novel feature into the domain of politics. Then for the first time in modern history the learned were beginning to compare the laws and customs of different nations; and the exaggerated accounts of travellers concerning barbarous tribes, naturally caused doubts as to the existence of natural principles of right.

The first book of the Ecclesiastical Polity is on the nature of laws in general. All things that are, have some operation not violent or casual; nor does any thing ever begin to exercise the same without some fore-conceived end for which it works. But no certain end could ever be attained unless the actions whereby it is attained were regular; that is to say, made suitable, fit, and correspondent to their end by some canon, rule, or law. All things, therefore, do work after a sort according to law.

By law eternal the learned for the most part do understand the order, not which God hath eternally proposed to himself in all his works to observe, but rather that which with himself he hath set down as expedient to be kept by all his creatures, according to the several conditions with which he hath endowed them. They who thus are accustomed to speak, apply the name of Law unto that only rule of working which superior authority imposeth; whereas we, somewhat more enlarging the sense thereof, term any kind of rule or canon whereby actions are framed, a law. And as natural agents considered in themselves have their law, which law directs them in the means whereby they tend to their own perfection, so likewise another law there is which teacheth them, as they are sociable parts united into one body — a law which binds them each to serve unto other's good, and all to prefer the good of the whole before whatsoever their own particular.

The laws of action are made to guide man's will. The will, properly and strictly taken, differs greatly from that inferior natural desire which we call appetite. The object of appetite is whatever sensible good may be wished for; the object of will is that good which reason doth lead us to seek. Affections, as joy and grief, and fear and anger, being as it were the sundry fashions and forms of appetite, cannot choose but rise at the sight of some things. Wherefore, it is not altogether in our power whether we will be stirred with affections or no. Whereas, actions which issue from the disposition of the will, are in the power thereof to be performed or stayed. Let reason teach impossibility in any thing, and the will of man doth let it go. A thing impossible it doth not affect, the impossibility thereof being manifest. There is in the will of man naturally that freedom whereby it is apt to take or refuse any particular object whatsoever being presented to it. Whereupon it follows, that there is no particular object so good, but it may have the show of some difficulty or unpleasant quality annexed to it in respect whereof the will may shrink and decline; if contrariwise, for so things are blended, there is no particular evil which hath not some appearance of goodness whereby to insinuate itself. For evil as evil cannot be desired.

The most certain token of evident goodness is, if the general persuasion of all men do so account it. And, therefore, a common received error is never utterly overthrown till such times as we go from signs unto causes, and show some manifest root or fountain thereof common unto all, whereby it may clearly appear how it hath come to pass that so many have been overseen. Wherefore, although we know not the cause, yet thus much we may know, that some necessary cause there is, whensoever the judgments of all men generally, or for the most part, run one and the same way, especially in matters of natural discourse; for of things necessarily and naturally done, there is no more affirmed than this, — they keep either always or for the most part one tenure, *"Η ἀεὶ ἢ ὡς ἐπὶ τὸ πολὺ ὡσαύτως ἀποβαίνει.* The general and perpetual voice of man is as the sentence of God him. self. For that which all men have at all times learned, nature herself must needs have taught. Infinite duties there are, the goodness whereof is by this rule sufficiently manifested, although we had no other warrant besides to approve them. A law, therefore, generally taken is a directive rule unto goodness of operation.

In goodness there is a latitude or extent whereby it comes to pass that even of good actions some are better than other some; whereas otherwise one man could not excel another, but all should be either absolutely good or be excluded out of the number of well-doers. Degrees of well-doing there could be none, except, perhaps, in the seldomness or oftenness of doing well. But the nature of goodness being thus ample, a law is properly that which reason in such sort defineth to be good that it must be done. And the law of reason or human nature is that which men by discourse of natural reason, have rightly found out themselves to be all for ever bound unto in their own actions. Laws of reason have these marks to be known by; such as keep them resemble most lively in their voluntary actions that very manner of working which nature herself doth necessarily observe in the course of the whole world. The works of nature are all behoveful, beautiful, without superfluity or defect; even so theirs, if they be found according to that which even the law of reason teacheth. Secondly, those laws are investigable by reason without the help of revelation, supernatural and divine. Finally, in such sort they are investigable, that the knowledge of them is general. The world hath always been acquainted with them, as Sophocles observes concerning a branch of this law; it is not of to-day or yesterday, but hath been no man knows how long since, —

*ού γάρ τι νŨν γε κάχθές άλλ' άεί ποτε*
*ζŨ ταŨτα, κούδείς οϊδεν έξ ő'του 'φάνŲ.*[26]

It is not agreed upon by one, or two, or few, but by all; which we may not so understand, as if every particular man in the whole world did know and confess whatsoever the law of reason doth contain; but this law is such that being proposed, no man can reject it as unreasonable and unjust. Again, there is nothing in it but any man having natural perfection of wit and ripeness of judgment may find out. Law rational, therefore, which men commonly use to call the law of nature, meaning thereby the law which human nature knoweth itself in reason universally bound unto, which also, for that cause, may be termed most fitly the law of reason, — this law comprehends all those things which men, by the light of their natural understanding, evidently know, or at least may know, to be good or evil for them to do.

Now the due observation of this law, which reason teaches us, cannot but be effectual unto their great good that observe the same. For we see the whole world and each part thereof so compacted that as long as each thing performeth only that work which is natural to it, it thereby preserves both other things, and also itself. Contrariwise, let any principal thing, as the sun, the moon, any one of the heavens or elements, but once cease, or fail

[26] Sophocles, Antigone.

or swerve, and who doth not easily conceive that the sequel thereof would be ruin both to itself and whatsoever dependeth on it? And, is it possible, that man being not only the noblest creature in the world, but even a very world in himself, his transgressing the law of his nature should draw no manner of harm after it? — Yea, tribulation and anguish unto every soul that doth evil.

It remains, then, to consider how nature finds out such laws of government as serve to direct even nature depraved to a right end. All men desire to lead in this world a happy life; that life is led most happily wherein all virtue is exercised without impediment or let. But in the world there has been always much wickedness — much misery. To take away all such mutual grievances, injuries, and wrongs, there was no way but only by growing unto composition and agreement among themselves by ordaining some kind of government public, and by yielding themselves subject thereto; that unto whom they granted authority to rule or govern, by them the peace, tranquillity, and happy estate of the rest might be procured. Men always knew that when force and injury was offered, that they might be defenders of themselves. They knew that however men may seek their own commodity, yet if this were done with injury unto others it was not to be suffered, but by all men, and by all good means, to be withstood. Finally, they knew that no man might in reason take upon him to determine his own right, and according to his own determination proceed in maintenance thereof; inasmuch as every man is towards himself and them whom he greatly affecteth, partial; and therefore that stripes and troubles would be endless, except they gave their common consent all to be ordered by some whom they should agree upon. Without which consent there were no reason that one man should take upon him to be Lord or judge over another; because, although, according to the opinion of some very great and judicious men, there is a kind of natural right in the noble, wise, and virtuous, to govern them which are of servile disposition; nevertheless, for manifestation of this their right, and men's more peaceable contentment on both sides, the assent of them who are to be governed seems necessary.

At the first, when some certain kind of regiment was once approved, it may be that nothing was then further thought upon for the manner of governing, but all permitted unto their wisdom and discretion which were to rule; till by experience they found this for all parts very inconvenient, so as the thing which they had devised for a remedy did indeed but increase the sore which it should have cured. They saw that to live by one man's will became the cause of all men's misery. This constrained them to come unto laws wherein all men might see their duties beforehand, and know the penalties of transgressing them. If things be simply good or evil, and withal universally so acknowledged, there needs no new law to be made for such things. The first kind, therefore, of things appointed by laws human containeth whatsoever being in itself naturally good or evil, is notwithstanding more secret than that it can be discerned by every man's present conceit, without some deeper discourse and judgment.

Besides that law which simply concerns men as men, and that which belongs unto them as they are men linked with others in some form of politic society, there is a third kind of law which teacheth all such several bodies politic so far forth as one of them hath public commerce with another. And this third is the law of nations; between men and beasts there is no possibility of sociable communion, because the well-spring of that communion is a natural delight which men hath to transpose from himself into others and to receive from others into himself; especially those things wherein the excellency of his kind doth most consist. Civil society doth more content the nature of man than any private kind of solitary living; because, in society this good of mutual participation is so much larger than otherwise. Herewith, notwithstanding we are not satisfied, but we covet to have a kind of society and fellowship even with all mankind, which thing Socrates intending to signify proposed himself a citizen not of this or that commonwealth, but of the world. And an effect of that very natural desire in us appears by the wonderful delight men have, some to visit foreign countries, some to discover nations not heard of in former ages, all to know the affairs and dealings of other people, and to be in league of amity with them.

Hooker has boldly laid down as an axiom of nature that natural desire cannot be utterly frustrate. In this sense it may fairly be contended that those which we term evil desires, in some indirect way tend to ultimate good; even as the existence of misery upon the earth is a spur to industry.

In the last section of the first book in the Ecclesiastical Polity it is explained why this digression on the nature of laws in general is prefixed. The drift and purpose of all this is even to show in what manner as every good and perfect gift, so this very gift of good and perfect laws, is derived from the Father of Lights, to teach men a reason why just and reasonable laws are of so great force, of so great use in the world; and to inform their minds with some method of reducing the laws, whereof there is present controversy, unto their first original causes, that so it may be in every particular ordinance, thereby the better discerning, whether the same be reasonable, just, and righteous, or not For nothing can be thoroughly understood or soundly judged of till the very first cause and principles from which originally it springeth be made manifest.

Of law there can be no less acknowledged, than that her seal is the bosom of God, her voice the harmony of the world; all things in heaven and earth do her homage, the very least is feeling her care, and the greatest is not exempted from her power; both angels, and men, and creatures, of what condition soever, though each in different sort and manner, yet with all uniform consent, admiring her as the mother of their peace and joy.

Mr. Hallam has pointed out that this celebrated sentence of law, concluding the first book of Hooker's Ecclesiastical Polity is in substance the same with the definition of Eternal Law by Suarez. — "Legem æternam esse decretum liberum voluntatis Dei statuentis ordinem servandum, aut generaliter ab omnibus partibus universi in ordine ad commune bonum, vel immediatè illi conveniens ratione totius universi, vel saltem ratione singularum specierum ejus, aut specialiter servandum a creaturis intellectualibus quoad liberas operationes earum." Hooker advanced those principles of government which were afterwards illustrated by Locke. He derives the origin of government from a primary contract, "without which consent there were no reason that one should take upon him to be Lord or judge over another; because although there be, according to the opinion of some very great and judicious men, a kind of natural right in the noble, wise, and virtuous, to govern them which are of servile disposition, nevertheless for manifestation of this their right, and men's more peaceable contentment on both sides, the assent of them who are to be governed seemeth necessary." And again he lays down that of this no man doubts, namely, that in all societies, companies, and corporations, what severally each man shall be bound unto, it must be with all their assents ratified. Against all equity it were that a man should suffer detriment at the hands of men, for not observing that which he never did, either by himself or others, mediately or immediately agree unto.

It has been maintained that the eighth book of the Ecclesiastical Polity, in which these liberal ideas on political society are promulgated chiefly, was interpolated or altered by the Puritans after his death. Mr. Hallam however, considers there is no foundation for this opinion The testimony that has been brought forward to throw a doubt over the authenticity of the three last books consists in those vague and self-contradictory stories which gossiping compilers of literary anecdote can easily accumulate, whilst the intrinsic evidence arising from the work itself seems altogether to repel every suspicion.

We now conclude the review of the jurists of the sixteenth century. The sixteenth century was remarkable for the variety and boldness of its speculations in moral and political philosophy. The adverse religious parties agitated all the problems of the state. The principle of the sovereignty of the people was supported by history, reason, the authority of the Scriptures, and was boldly pursued into its furthest consequences. The idea of monarchy was limited by the idea of liberty of conscience. The Utopists questioned the essential principles of society, and asserted — some in ingenious and chimerical books, some with arms in their hands — unknown forms of social government. The doctrine of tyrannicide was advocated by the most advanced writers. Their works in the succeeding century were used as justificatory pieces by the executioners of Charles I. All the questions which still agitate modern times were discussed in this century. The rights and duties of property were enounced. Slavery received its final condemnation in Europe. The ideas of political and religious liberty were originated.

Made in United States
North Haven, CT
04 November 2026

21770788R00163